REGIONAL ITALIAN COOKING

MAP OF ITALY

1 inch = approx. 150 statute miles

0 50 100 150 200
Kilometers

——————— National borders
– – – – – – Regional borders
(Equivalent to states)

REGIONAL ITALIAN COOKING

From the Alps to the Mediterranean

WILMA REIVA LaSASSO

COLLIER BOOKS
A Division of Macmillan Publishing Co., Inc.
NEW YORK
COLLIER MACMILLAN PUBLISHERS
LONDON

Library of Congress Catalog Card Number: 58-6731

Regional Italian Cooking, originally published as
The All-Italian Cookbook, is also published in a
hardcover edition by Macmillan Publishing Co., Inc.
First Collier Books Edition 1974

Printed in the United States of America

DEDICATION

To the memory of my beloved father, Dominic P. Reiva, a native of Piemonte (Piedmont), Italy, I dedicate this book, remembering his constant encouragement.

In looking over the years of my trials as an amateur, I marvel at the patience Papa had in sampling what I had prepared. Many times the herbs were not too well blended, or there was too much oil in the salad; yet he was always ready to try my next experiment. Just three months before he died he said, "Busybody! Someday you make a cookbook for Italy!" This, at the time, brought joyous laughter. But on the morning that God took him, this phrase stood before my eyes, making me realize that I had a challenging goal ahead.

IN RECOGNITION

Space does not allow detailed acknowledgment of my debt to the wide circle of friends and acquaintances who generously aided and inspired the writing of this book. No writer was ever more serious than I, as I interviewed men and women from Italy to learn of their favorite recipes, then recreated the dishes through experimental cookery.

Besides my father, Dominic P. Reiva, who was my first and most helpful critic, and my beloved mother, Maria B. Reiva, my first teacher of cookery—both natives of Piemonte, Italy—I shall name here only my dear husband, Lawrence LaSasso, whose paternal grandparents came from southern Lucania.

To this background and to these people I humbly acknowledge my debt for incentive and continuing inspiration.

PREFACE

More than twenty million Americans can trace the origin of one or both parents to the "bel paese" (beautiful country) which is Italy. Characteristic Italian dishes were at first confined to these people, but today, with more world travel—including that of our servicemen—and more world-wide feeling, there has developed an unprecedented interest in foreign food, and Italian cooking has come to be one of the most highly esteemed of all.

To those who share my ancestry and to all others who find Italian food appealing, I offer the recipes in this book, with notes on the historical origins of many of the dishes.

INTRODUCTION

Lovers of Italy have marveled at the distinctive customs, music, folklore, and arts that characterize the diversified regions of the country—from the rustic chivalry of the proud, fiery, and intensely loyal Sicilian to the suave graciousness of the gentle, calm, and modern Lombard.

Connoisseurs of the "bel paese" have, to an equal degree, admired the savory Italian dishes, all having the peculiarly Italian subtle dash of a pungent cheese, whether prepared with the northern love of wines and brandies or with the southern preference for olive oil and garlic. But often they are unaware of the history and folklore that are in the background of their favorite recipe, nor can they identify the region to which it is indigenous.

Until the end of the nineteenth century, communications in Italy were poor, so that local customs and types of food remained close to their place of origin. Afterward, when Italy became a modern country, regional ways spread throughout the peninsula. Now it is difficult to find out which city gave origin to certain ways of preparing food; but immigrants from Italy to the United States before 1900 brought their own regional customs and jealously retained them.

For my interviews in preparation for this book, I carefully chose such people, many of whom are no longer living. Proudly they told me of their traditional ways with food. Proudly and with humility I learned from them.

Italian dishes vary from province to province, yet all have certain peculiarities and characteristics native to their country. While in the north butter is most frequently used for basic cooking, and in the south olive oil and salt pork are more common, everywhere the blending of herbs is important and similar. For example, rosemary leaves are used mainly with pork, veal, and wild meats; sweet basil, "queen of the kitchen," is used universally.

Americans speaking of macaroni and spaghetti products tend to confuse them. Macaroni, spaghetti, spaghettini (finer spaghetti), capellini (fine hair spaghetti), tagliatelle (noodles), lasagne (very wide noodles), and many other sizes and styles are all *pasta* (dough) rolled out and cut into different forms. Ravioli, cappelletti, agnellotti, and tortellini are little thin forms of dough folded over a filling. (Note the picture chart of the varieties of *pasta asciutta*, or dry noodle-type dough, page 26.)

Gourmets in all parts of Italy will insist that spaghetti or any elongated pasta be cooked whole and not broken up as is commonly done in America. The more sophisticated feel that spaghetti tastes best when eaten by the fork-and-spoon method. To such persons, use of a knife would be all but sacrilege. The technique is simple and artful. Taking a fork in the right hand and a tablespoon in the left, the diner twists the spaghetti in the spoon with the fork—only a small quantity at a time. Some persons use only a fork, twisting two strands at a time on the plate.

Italian chefs are noted for their clever way of forcing the long strips of spaghetti into the boiling water. The trick is to push one end of a handful into the water, letting it gradually wilt and sink until it is completely covered. The secret, of course, is to use a large kettle with plenty of water boiling rapidly before the spaghetti is immersed.

One must be very careful with spaghetti or any other form of pasta not to overcook. It is most palatable when served in the *al dente* (chewy) stage.

Italian connoisseurs have a simple way of judging their familiar foods. Some claim that a raw pear should be eaten with cheese to bring out the pear's true flavor. Others say that cheese eaten with wine will enhance the wine's bouquet.

Among the many proverbs and maxims about savory food with which Italian people effervesce, one of the most common is *fa companatico* ("it goes well with bread"). In other words, food that is tasty and expensive can well be economical because it is tastier with bread. Starches (pizza, potatoes, pasta, pie) are not "companatico," but well-flavored cheese, salami, walnuts, and sausage are "companatico."

Italian cooks are characteristically eager to prepare food with appetizing taste as well as attractive appearance. Even without using superior cuts of meat or expensive vegetables, a good cook with ambition and time can make any meat or vegetable tasty if patience, ingenuity, and wisdom go into its preparation.

ITALIAN CUISINE
(An Introduction)

To enable the homemaker to derive the greatest possible enjoyment from the use of this cookbook, the following glossary of definitions, explanations, and translations has been prepared. Used as a point of departure for those of divers ancestries, these pages will serve as a guide to the terminology of the individual recipes and instructions.

I. THE ORDER OF THE MEAL

The typical Italian meal generally consists of seven courses:

An **"Aperitivo"**—(apéritif—welcoming drink before dinner): chilled vermouth or an "Americano" (cocktail) is served.

First course—**"Antipasto"** (before meal): a platter of attractive appetizers

Second course—choice of **"Minestra"** (light soup), **"Minestrone"** (heavy soup), **"Risotto"** (rice dish), or **"Pasta Asciutta"** (cooked noodle-type dough with sauce)

Third course—**"Primo Piatto"** (main course: meat, fish, poultry, or wild game, and
   "Contorno" (accompaniment to the main course): vegetables, salad, and potatoes

Fourth course—**"Scelta di Formaggi"** (attractive platter of varied cheeses)

Fifth course—**"Dolce"** (dessert)

Sixth course—**"Frutta"** (fresh fruit)

Seventh course—**"Caffè"** (coffee): small cup of strong coffee, usually with sugar, but *no* cream

II. CONDIMENTO
(*Seasoning*)

An Italian cook does not speak of herbs, but refers to the seasoning, whatever it may be, as "un buon odore," meaning "just enough seasoning to give *a good odor*." Seasoning must be used to satisfy the taste. The following basic rules may be used as a guide:

1 tablespoon minced fresh seasoning is equivalent to ½ teaspoon dried or ¼ teaspoon powdered

Bay leaf: Use sparingly in veal, pork, lamb, wild game, poultry, stuffings, soups, and sauces.

Black pepper: Freshly ground is best.

Capers: Fish, garnishes, sauces, salads, and appetizers.

Celery leaves: When crisping celery stalks for table use, it is wise to dry the leaves for future use in sauces, meats, soups, stuffings, and stews.

Chili pepper: Strong and hot; useful in sauces, meats, soups, stuffings, and appetizers.

Cinnamon: For sausage, stuffings, and desserts.

Cloves: Freshly ground are best. Used in sausage, veal, pork, lamb, wild game, stuffings, sauces, and desserts.

Fennel: Mild licorice flavor; used in pastries, sausage, and sauces.

Garlic: For "un buon odore." In a salad, rub the bowl with a clove; in a roast, cut slits and insert a clove for cooking and remove before serving; in a sauce, cook the whole cloves and remove when done.

Leek: A very refined cousin to the onion.

Mint: Used in veal, pork, lamb, beverages, vegetables, salads, sauces, and stuffings.

Mushrooms: Used in soups, sauces, meats, vegetables, and garnishes.

Nutmeg: Used in sausage, stuffings, and desserts.

Onion: Sauté only till delicate or golden brown for ideal seasoning.

Origano (marjoram; but not the kind known as "sweet" marjoram): Use sparingly in salads, veal, pork, wild game, lamb, and snacks.

Parsley: Italian parsley is best for seasoning, while the curly parsley is more effective as a garnish.

Rosemary: A pungent flavor used with veal, pork, lamb, wild game, poultry, stuffings, and sauces.

Saffron: Aromatic and colorful (yellow). Use sparingly in soups, sauces, rice, and pastries.

Sage: Use sparingly in sauces, wild game, poultry, snacks, and stuffing.

Sweet basil: The "queen of the kitchen" can be used in all cookery and is used in all Italian regions.

Sweet marjoram: Use sparingly in meats, fish, stuffings, soups, and sauces.

Thyme: Use sparingly in soups, sauces, stuffings, wild game, and fish.

III. FORMAGGIO
(for máh jo)
(*Cheese*)

Caciocavallo (ca cho ca vál lo)—a smoked cheese originating in southern Italy, made from matted curds softened in hot water; often molded into the shape of an Indian club or ten-pin; used for seasoning

Fontina (fon té na)—a cheese originating in Piedmont

Gorgonzola (gor gon zó la)—a blue pressed-milk cheese resembling Roquefort

Mozzarella (moh tsa rél la)—an unripened cheese for seasonings, snacks, and appetizers

Parmigiano (par me jáh no)—Parmesan, a large, hard, dry pressed cheese of mild sweetish flavor, with an even distribution of small gas holes. Made from skimmed or partly skimmed milk, it is high in casein. It is ripened for two or three years before being grated for seasoning.

Provolone (pro vo ló ne)—a smoked cheese used for seasoning

Ricotta (ri cót ta)—a soft, fresh cottage cheese*

Romano (ro máh no)—a hard, sharp ewe's-milk cheese resembling Parmesan; also called Pecorino

Scamorza (sca mór tsa)—an unripened cheese used for seasonings

* See Chapter XIII for recipe.

IV. VARIETA DI PASTA
*(Varieties of Noodle Dough)**

cappelletti (ca pel lét te)—little hats with stuffing (also known as tortellini)

capellini (ca pel leé ne)—"fine hair"—a very thin pasta

conchiglie (con keél yay)—sea shells

ditali (de táh le)—thimbles of macaroni

ditalini (de tah leé ne)—small cuts of macaroni

farfalle (far fáhl lay)—butterfly noodles

ferretti (fer rét te)—little irons

fuselli (foo sél le)—spindles

lasagne (la sáhn yay)—wide noodles

lasagnette (la sah nyét tay)—narrow noodles

limoncini (le mohn chée ne)—lemon slices

lumache (loo máh kay)—snails

maccheroni (mah ker óh ne)—macaroni

mostaccioli (mos tah chó le)—pasta cut like a mustache

pasta asciutta (pás ta   ah shoó ta)—noodle-dough variations

pastina (pas tée nah)—midget form of noodle-type dough

ravioli (rav yó le)—miniature pillows with stuffing

rigatoni (ri gah tóh ne)—striped noodles

semini (séh mi ne)—seed-shaped noodles

spaghetti (spa gét te)—solid cords of pasta

spaghettini (spa geh teé ne)—fine spaghetti

stelline (stel lée ne)—star-shaped noodles

vermicelli (ver mi chél le)—a very thin spaghetti

* See picture page of pasta shapes.

V. REGIONI ITALIANE *

Italian name	*English equivalent*
Abruzzi [1]	Abruzzi
Alto Adige [2]	Alto Adige
Calabria	Calabria
Campania	Campania
Emilia	Emilia
Lazio	Latium
Liguria	Liguria
Lucania [3]	Lucania
Lombardia	Lombardy
Le Marche	Marches
Piemonte	Piedmont
Puglia	Apulia
Sardegna	Sardinia
Sicilia	Sicily
Toscana	Tuscany
Umbria	Umbria
Val d'Aosta [4]	Valley of Aosta
Venezia Euganea	
Venezia Giulia e Trieste	

* See Frontispiece for map.

[1] Abruzzo e Molise.

[2] The provinces of Alto Adige (capital: Bolzano) and Trentino (capital: Trento) are together known as the region of Alto Adige, which is synonymous with Venezia Tridentina. The people of Alto Adige are known as Tirolese, derived from Tirolo, a name unofficially applied since part of the Austrian Tirol was ceded to Italy by the Treaty of St.-Germain, 1919.

[3] Basilicata is a synonym.

[4] Formerly considered a part of Piedmont.

CONTENTS

(Recipes in each chapter are in alphabetical order by Italian name. Each recipe has been prepared by the author, and tested in her home. All are based on yields of six portions.)

CHAPTER I

ANTIPASTI
Appetizers

The antipasto is prepared according to individual taste, pocket-book, and artistic ability. It is a large platter of varied appetizers, decorated with edible garnishes of carrot strips, celery, olives, radishes, artichoke hearts, parsley, water cress, green onions, slices of hard-boiled egg, and the like. One can add miniature sandwiches (crusts removed), with fillings as desired, from the many recipes in this chapter.

Readers who wish to keep some choice appetizers in the larder will find a selection among the following recipes in Chapter XII, Cibi Conservati (Preserved Foods):

Caponata (canned appetizer, Sicilian style)
Cavolfiore marinato in barattolo (pickled cauliflower in jars)
Ceci (Chick-peas, also known as garbanzo beans)
Cetriolini alla senape (mustard pickles)
Cetriolini sotto aceto (dill pickles)
Funghi sotto aceto (pickled mushrooms)
Lupini salati (salted lupine seeds)
Peperoni rossi sotto aceto (pickled cherry peppers)
Peperoni ungheresi sotto aceto (pickled Hungarian yellow-wax peppers)
Trippa marinata (pickled tripe)
Verdure marinate in barattolo (pickled vegetables)

ANTIPASTO VARIATO

Varied Appetizer   *All Regions*

On a large platter, or individual serving plates attractively arrange
thin slices of salami
**finger-length rolls of thin slices of prosciutto or boiled
ham pinned with toothpick**
filets of anchovies, drained of oil
artichoke hearts in oil or vinegar, drained
black and green olives
strips of crisp red and green peppers
pickled cherry peppers
crisp green onions
florets of cauliflower

With artistic imagination, garnish with sprigs of parsley, crisp
water cress, slices of hard-boiled egg, and the like.

BURRI VARIATI PER ANTIPASTI

Butter Variations for Appetizers   *Northern Regions*

To ½ cup soft **butter** add your choice of one of the following:

½ **teaspoon dry mustard**
5 **filets of anchovies (drained and minced) and 3 drops of
vinegar**
2 **tablespoons caviar**
¼ **pound Gorgonzola cheese and ½ teaspoon pepper**
½ **cup minced prosciutto or lean boiled ham**
¼ **cup red salmon, minced into a paste, and ½ teaspoon
pepper**
½ **cup minced tuna, drained of oil, 1 tablespoon minced
fresh parsley, and 1 teaspoon minced onion**

Whip until creamy. Spread on fancy shapes of bread, toasted
medallions, or snack crackers, or fill midget sandwiches.

CAVOLFIORE E GAMBERI

Cauliflower and Shrimp   *Abruzzi*

Parboil the florets of **cauliflower,** and drain. Dip into well-beaten **egg,** and toss into **flour.** Deep-fry in **oil.** Repeat the procedure with the **shrimp.** Place cauliflower in center of platter, and surround it with the shrimp. Serve with **Maionese** or **Salsa Verde** (Chap. VI).

CECI ALL' OLIO

Chick-Peas in Oil   *Calabria*
Christmas delicacy

Use either canned chick-peas or the home-treated kind as in recipe for Ceci (Chap. XII). Drain the **chick-peas** from the juice. Sauté them in a little **olive oil** with chopped **garlic.** When delicately browned, drain, **salt** and **pepper** to taste, and place in a relish compote.

CROSTINI ALLE RIGAGLIE

Toasted Medallions with Giblet Sauce   *Toscana*

Cut thinly sliced **bread** into small medallions or triangles the size of silver dollar; place in 300° oven till golden-brown.

Prepare a giblet sauce of **chicken livers** and **gizzards** ground fine, minced **parsley** and **salt, pepper,** and **hot pepper** to taste.

Sauté in **butter** till tender; add enough fine **bread crumbs** to thicken. Whip the thickened sauce into a paste. Spread evenly on toasted medallions. Garnish with a tiny strip of **pimento.**

FORMAGGIO TONNATO

Cheese-Tuna Roll   *Piemonte*

- 1 **cup finely-chopped fresh parsley**
- 1 **pound ricotta or other cream cheese**

¼ **pound Gorgonzola cheese**
2 **tablespoons minced chives, onion, or 1 tablespoon onion juice**
1 **cup minced walnuts or pignons**
1 **seven-ounce can tuna with oil**
½ **teaspoon pepper**
¼ **teaspoon cayenne pepper**

To only 2 tablespoons of the chopped parsley add the rest of the ingredients, and whip into a thick smooth consistency. With the aid of wax paper, form the mixture into a roll (diameter of a fifty-cent piece). Spread the rest of the chopped parsley out on another piece of wax paper. Roll the form into the parsley. Place in refrigerator for at least 4 hours before using. To serve, either slice and place on toasted medallions or snack crackers, or place the decorative roll on a platter and allow each person to serve himself.

LINGUA PICCANTE

Spiced Tongue   *Lombardia*

2 **pounds tongue (veal preferred)**	1 **large onion**
3 **quarts cold water**	1 **tablespoon sweet basil**
½ **cup vinegar**	1 **tablespoon minced garlic**
2 **tablespoons salt**	¼ **cup minced fresh parsley**
1 **tablespoon sugar**	1 **teaspoon crushed origano**
2 **bay leaves**	**salt and pepper**
	¼ **cup olive oil**

1 **teaspoon wine vinegar**

Soak tongue in the cold water with vinegar, salt and sugar overnight. Drain off all the liquid but 1 pint. Add fresh water, and bring to the boiling point. Drop tongue into the boiling liquid, and add bay leaves, large onion, and sweet basil. Let simmer until tender, about 2 hours. Drain, peel, and slice. Place on platter. Sprinkle with minced garlic, parsley, origano, salt and pepper to taste. Pour a thin coat of olive oil over all, and add a dash of wine vinegar. Let marinate for at least 4 hours before serving.

MEDAGLIONI DI MOZZARELLA

Medallions of Mozzarella Cheese   *Campania*

Cut medallions (diameter of fifty-cent piece and ½ inch thick) of **mozzarella** or other cheese. Roll each piece of cheese in **flour,** well-beaten **egg,** and fine **bread crumbs;** deep-fry in **olive oil** (¼ inch oil in skillet) until golden-brown on both sides.

TARTINE VARIATE

Toasted Midget Sandwiches with Varied Fillings   *Toscana*

Make miniature **sandwiches** (crusts removed) with **fillings** selected from Burri Variati per Antipasti. Sauté the sandwiches in a small skillet, using 2 tablespoons **butter** to each 3 tablespoons of **oil,** until golden-brown on both sides.

UOVA RIPIENE

Stuffed Eggs   *Emilia*

Be sure the eggs are at room temperature *before cooking.* Place in a pan, covered by 1 inch of cold water. When boiling point is reached, reduce the heat and let them simmer. Stir them often in the beginning, so that the yolk will be centered. Simmer 20 minutes. Transfer the eggs to cold water immediately (they will peel much more easily, and the yolk will not turn black). Peel when cool. Cut each egg in half; remove yolks to a bowl.

Stuffing (Three Variations)

I.   **6 egg yolks**
    1 teaspoon prepared mustard
    1 tablespoon minced capers
    salt and pepper to taste
    1 tablespoon soft butter
    1 teaspoon olive oil

II.   6 egg yolks
      ¼ cup tuna, minced
      salt and pepper to taste
      1 tablespoon soft butter

III. 6 egg yolks
      ¼ cup chopped boiled ham
      1 tablespoon soft butter
      salt and pepper to taste

Whip the stuffing until creamy. Place in pastry tube and squeeze into the individual egg-white halves, in a rose or other design. Garnish tops with dot of pimento, chopped dill pickle, ½ anchovy, sprig of parsley, olive slice, dash of paprika, or other colorful item.

VITELLO TONNATO

Veal-Tuna Appetizer   *Piemonte*

      2–pound roast of lean veal
      2 bay leaves
      salt and pepper
      2 cups chopped fresh parsley
      6 cloves garlic, minced, or 1 cup minced onion
      1 tablespoon finely-crushed rosemary leaves
      2 six-ounce cans solid-pack tuna
      ¾ cup olive oil combined with tuna oil
      2 tablespoons wine vinegar

Boil the veal roast in as little water as possible, with bay leaves, salt and pepper added for seasoning. When meat is tender drain, saving broth, and cut into pieces about ¼ inch thick and 2 or 3 inches square. In a small crock or deep bowl place a layer of veal, chopped parsley, garlic or onion, salt and pepper to taste, dash of rosemary, olive oil, and a dash of wine vinegar; then a layer of pieces of tuna. Repeat the procedure until all is used. Pour ½ cup broth and the last of the oil over all. Let marinate in a cool place at least 4 hours before serving. Using a pie server or spatula, transfer to a large platter with garnish of olives, artichoke hearts, or whatever is desired.

CHAPTER II

MINESTRE AND MINESTRONI
Light Soups and Heavy Soups

ACQUA E SALE

Water and Salt Soup   *Lucania*

2 cups chopped onion
¼ cup olive oil
1 cup mashed tomato
   (optional)
¼ cup chopped parsley
1½ quarts water with salt and
   pepper to taste
1 egg per person served
2 slices stale bread or toast per person served

In a kettle, sauté the onions in oil till golden-brown. Add the tomatoes, parsley, salt and pepper, and let simmer ½ hour, stirring occasionally. Add the water, stir, and let cook another 10 minutes. Let soup reach a good rolling boil; carefully break the eggs (one at a time) into the broth to poach. Serve in soup bowls, over hard stale bread or toast. Top with grated **Romano cheese,** if desired.

BENEDETTA

Benediction Soup   *Campania*
Served on Easter Sunday in Naples

1 leg of lamb (meat removed from bone and diced)
1 cup minced fresh parsley
  salt and pepper

2 eggs, well beaten
½ cup grated Romano cheese
½ cup Easter Water, from the Holy Saturday blessing

Place the diced meat in a large kettle. Cover with enough cold water to reach 3 inches above the meat. Salt and pepper to taste. Bring to boiling point, reduce heat, and let simmer till tender. Add the chopped parsley, and let simmer another 10 minutes. When ready to serve stir constantly while adding the well-beaten eggs and grated cheese. Add the Easter water; stir well and serve.

BRODO ALLA ROMANA

Broth, Roman Style   *Lazio*

Choose a good-sized veal or beef knuckle, shank, or short ribs, or a disjointed capon or stewing hen. Place the **meat** in a large kettle of cold water. Bring it to the boiling point; let it boil for ½ hour. Skim off the top. Add the following seasonings and vegetables:

1 cup finely-chopped celery
2 large onions, chopped
1 cup chopped carrots
3 tomatoes, blanched and cubed; or 1 cup canned tomatoes (optional)
   salt and pepper to taste

Cover, and let simmer at least two hours—longer if possible. Strain before using.

BUSECCA

Tripe Soup   *Lombardia*

2 pounds honeycomb tripe, washed well, parboiled, and washed again
2 medium-sized onions, minced
½ cube butter and 2 tablespoons olive oil
2 quarts rich broth (chicken, beef, or veal shank)
½ cup minced celery
1 cup minced carrot
1 cup minced potato

¼ cup minced parsley
¼ cup rice
  salt and pepper

Cut the parboiled tripe into small strips, 1 inch long. Boil in water till tender; drain. In a skillet, sauté the onions in the butter and oil. When onions are delicately brown, add the tripe, and when both are golden-brown, add them to the rich broth. Add the minced vegetables, salt and pepper to taste, and rice. Cook until rice reaches the chewy stage (*al dente*). Serve topped with grated **Parmesan cheese.**

CANEDERLI IN BRODO

Tirolese Dumplings in Broth   *Alto Adige*

Prepare a rich **broth,** chicken preferred. Prepare one of the following dumplings:

I. ½ **loaf stale Italian bread diced, soaked in water, and squeezed**
   1 **cup buttermilk, milk, or water**
   2 **eggs, well beaten**
   3 **slices salami, chopped fine**
   2 **tablespoons minced parsley**
   2 **tablespoons minced onion**
     salt and pepper to taste
   4 **slices bacon, chopped fine and placed over slow flame till melted (transparent) and curds are formed**
   3 **tablespoons flour**

II. ½ **loaf stale Italian bread, diced and soaked in a little broth**
   8 **thin slices of sausage (salami or luganighe), chopped fine**
   4 **eggs, well beaten**
   1 **cup flour (more if necessary)**
   1 **tablespoon minced chives or onion**
   2 **tablespoons minced parsley**
   2 **tablespoons grated Parmesan cheese**
   ½ **teaspoon salt**

III.   2 cups bread crumbs
       ½ cup broth
       ½ pound ground calf liver
       ¼ cup minced onion
       ¼ cup minced parsley
       2 eggs
         salt and pepper to taste
       ½ cup flour

Mix all ingredients together. With a tablespoon place enough batter in a cup, rinsed with cold water, to form a dumpling the size of a golf ball. Drop the dumplings one at a time into rapidly boiling water. Cover and let boil about 6 minutes. Drain, and serve 2 or 3 in each soup bowl of broth.

CAPPELLETTI IN BRODO

Little Dough Hats in Broth   *Emilia*
         The little hats originated in Romagna, in the re-
         gion of Emilia; however, all Italy now enjoys them.

Prepare **Pasta Asciutta** (Chap. III), and roll out thin as a dime. With a glass or cooky cutter, cut dough disks 3 inches in diameter. In the center of each disk place 1 teaspoon of the following mixture:

   1½ cups ground cooked pork, veal, or chicken breast—
         chicken preferred
    ½ cup grated Parmesan cheese
    ¼ cup minced fresh parsley
    1 large egg
    1 cup ricotta
      salt and pepper to taste
    ½ cup cooked spinach, well drained, squeezed, and
         chopped
      dash of nutmeg

Fold each filled disk into a half-moon. Pinch the edges together, and roll the complete double edge back; bring the extreme points together, and press securely to form a little sombrero. Place them on a slightly floured board, and cover with a clean dish towel until partially dry. Drop them into rapidly boiling broth. Let boil until they come to the surface and are tender, 6 to 8 minutes. Serve 6 or 8 cappelletti with broth in individual soup bowls, topped with grated **Parmesan cheese** for those who desire it.

CUCIA

St. Lucy Soup　　　　　　　　　　　　　　　　*Southern regions*

> Cucia *is a dialect word meaning eyesight. Whole*
> *grains are supposed to give strength to eyes. This*
> *soup is the only food taken on December 13, the*
> *feast day of St. Lucy, the patron saint of eyes.*

Calabrian Style

**2 pounds whole-grain dried wheat (preferably not more
　　than one year old)
1 gallon water
　salt to taste**

Place in large kettle and let boil slowly 12 hours, stirring occasionally. Serve with **milk** and **sugar.**

Potenzese Style

In Potenza Cucia is not cooked as a soup, but in the form of a snack, similar to our popcorn. In a large kettle place equal portions of freshly-dried

field corn	**lentils**
chick-peas	**whole wheat**

Cover completely with cold water and let boil slowly about 8 hours, adding water as necessary and stirring occasionally, till tender. When done season with salt and pepper to taste. Serve in small bowls as a snack.

Sicilian Style

2 pounds whole-grain	**3 bay leaves**
dried wheat	**2 gallons water**
1 pound chick-peas	**1 tablespoon salt**

Place in large kettle and let boil slowly 12 hours, stirring occasionally. Serve with **honey** or **sugar.**

FRIGOLOTTI

Tirolese Egg Soup   *Alto Adige*

1 cup flour	½ teaspoon salt
1 egg	1 pint milk
	1 pint water

Beat egg and salt; add flour. Work with fork, forming into granules. Bring the milk and water to the boiling point in a saucepan. While rapidly boiling, add the frigolotti mixture and stir constantly. Tiny chunks of **Swiss cheese** may be added if desired.

MINESTRA DI FAGIOLI

Florentine Bean Soup   *Toscana*

1 pound navy beans, cooked till tender and passed
    through a sieve, with juice added *
3 cloves garlic
3 tablespoons olive oil
3 tablespoons tomato sauce
1 teaspoon crushed rosemary leaves
    salt and pepper to taste
2 cups ditali **

Sauté the garlic in oil till delicately brown; discard the garlic. Add the seasoned oil and rosemary leaves to the beans and juice. Add the tomato sauce, salt and pepper. Stir well, and let simmer 20 minutes. Add the ditali, and let cook another 15 minutes.

MINESTRINA CON FEGATINI DI POLLO

Thin Soup with Chicken Giblets   *Lombardia*

1 hen, disjointed	¼ cup chopped parsley
3 quarts cold water	½ cup fine pastina
2 stalks celery	salt to taste

Place hen in cold salt water; bring to boiling point and let cook ½ hour. Skim off top; add celery and parsley. Cover and let simmer

° See Chapter VIII, D, Fagioli Rifatti.
°° See picture page, "Varietà di Pasta."

2 or 3 hours, till done. Remove chicken, and use as desired. Strain broth. Chop giblets very fine, and add to broth. Add pastina and boil rapidly for 6 minutes, or until it is done.

MINESTRONE ALLA MILANESE

Heavy Vegetable Soup, Milanese Style   *Lombardia*

    Lombardy, in the plains region of northern Italy, is known for its wonderful vegetables. From early spring throughout the summer, minestrone is on the daily menu.

- ½ **cup minced onion**
- 2 **tablespoons minced sweet basil**
- 2 **tablespoons minced parsley**
- ¼ **cup butter**
- 2 **quarts water**
- 4 **finely-diced new potatoes**
- 2 **cups finely-diced zucchini**
- 2 **cups finely-chopped Swiss chard**
- 1 **cup chopped celery**
- ½ **pound cut green beans**
- 1 **cup shredded young Savoy cabbage**
  salt and pepper
- ½ **cup rice**

Sauté the onion, basil, and parsley in butter. When golden-brown add 2 quarts water, and let simmer ½ hour. Add the vegetables and salt to taste. When the vegetables are half cooked, add the rice and let cook until done, about 20 minutes. Add pepper to taste when ready to serve.

MINESTRONE AL PESTO

Heavy Soup with Basil Sauce   *Liguria*

Prepare **Pesto** (Chap. VI).
Prepare the following soup:

¼ **cup minced onion**	2 **cups cubed potatoes**
¼ **cup minced celery**	½ **pound lasagnette**

1 tablespoon olive oil	3 quarts water
1 cup dried beans or 1 pound fresh string beans (Italian preferred)	salt and pepper

Sauté the minced onion and celery in the olive oil. When golden-brown add the dried beans (which have soaked in water at least 4 hours) or the fresh beans, potatoes, and 3 quarts of water. Salt and pepper to taste, and let cook for 2 hours. Ten minutes before serving, add the noodles and sweet basil sauce and let cook rapidly. Serve topped with grated **Parmesan cheese.**

MINESTRONE CALABRESE

Heavy Soup, Calabrian Style   *Calabria*

Choice of 1 pound of endive, spinach, chicory, dandelion greens, Savoy cabbage, or Swiss chard
Choice of 1 pound of pork hock, spareribs, neck bones, Italian sausage, pigs' tails, or pigs' feet
1 cup chopped onion
¼ cup chopped parsley
¼ cup sweet basil, chopped
2 small chili peppers, crushed
¼ cup lard or bacon drippings
  salt and pepper to taste
2 large potatoes, peeled and cubed

Brown the onion, parsley, sweet basil, and chili peppers in the bacon drippings. Add the meat, and brown well. Add 1 quart water, salt and pepper. Let simmer till meat is almost tender. Add the potatoes and fresh chopped greens. Let cook another 20 minutes.

MINESTRONE DI NAPOLI

Heavy Vegetable Soup, Neapolitan Style   *Campania*
A favorite of Enrico Caruso, world-renowned tenor

2 quarts fresh garden vegetables (Windsor beans, peas, broccoli, endive, cauliflower, turnip greens, broken into bite-size pieces)

¼ **cup butter and 3 tablespoons olive oil**
1 **quart beef broth**
   salt and pepper to taste

Sauté all the vegetables in the butter and oil. Add the beef broth, salt and pepper and boil 15 minutes, until vegetables are cooked. Serve over Crostini (Chap. X).

MINESTRONE DI PASTA E FAGIOLI
(Dialect name, Pasta Fazula)

Heavy Soup of Macaroni and Beans   *Campania*

Wash and soak overnight (in 2 quarts water) 1 pound dried pinto or navy **beans.** Cook beans in the same water. Prepare the sauce as follows:

Sauté ½ cup chopped **salt pork,** bacon, or ham with 1 clove minced **garlic** or 2 tablespoons minced onion and a dash of **chili pepper.** Add to the beans, and let cook until tender. Just before serving, add 1 pound cooked and strained **ditalini,** and let simmer 5 minutes. Stir well, and serve topped with grated **Romano cheese, salt** and **pepper.**

MINESTRONE DI RISO E PISELLI

Heavy Soup of Rice and Peas   *Venezia*
A favorite of Pope St. Pius X

2 **cups fresh or canned peas, or dried split peas (dried**
   split peas should be soaked in water overnight)
¼ **pound minced bacon or ham**
¼ **pound minced salt pork**
1 **cup rice**
½ **cup minced onion**
¼ **cup minced celery**
   salt and pepper to taste
2 **quarts broth**

Place the peas and minced bacon or ham in a kettle with just enough boiling water to cover. In the meantime sauté the salt pork;

when well rendered, add the rice, and brown well. Add the minced onion, celery, salt and pepper (very little salt because of salt pork). When delicately brown, add the broth, stirring constantly till rice is tender. Add the peas, and stir well. Serve topped with grated **Parmesan cheese** if desired.

PAMPESTO

Cracker Soup   *Piemonte and Venezia*

Place 2 tablespoons **butter,** ¼ teaspoon **salt,** and 2 cups **cold water** in a saucepan, over a high flame. When water is boiling and butter is melted, add 1 cup **cracker crumbs.** Lower flame, and let simmer ½ hour, stirring occasionally. Serve topped with grated **Parmesan cheese.**

PANATA

Bread Soup   *Piemonte and Venezia*

Place 2 tablespoons **butter,** ¼ teaspoon **salt,** and 2 cups **cold water** in a saucepan, over a high flame. When water is boiling and butter is melted, add 4 slices of hard, stale **Italian bread.** Let simmer 45 minutes, stirring occasionally. If desired, add a well-beaten **egg** just before serving, and stir well. Top with grated **Parmesan cheese** and melted **butter.**

SCRIPPELLE AL BRODO

Rolled Pancakes in Broth   *Abruzzi*
           Traditional in Abruzzi on the Sunday before Lent

A scrippella is a large paper-thin pancake (8-inch diameter) very similar to the French crêpe Suzette. The following ingredients will provide batter for 30 pancakes:

    6 eggs   **2 cups flour**
           ½ teaspoon salt

Beat the eggs and salt thoroughly. Gradually adding the flour, beat constantly until smooth. Continue beating, and add enough *cold* water to make a thick-milky texture. In an 8-inch skillet, over a slow fire, rub a piece of fresh **pork fat** (unrendered leaf lard). Remove the fat, and with a tablespoon drop enough batter into the center of the pan to run to the edges in such a manner that you may see the bottom of the pan. Cook over low heat until a delicate brown. Pick the pancake up on edge with the thumbs and forefingers, and flip it over for another delicate brown color. When all the scrippelle are made, sprinkle each with 1 tablespoon grated **Parmesan cheese** and a dash of **cinnamon.** Roll up loosely, and place 3 side by side in an individual soup bowl. Place a second layer in the opposite direction, as if arranging a cord of wood. Pour rich **broth** over them, and serve.

If desired, the scrippelle may be made in a 12-inch frying pan. Place these large rolls in a large tureen, and cover with rich broth.

TORTELLINI IN BRODO

Little Dough Rings with Stuffing in Broth   *Emilia*

Have in readiness 2 quarts rich **chicken broth.**

Prepare **Pasta Asciutta** (Chap. III), and roll it out thin as a dime. Cut into 2½-inch squares. In center of each square place ½ teaspoon of the following mixture:

- ½ **cup ground cooked pork meat**
- ½ **cup ground cooked beef**
- ½ **cup cooked spinach, well drained, squeezed, and chopped**
- 1 **cup ricotta**
- 3 **tablespoons grated Parmesan cheese**
  salt and pepper to taste
- 1 **egg**
  pinch of nutmeg

Fold each square of dough diagonally, making a triangle. Press edges together, fold point back, twist around fingertip and pinch ends together, forming a filled ring. Place rings on large pastry board, and cover with dish towel to dry at least 2 hours before serving. Drop them into rapidly boiling chicken broth. Let it boil until they come to the surface and are tender, 5 to 8 minutes.

ZUPPA ALLA CALABRESE

Calabrian Soup   *Calabria*

> *Locally known as Tre Giorni (Three Days), be-*
> *cause it is served on the Sunday before Lent.*

- **2 pounds pork shoulder or loin (in one piece)**
- **1 pound ground veal or beef**
- **3 cups fine bread crumbs**
- **½ cup grated Parmesan or Romano cheese**
- **3 eggs**
- **2 tablespoons chopped parsley**
- **salt and pepper to taste**
- **1 cup parboiled Swiss chard, endive, or dandelion greens**

Boil the piece of pork in enough salt water to make a rich broth.
When cooked, remove and grind it. Add the ground veal or beef,
bread crumbs, grated cheese, eggs, parsley, salt, pepper, and 1 cup
of the broth. Mix well, and form into small meat balls. Drop them
into the broth. Also add the precooked greens. Let simmer ½ hour.

ZUPPA ALLA ROMANA

Roman Soup   *Lazio*

Have in readiness 3 quarts rich **chicken broth.**
Prepare meat balls:

1 pound ground veal	**2 eggs**
1 cup bread crumbs	**¼ cup chopped parsley**
salt and pepper to taste	

Mixture for final soup base:

- **3 eggs**
- **4 tablespoons grated Romano cheese**
- **juice of 1 lemon**

Form the meat mixture into walnut-size balls. Drop them into
the boiling broth, and let cook ½ hour.

In a cup, beat the eggs, lemon juice, and cheese, and mix thoroughly. A few minutes before serving, add this egg mixture to the boiling broth, stirring constantly.

ZUPPA DI CASTAGNE

Chestnut Soup   *Piemonte*

Boil 2 cups **dried chestnuts** in a saucepan, in enough water to cover, for 10 minutes. Drain, and remove skins. Drop the nuts into 2 quarts fresh boiling water, and let simmer about 2 hours. Add ½ cup **rice** and ½ teaspoon **salt.** When rice is cooked, add 2 cups **milk** and let come to the boiling point.

ZUPPA DI CAVOLO E BROSTINCIANA

Cabbage and Sparerib Soup   *Lucania*

2 **pounds lean spareribs**	2 **small chili peppers (op-**
1 **medium onion, diced**	**tional)**
1 **clove garlic, minced**	2 **heads Savoy cabbage**
salt and pepper to taste	2 **potatoes, peeled and sliced**

In a large kettle, braise the spareribs until the lard is rendered. Add the onion and garlic. When delicately brown, add salt, pepper, and chili pepper. Add the Savoy cabbage leaves, and cover with water. Add the potatoes, and cook together until the meat is tender.

ZUPPA DI CECI

Chick-Pea Soup   *Puglia*
Served on Christmas Eve

Roll 1 pound dried **chick-peas** in salt, and drop them into warm water to soak 1 hour. Drain, and place in pan with 3 quarts warm fresh water. Let cook 2½ hours. Add ½ cup **butter,** 1 cup sliced **mushrooms,** 1 **sage** leaf (or ¼ teaspoon powder), 3 or 4 **celery** leaves, 1 clove **garlic,** minced, and 1 **tomato,** blanched and diced. **Salt** and **pepper** to taste, and continue cooking another ½ hour. Serve over Crostini (Chap. X).

ZUPPA DI FAGIOLINI VERDI

Green-Bean Soup   *Liguria*

2 pounds green beans	1 sprig sweet basil
3 quarts water	½ cup minced celery
2 potatoes, peeled and cubed	1 zucchini, diced
1 tomato, blanched and cubed	2 tablespoons chopped salt pork
	1 tablespoon butter
	3 cloves garlic, chopped

Drop the washed and cut green beans into 3 quarts boiling water. Add cubed potatoes, tomato, sweet basil, celery, and diced squash. Cook until done. Then, with a mortar and pestle, pound and mash the salt pork, butter, and garlic until creamy. Sauté the mixture slowly until well liquefied and blended. Add to the soup. Stir well, and serve.

ZUPPA DI LENTICCHIE

Lentil Soup   *Campania*

Soak 1 cup **lentils** in 1 quart water overnight. Drain in the morning, and add 2 quarts cold water. Boil until tender.

In a skillet with ¼ cup **olive oil,** sauté:

1 cup chopped onion	¼ cup chopped parsley
1 clove garlic, minced	¼ cup chopped celery
salt and pepper to taste	

When all is well browned, place in kettle and add 2 cups of the lentil broth and 1 cup blanched, chopped tomatoes. Bring to the boiling point, and add the rest of the lentils and liquid. Cook together 15 minutes. Serve the soup immediately as is, or, if desired, pass it through a sieve before serving.

ZUPPA DI ORZO

Barley Soup   *Alto Adige*

1 pound smoked pork (or ham, bacon, or knuckles)
1 cup dried pinto beans

¼ **cup barley (more if desired)**
¼ **cup chopped leek or onion**
　salt and pepper to taste
¼ **cup chopped parsley**
3 **quarts water**

Place all ingredients in a large kettle. Bring to the boiling point, and let simmer ½ hour. Skim off the top, and continue simmering for 3 or 4 hours, till beans are done.

ZUPPA DI PANE E CAVOLO

Soup of Bread and Cabbage　　　　　　　　　　　　　*Piemonte*
　　A delicacy prepared in Piedmont at butchering time

2–**pound piece of lean pork**
1 **large head of Savoy cabbage**
2 **loaves stale Italian bread, sliced**
1 **cup grated Parmesan cheese**
1 **cluster garlic (4 or 5 cloves), sliced**
½ **cup butter**
　salt and pepper to taste

Boil the pork in enough water to cover. When almost done, add cabbage leaves and boil a few minutes to wilt. In a roasting pan, alternate a layer of cabbage leaves with one of stale bread slices topped with grated cheese, salt, pepper, garlic slices, dabs of butter. Repeat until all is used, ending with bread, cheese, salt, pepper, garlic slices, and dabs of butter. Pour the pork broth over all and bake in 350° oven 1½ to 2 hours, till liquid is well absorbed and top is golden-brown. Serve the pork sliced on a platter. If desired, use chicken broth and onion instead of pork broth and garlic. For a meatless broth, use ½ cup butter melted in 1 quart water, with onion for seasoning.

ZUPPA DI PASTA GRATTATA

Soup with Grated Dough　　　　　　　　　　　　　　*Abruzzi*

Have 2 quarts **chicken broth** in readiness.

Prepare a **Pasta Asciutta** (Chap. III), adding enough extra flour to form a hard ball. Grate it on a cheese grater, to form ricelike kernels. Toss the kernels into the rapidly boiling broth, and cook slowly, stirring occasionally, for about 15 minutes. In a cup, beat 2 tablespoons grated **Romano cheese** with 1 **egg**. While broth is rapidly boiling, add the egg-cheese mixture, stirring constantly, for 1 minute. Each kernel of cheese will be coated with egg, which adds a rich body to the soup.

ZUPPA DI RADICCHI DI CAMPO

Dandelion Greens in Soup   *Lucania*
A very special soup for Easter time in Potenza

- **2 quarts rich chicken broth**
- **1 pound young spring dandelions, parboiled and chopped**
- **3 eggs**
- **½ cup grated Romano cheese**
- **salt and pepper**

Add the dandelion greens to rapidly boiling broth. Beat the eggs and cheese together, and add to the still rapidly boiling soup, stirring constantly. Salt and pepper to taste.

ZUPPA DI RISO AL LATTE

Rice Soup with Milk   *Toscana*

- **¼ cup minced onion**
- **¼ cup butter**
- **3 cups milk**
- **½ cup rice**
- **2 tablespoons minced parsley**
- **pepper**
- **3 tablespoons grated Parmesan cheese**

Sauté the onions in butter until delicately brown, add the milk, and let simmer. In the meantime cook the rice in salt water till done to the chewy stage (*al dente*). Strain and add to the milk mixture. Add the parsley, pepper to taste, and the grated cheese. Stir well and serve over Crostini (Chap. X).

ZUPPA DI RISO E CAVOLO

Rice and Cabbage Soup   *Venezia*

½ cup minced onion	4 potatoes, cubed
¼ cup butter	salt and pepper to taste
1 head cabbage, shredded	½ cup rice
3 quarts water	2 tablespoons grated cheese

Sauté the onion in butter. Add the cabbage and cook a little longer. Put into a large kettle, and rinse out the frying pan to be sure to get all the seasoning. Add the water, potatoes, salt and pepper, and let cook till almost done. Add the rice, and continue cooking 20 minutes, stirring occasionally. Stir in the grated cheese and serve immediately.

ZUPPA DI SANT' ANTONIO

Soup for St. Anthony   *Venezia*
For the Feast of St. Anthony of Padua, June 13

2 quarts rich chicken broth   1 cup chopped fresh spinach

Batter

4 eggs, well beaten	½ teaspoon salt
3 tablespoons flour	½ teaspoon baking powder

Whip into a very thin, creamy batter. With a teaspoon, let little balls of batter fall drop by drop into deep hot fat. When light brown, drain on absorbent paper. Add the dough balls and spinach to the boiling chicken broth, and let cook 5 minutes. Serve topped with grated **Parmesan cheese.**

ZUPPA SANTE

Soup "To Health"   *Lazio*

1 pound fresh greens (sorrel, spinach, Swiss chard, fennel) sliced like noodles

    1 cup shredded carrot
    ½ cup butter
       salt and pepper to taste
    2 quarts rich broth (chicken preferred)
    3 cups Crostini (Chap. X)
    1 cup finely-diced scamorza cheese

Place the greens, carrots, butter, salt and pepper in a covered pan over a slow fire, and let simmer in their own juice for 15 minutes, stirring carefully if necessary. Add to the rapidly boiling broth, stirring well, but carefully. In each soup bowl place crostini and scamorza cheese. Cover with a serving of soup.

ZUPPA SPOSALIZIO

Wedding Soup   *Abruzzi*

Prepare 3 quarts strained, rich **chicken broth,** with seasoning of only salt and chopped celery.

Prepare tiny meat balls:

1 pound ground beef	2 teaspoons salt
1 pound ground veal or pork	1 scant teaspoon pepper (freshly ground, preferred)
2 eggs	3 tablespoons minced parsley
1 cup fine bread crumbs	½ cup broth

With hands, mix the meat-ball mixture thoroughly. Wet the palms of the hands and form tiny balls, the size of a marble or smaller. Brown in **lard,** drain onto absorbent paper.

Then prepare tiny dough balls:

Mix a soft noodle **dough** as in Pasta Asciutta (Chap. III). Instead of rolling it out to paper-thinness, pinch off lumps of golf-ball size, one at a time, and, with the palms of the hands roll into pencil-size strips. Cut these into pea-like chunks, and deep-fry in **lard.** Drain onto absorbent paper.

Before serving, drop the browned meat balls and dough balls into the chicken broth, and cook, not boil, ½ hour.

CHAPTER III

PASTE ASCIUTTE
Noodle-Dough Variations

Pasta asciutta (singular form) is the basic recipe from which all the noodle doughs are made. It can be found on page 37. *Paste asciutte* (plural) is the over-all name signifying all the different variations (macaroni, vermicelli, spaghetti, and the like) which may be created from *pasta* (dough). Many of the forms may, of course, be purchased ready made.

The paste asciutte in this chapter may be prepared to serve with the sauce accompanying any of the following dishes, which are found in other chapters:

Baccalà alla Marinara (Codfish, Mariner Style)
Braciola alla Calabrese (Meat Roll, Calabrian Style)
Braciola alla Siciliana (Meat Roll, Sicilian Style)
Braciola con Pelle di Maiale (Roll of Pork Skin)
Coniglio in Umido di Bergamo (Rabbit Stew, Bergamo Style)
Cuore in Umido (Heart Stew)
Golasch (Tirolese Stew)
Il Pesto (Sweet Basil Sauce)
Pollo alla Cacciatora (Chicken, Hunter Style)
Pollo in Bianco (Chicken in White)
Pollo in Umido (Chicken Stew)
Polpettine di Palombo con Salsa (Halibut Balls with Sauce)

VARIETÀ DI PASTA
(*Varieties of noodle dough*)

CAPELLINI (fine hair).

SPAGHETTINI (fine spaghetti)

SPAGHETTI (spaghetti)

RIGATONI (striped pattern)

MOSTACCIOLI (mustache)

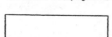
FERRETTI (little irons)

LASAGNE (very wide noodles)

FUSELLI (spindles)

FARFALLE (butterflies)

RAVIOLI
(miniature pillows with stuffing)

TORTELLINI or CAPPELLETTI
(little hats with stuffing)

CONCHIGLIE
(sea shells)

LIMONCINI
(lemon slices)

LUMACHE
(snails)

PASTINA (miniature noodle cuts)

DITALI (thimbles) STELLINE (stars) SEMINI (seeds)

Polpettine di Tonno con Salsa (Tuna Balls with Tomato Sauce)
Polpettone alla Lombarda (Meat Loaf, Lombard Style)
Pomarola (Meatless Tomato Sauce)
Ragù alla Bolognese (Tomato Sauce, Bologna Style)
Ragù con Fegato di Pollo (Tomato Sauce with Chicken Liver)
Salsa alla Marinara (Mariner's Sauce)
Salsa alle Rigaglie di Ancona (Giblet Sauce, Ancona Style)
Salsa con Polpettine (Tomato Sauce with Tiny Meat Balls)
Salsa Parmigiana (Basic Tomato Sauce)

For the cook who desires more intricate preparations, the following recipes are offered:

AGNELLOTTI

Little Pillows ("Little Lambs") with Stuffing   *Piemonte*
Similar to ravioli, but smaller

Sauce

In a Dutch oven or similar kettle, brown a disjointed **fryer**, or 1½ pounds **stew meat** (beef or veal or a combination of both), in ½ cup **shortening**. When light brown add 2 tablespoons minced **onion** and 1 clove **garlic**. Also add ¼ cup chopped **celery**, ¼ cup fresh **parsley**, 2 tablespoons **tomato paste**, 1 cup sliced **mushrooms**, 3 cups **water**, and **salt** and **pepper** to taste. Cover, and let simmer 2 hours. Discard clove of garlic.

Stuffing

1½ cups ground cooked chicken or veal roast
1 cup minced, cooked, strained spinach
1 tablespoon minced parsley
1 large egg
2 tablespoons grated Parmesan cheese
salt and pepper to taste

Dough

4 cups flour
3 eggs
1 tablespoon melted butter or olive oil
¼ cup water, if necessary

Work into a soft noodle dough, and let rest (covered with a bowl) for ½ hour. Roll out paper-thin and cut into 2-inch strips. Place ½ teaspoon filling on strips of dough at 1¼-inch intervals. Fold dough over, and, with pastry cutter or knife, cut each little filled pillow; press the three edges together with a fork. Place the pillows on a large flat surface and cover with a towel. One-half hour before serving, carefully drop the agnellotti into a large kettle of rapidly boiling salted water, and boil 8 to 9 minutes, until dough is tender. Strain, and place on platter. Cover with sauce, and top with grated **Parmesan cheese**.

CANNELLONI

Noodle-Dough Tubes with Stuffing   *Lazio*

Sauce

¼ cup minced onion	1 pound ground beef
1 cup minced celery	salt and pepper to taste
½ cup minced carrot	1 cup tomato sauce
¼ cup butter	½ cup water
½ cup dry wine	

Sauté the onion, celery, and carrot in the butter. When golden-brown add the meat, salt, and pepper; stir while meat is browning. Add the tomato sauce, water, and wine. Let simmer 1 hour.

Stuffing

1 cup cooked, strained, chopped spinach
2 eggs
1 cup grated Parmesan cheese
1½ cups ground cooked chicken, veal, or pork
salt and pepper to taste

Dough

4 eggs
4 cups flour
2 tablespoons water

Work and knead the dough into a smooth noodle texture Roll out paper-thin, and cut into 4-inch squares. Drop into a large kettle of rapidly boiling salt water, and boil 5 minutes, until almost tender. Drain on a large dish towel. Place 1 tablespoonful of stuffing on each square of parboiled dough. Roll up, and lay side by side in a large buttered casserole or roaster. Cover with sauce, salt, pepper, and grated **Parmesan cheese**. Place in 375° oven for 20 minutes.

CANNELLONI AL BURRO

Noodle-Dough Tubes with Stuffing and Butter   *Lazio*

Prepare the dough of the preceding recipe, with the following stuffing:

- **1 pound ricotta**
- **1 cup grated Parmesan cheese**
- **1 clove garlic, minced (optional)**
- **¼ cup minced parsley**
- **2 eggs**
  salt and pepper to taste

Place 1 tablespoonful of stuffing on each square of parboiled dough. Roll up, and lay side by side in a large buttered casserole or roaster. Sprinkle abundant grated Parmesan cheese over all, and cover with ½ cup melted butter. Place in 375° oven for 20 minutes.

CAPELLINI CON AGLIO, OLIO E ACCIUGHE

Fine Noodles with Garlic, Oil and Anchovies   *Southern Regions*
Served on Fridays and vigils of feasts, particularly
Ash Wednesday and Christmas Eve

**1 pound capellini or ver-   ⅓ cup olive oil
micelli   3 cloves garlic, minced
          1 small can anchovies**

Drop the noodles into rapidly boiling salt water, and stir well. Boil about 5 minutes, to the chewy stage (*al dente*). In the meantime, sauté the garlic in the oil. When delicately brown, add the anchovies. Mix, and pour over the strained, cooked, fine noodles.

CASUNSEI
(Dialect for Ravioli)

Small Noodle-Dough Pillows with Stuffing   *Lombardia*
Found only in Bergamo

Prepare **Coniglio in Umido di Bergamo** (Chap. VII, D), or one of the other dishes listed at the beginning of this chapter.

Prepare the little stuffed pillows in the same manner as **Ravioli,** but use the following stuffing:

- ½ **cup minced onion**
- ½ **pound ground veal**
- ¼ **cup butter**
- ¼ **cup minced sweet basil**
  salt and pepper to taste
- ¼ **cup ground seedless raisins**
- ¼ **cup grated Parmesan cheese**
- ¼ **cup amaretti (macaroon) crumbs or bread crumbs**
- 1 **egg**

Sauté the onions and ground veal in the butter. Remove from fire, and add the other ingredients. Mix thoroughly. Proceed as in making the ravioli. When cooked, serve with sauce and grated **Parmesan cheese.**

DITALI CON RICOTTA

Small Cuts of Macaroni with Cottage Cheese   *Umbria*

1 **pound ditali or elbow macaroni**	1 **pound ricotta** **salt and pepper**

Drop the ditali or elbow macaroni into rapidly boiling salt water, and allow to cook to the chewy stage (*al dente*). Drain, saving ½ cup of the water to add to the ricotta. With a fork, mix the cheese well into fine granules. Add salt and pepper to taste. Mix thoroughly with the cooked, strained ditali.

DITALI CON SALSA DOLCE

Small Cuts of Macaroni with Sweet Sauce *Sicilia*

- 1 cup chopped onion
- 2 cloves garlic, minced
- ¼ cup chopped sweet basil
- ¼ cup chopped parsley
- 3 tablespoons olive oil
- 1 pound ground beef
  salt and pepper to taste
- 2 small cans tomato paste diluted in twice the quantity of water
- 1 pound ditali or elbow macaroni
- 1 pound ricotta
- 3 tablespoons honey

Sauté the onion, garlic, basil, and parsley in the oil. When golden-brown, add the meat, salt, and pepper and cook till well browned. Add the tomato paste and water, and let simmer 1 hour. Drop the ditali or elbow macaroni into rapidly boiling salt water, and cook to *al dente* (chewy) texture. Stir the mashed ricotta into the sauce; add 3 tablespoons honey, and stir well. Serve over the cooked, strained ditali. Top with grated **Romano cheese.**

FARFALLE AL FORNO

Baked Noodle-Dough Butterflies *Abruzzi*

- 1 preparation of Salsa con Polpettine (Chap. VI)
- 2 pounds farfalle
- 2 cups grated Parmesan cheese
  salt and pepper

Drop the dough butterflies into a large kettle of rapidly boiling salt water, and let cook to the *al dente* (chewy) stage. Drain. In a large butter-lined casserole or roaster place alternating layers of

cooked, strained farfalle
tiny meat balls and sauce
grated Parmesan cheese
salt and pepper to taste

Pour remaining sauce over all. Sprinkle with grated cheese. Bake in 375° oven 20 minutes.

FERRETTI

Spiral Macaroni   *Lucania and Sardegna*

Prepare a main dish and sauce from the list at the beginning of this chapter.

Work 3 large **eggs** and 4 cups **flour** into a smooth, springy noodle dough. Poke the dough with fingertips; if it springs back, it is of the proper consistency. Pinch off a walnut-size piece, place on a pastry board, and use a long **knitting needle** as a rolling pin. With pressure of your fingertips, roll each piece out to the full length of the needle; then slip it off the needle, and shake into noodle length. When all are made, cover with towel till 15 minutes before serving. Drop the noodles into a large kettle of rapidly boiling salt water; cook to the chewy stage (*al dente*). Strain, and serve with **sauce,** topped with grated **Romano cheese.**

FETTUCCINE AL BURRO

Narrow Homemade Noodles in Butter   *Lazio*

> **3 eggs**
> **3 tablespoons water, or white wine**
> **4 cups flour (more if necessary)**

Work into a fine noodle dough. Roll out to thinness of dime, and cut into ¼-inch strips. Drop strips into a large kettle of rapidly boiling salted water. Cook to the *al dente* (chewy) stage. Strain, and serve with grated **Parmesan cheese** and abundant melted **butter.**

GNOCCHI DI PATATE

Potato Dumplings   *Alto Adige*
> *Even though the gnocchi (nyók ke) originated in*
> *Tirol, other regions prepare them and serve with*
> *a tomato sauce.*

4 large potatoes, boiled and mashed	**1 large egg**
	1 teaspoon salt

2 cups flour, more if necessary

Mix together, and work into a noodle dough. Form into rolls like bread sticks. Cut into 1-inch pieces. With the thumb, roll each one on a cheese grater to create stripes, and form like a sea shell. Drop them into a kettle of rapidly boiling salted water. When they come to the surface, boil 2 or 3 minutes. Strain, and serve with abundant grated **Parmesan cheese** and abundant melted **butter.**

GNOCCHI DI SEMOLINO

Cream of Wheat Dumplings   *Lazio*

1 quart milk	1 teaspoon salt
¼ cup butter	2 eggs
½ cup cream of wheat	1 cup grated Parmesan cheese

Place milk and butter in saucepan, and bring them just to boiling point. Add cream of wheat, and cook slowly for 15 minutes, stirring constantly. When cool, add salt and one egg at a time, beating thoroughly. Dampen a marble or metal table top, and spread a ⅛ inch layer of the cooked cream of wheat over the area, to set for three hours. Cut little disks with a small whisky glass, and arrange them in layers to resemble a volcano in a butter-lined casserole, with sprinklings of grated cheese to separate the layers. Place in 375° oven for 15 minutes, or until golden-brown.

LASAGNE AL FORNO

Baked Lasagne   *Abruzzi*
          Served in Abruzzi on the Feast of St. John the
          Baptist, June 24

Prepare **Salsa con Polpettine** (Chap. VI). Purchase 1 pound **lasagne** or prepare **Pasta Asciutta,** cutting the noodles 2 inches wide. Prepare the following ingredients to place between layers of noodles:

1 pound scamorza or mozzarella cheese, diced
½ pound boiled ham or Italian sausage, chopped (optional)
6 hard-boiled eggs, chopped (optional)

1 pound ricotta, crumbled
1 cup grated Parmesan or Romano cheese
salt and pepper to taste

Cook the wide noodles in a large kettle of rapidly boiling salt water till half done; drain. In a well-buttered roaster place a layer of parboiled noodles, a layer of scattered cubes of scamorza or mozzarella cheese, chopped ham or sausage, hard-boiled egg, crumbles of cottage cheese, grated cheese, salt and pepper, and a layer of tomato sauce with tiny meat balls. Repeat procedure, ending with the remaining sauce. Bake ½ hour, uncovered, in a 375° oven.

LASAGNE CON CAVOLFIORE

Wide Noodles with Cauliflower   *Sicilia*
A dish of baked lasagne, served cold

Follow the directions for **Lasagne al Forno,** but use the following ingredients between the layers:

1 large head cauliflower, parboiled and diced
1 pound ricotta, creamed with 4 well-beaten eggs and
    crumbled
1 cup grated Romano cheese
salt and pepper to taste

After baking, cool, turn out onto a platter, and slice.

LASAGNE VERDI ALLA BOLOGNESE

Green Noodles, Bologna Style   *Emilia*

6 eggs   **4 cups flour**
1 cup cooked spinach, strained and chopped

First make two sauces: **Ragù con Fegato di Pollo** and **Besciamella** (Chap. VI).

Work and knead eggs, spinach, and flour into a smooth fine dough. Roll out ⅛-inch thick, and cut into 5-inch squares, leaving 1 large piece of dough for top of casserole. Parboil the noodle squares, and drain. In a butter-lined casserole place 2 or 3 of the noodle squares, tomato sauce, white sauce, grated **Parmesan cheese.** Repeat these layers, covering the top with the large piece of noodle dough. Bake in 375° oven ½ hour. Remove, and discard the noodle covering.

MACCHERONI CON CARCIOFI

Macaroni with Artichokes *Sicilia*

Stuffing

½ **pound ground beef**
¼ **pound ground pork**
¼ **cup minced parsley**
3 **tablespoons grated Romano cheese**
3 **tablespoons currants, chopped**
3 **tablespoons pignon nuts, sliced**
 salt and pepper to taste

Mix stuffing thoroughly.

Remove stems from 6 **artichokes.** With force, pound each artichoke on the table to open the bud. Poke center with knife handle, making place for stuffing. Stuff each artichoke, and dip the top into well-beaten **egg.** Dip into a skillet with a bit of hot **oil,** to seal the stuffing. Place all prepared artichokes on a plate while preparing the following **sauce:**

Sauté 2 cups minced **onion** in 3 tablespoons **olive oil.** When golden-brown add 2 small cans **tomato sauce** and 2 cups water. Stir well; salt and pepper to taste. Simmer 45 minutes.

Set the stuffed artichokes in the sauce, and place the lid on the kettle. Cook slowly another 30 minutes, or until a leaf can be readily pulled out from an artichoke. Serve artichokes individually. Serve sauce with boiled, strained **macaroni,** topped with grated **Romano cheese.**

MACCHERONI CON PATATE
La Casseruola (The Casserole)

Macaroni and Potatoes *Puglia*

Prepare **Salsa Parmigiana** (Chap. VI).
Parboil ½ pound **macaroni,** broken into 3-inch pieces.

Peel and slice 3 large **potatoes.**

In a butter-lined casserole place a layer of parboiled, broken macaroni, a layer of sliced potatoes, salt and pepper to taste, tomato sauce, and grated **Romano cheese.** Repeat procedure until all is used. Cover with water. Bake in 375° oven 1 hour, till done.

MAGLIETTE CON FORMAGGIO

Elbow Macaroni with Swiss Cheese   *Alto Adige*

1 cup minced onion	**1 pound elbow macaroni**
¼ cup butter	**1 pound grated Swiss cheese**

Sauté the onion in butter till delicately brown. Boil the macaroni in rapidly boiling salt water till tender; strain, and add to the onion. Stir well, and add the grated Swiss cheese. Stir well, and serve.

MANICOTTI RIPIENI

Little Muffs with Stuffing   *Campania*
Also known as banana spaghetti

Dough	Filling
4 eggs	**1 pound mozzarella cheese**
1 cup water	**½ pound ricotta**
1 cup flour	**1 teaspoon salt**
1 teaspoon salt	**2 eggs**

First make **Ragù alla Bolognese** (Chap. VI) or other desired tomato sauce.

For the dough, beat eggs, water, flour, and salt well; cover, and let rest 2 or 3 hours. Fry by spoonfuls, like pancakes, in a skillet with very little lard. Stack the muffs up like Mexican tortillas.

For the filling, cut mozzarella cheese into thin slices. Cream ricotta thoroughly with salt and eggs.

Place 1 slice of mozzarella cheese and 2 tablespoons of ricotta mixture on each pancake. Roll up, and place side by side in a large butter-lined roaster. Cover with sauce, and place, uncovered, in a 375° oven for ½ hour.

PAPPARDELLE CON MOLLICA E NOCI

Homemade Noodles with Crumbs and Nuts   *Puglia*
Served on Palm Sunday in Bari

Prepare **Pasta Asciutta,** roll it out thin as a dime, and cut into noodles 1 inch wide.

Prepare **Salsa Parmigiana** (Chap. VI).

Have ready: **2 cups bread crumbs**
               2 cups pignon nuts
               3 tablespoons olive oil

Drop noodles into a large kettle of rapidly boiling salt water, and cook to the chewy stage (*al dente*). In the meantime, toast bread crumbs in a pan over a very low flame, stirring constantly; when delicately brown add nuts, and continue stirring till these are thoroughly heated. Add olive oil, and stir well. Place cooked, strained noodles in a large platter. Pour sauce and nut mixture over all. Serve immediately.

PAPPARDELLE DI SAN GIUSEPPE

Noodles for St. Joseph   *Lucania*
Served on the Feast of St. Joseph, March 19

Prepare **Pasta Asciutta,** and roll out to noodle-thinness; cut in desired widths. Many times the people of Potenza prepare Ferretti in preference to noodles.

Place in a large frying pan:

¼ **cup hot olive oil**	1½ **cups fine bread crumbs**
1 **cup chopped walnuts**	¼ **cup sugar**

Stir until delicately brown. Remove from fire, and mix well into the cooked and strained noodles or spiral macaroni.

PASTA ASCIUTTA

Noodle-Type Dough   *All Regions*

In a noodle dough, consistency depends upon the type of flour and size of eggs used. In other words, judgment must be used as to

whether or not to add water. Because salt makes the dough tough
and more difficult to roll, I suggest adding it later, to the cooking
water.

| 4 cups flour | 1 tablespoon melted butter or |
| 3 large eggs | olive oil |

Mix thoroughly, and work into a soft dough, adding more flour or
water as necessary. Place a bowl over the dough, and let rest ½ hour
(it will roll much more easily into paper-thin form). Use as desired.

PASTA CON LATTE

Macaroni with Milk   *Campania*

> *Served in Naples on the Feast of the Assumption,*
> *August 15. There is a tradition that the milk from*
> *heaven goes into the wheat kernel on this day,*
> *when the fields are blessed and the people sing*
> *the Litany of the Saints.*

Parboil ½ pound of **macaroni** (or narrow noodles or spaghetti) in
rapidly boiling salt water; strain, place in saucepan, and cover with
milk. Cook slowly, stirring until thick. Sprinkle with **sugar** and
cinnamon.

RAVIOLI

Miniature Pillows of Noodle Dough, with Stuffing   *Liguria* °

Sauce

**1 large spring chicken cut into serving pieces, or 2
pounds of beef and veal stew meat**
½ cup butter and 4 tablespoons olive oil

° For all that I know of Ligurian cooking I am deeply grateful to my friend
Rosie Cordano, a native of Genoa.

½ cup minced onion and 1 clove garlic, minced
 salt and pepper to taste
 dash of nutmeg
¼ cup chopped celery
¼ cup chopped parsley
3 tablespoons tomato paste diluted in 3 cups water and
 1 cup diced tomatoes

Brown chicken or meat in oil and butter. Add onions and garlic. When delicately brown add the other ingredients, cover, and simmer 2 hours.

Stuffing

1 cup cooked spinach, strained and chopped
2 tablespoons minced parsley
1 tablespoon minced sweet basil
1 clove garlic, minced
2 cups ground cooked chicken or veal
1 set brains (optional—parboiled, veil removed, browned
 in butter and chopped)
½ cup bread crumbs
2 eggs
2 tablespoons olive oil
½ cup grated Parmesan cheese
 salt and pepper to taste

Mix all ingredients thoroughly into a blended stuffing.

Prepare **Pasta Asciutta** and roll out thin as a dime. If a ravioli rolling pin is available, spread stuffing over *half* of the noodle dough. Completely cover this with other half of the dough. With ravioli rolling pin, press into miniature pillows. With a pastry cutter, cut them individually. If a ravioli rolling pin is not available, cut the noodle dough into circles with a biscuit cutter or medium-size glass. Place 1 teaspoonful of the stuffing on half of each disk; fold each half over, and press edges together with a fork. Place pillows on a large flat surface, and cover with a towel. One-half hour before serving, drop the ravioli carefully into a large kettle of rapidly boiling salt water, and boil 8 or 10 minutes, until tender. Strain, and place on platter or individual soup plates. Cover with sauce and grated Parmesan cheese. Serve chicken or meat from sauce, separately on a platter.

RAVIOLI DI RICOTTA

Miniature Pillows of Noodle Dough, with Cheese   *Abruzzi*

From **Pasta Asciutta** form and cut the pillows as in the recipe for Ravioli, but use the following stuffing:

1 pound ricotta	½ cup minced parsley
½ teaspoon sugar	½ cup grated Romano cheese
2 eggs	salt and pepper to taste
	butter

Serve with a sauce from one of the dishes in the list at the beginning of this chapter; or top with abundant grated Romano cheese and abundant melted butter.

SPAGHETTI CON SARDINE

Spaghetti with Sardines   *Sicilia*
         Served in Palermo on the Feast of St. Joseph,
         March 19

1 pound fresh fennel	1 eight-ounce can sardines in
2 cups chopped onion	tomato sauce
½ cup olive oil	1 pound spaghetti
4 cloves garlic, minced	1 head cauliflower
2 small cans tomato paste	1 cup fine bread crumbs

Split each sardine, remove middle bone, and break fish into 4 pieces. Cut cauliflower into small florets, parboil, and brown in ¼ cup olive oil with 2 cloves garlic, minced. Toast bread crumbs in a pan over slow fire until delicately brown, stirring constantly; then add 1 tablespoon oil and stir.

Boil fennel 5 minutes in plenty of salt water. Drain (save water to boil spaghetti), and chop fine. Sauté onion in oil; when delicately brown add the garlic. When golden-brown add the chopped fennel and tomato paste and 2 cups of the fennel water. Simmer 45 minutes. Add the sardines to the sauce. Simmer another 10 minutes. Bring the fennel water to a rapid boil, add the spaghetti, and boil it till tender. Strain, and place layers on a large platter in order as follows: cooked spaghetti, sauce, cauliflower, toasted bread crumbs, till all is arranged.

SPAGHETTI FURIOSI

Furious Spaghetti   *Campania*

Prepare **Salsa Parmigiana** (Chap. VI). When thick, add the following ingredients:

> 2 **cans tuna, sliced**
> ½ **cup black olives, pitted and chopped**
> ½ **cup green olives, pitted and chopped**
> ¼ **cup capers, drained of liquid**
> 1 **small can anchovies, cut in halves**
> 1 **teaspoon black pepper (freshly ground preferred)**
> 1 **tablespoon crushed chili pepper**

Cook another five minutes. Serve over 1 pound boiled and strained **spaghetti.**

TAGLIERINI (or TAGLIATINI) VERDI ALLA GENOVESE

Green Noodles, Genoa Style   *Liguria*

> 1 **cup cooked spinach, strained, squeezed, and chopped**
> 2 **tablespoons spinach juice**
> 2 **large eggs**
> 3 **cups flour (more if necessary)**

Work and knead into a smooth noodle dough. Roll out paper-thin, and cut into ¼-inch strips. Cook in rapidly boiling salt water till tender. Strain and serve with a **sauce** from the list at the beginning of this chapter, or with abundant grated Parmesan cheese and abundant melted butter.

TORTELLINI AL BURRO

Little Dough Rings with Stuffing and Butter   *Emilia*

Prepare **Pasta Asciutta** and roll out paper-thin. Cut into 2½-inch squares. In center of each square place ½ teaspoon of the following mixture:

> 1 **cup ground, cooked chicken breast or pork meat**
> 1 **cup cooked spinach, strained, squeezed, and chopped**
> 2 **cups ricotta**
> ½ **cup grated Parmesan cheese**
>   **salt and pepper to taste**
> 1 **egg**
>   **dash of nutmeg**

Fold each square of dough diagonally, making a triangle; pinch points together and fold back. Wrap the whole around the forefinger like a ring, and pinch the ends together. The first few rings seem complicated; however, they are mastered quickly with a little patience. Place rings on large pastry board, and cover with towel to dry at least 2 hours before serving. Drop them into rapidly boiling salt water. When they come to the surface and are tender (5 to 8 minutes), carefully remove with wire strainer. Top with abundant grated **Parmesan cheese** and abundant melted **butter.**

TORTELLINI AL RAGU E PANNA

Little Dough Rings with Sauce and Cream   *Emilia*

Prepare Ragù e Panna by first making **Ragù alla Bolognese** (Chap. VI), then boiling 1 pint rich milk, letting it cool, removing the skim, and folding it lightly into the sauce, to create a marbled effect. Serve over **Tortellini al Burro,** above.

TORTELLONI DI VIGILIA

Large Dough Rings with Meatless Filling   *Emilia*
      A Bolognese specialty for Christmas Eve, greatest
      fast day of the year

Prepare **Tortellini al Burro.** However, make the rings 1 inch larger, and stuff with the following ingredients: 3 cups **ricotta,** ½ cup chopped **parsley,** 1 clove **garlic,** minced, 1 cup grated **Parmesan cheese,** 1 **egg, salt** and **pepper** to taste.

TIMBALLO DI MACCHERONI

Timbale of Macaroni   *Abruzzi*

Also known as Pasticcio di Maccheroni (Mixture of Macaroni)

Prepare **Salsa con Polpettine** (Chap. VI).
Prepare **Besciamella** (Chap. VI).
Parboil 1 pound of **macaroni,** broken into 1½-inch pieces.

Pie Dough

1½ cups butter	1 cup sugar
3 cups flour	3 egg yolks
1 teaspoon grated lemon rind	

Roll out two-thirds of the dough, and line a deep casserole. In this place a layer of strained, parboiled macaroni, a layer of sauce, white sauce, and another layer of macaroni. Sprinkle with grated **Parmesan cheese, salt** and **pepper** to taste. Repeat until all is used. Roll out rest of dough, and cover casserole with it, sealing the edges so that the mixture is completely encased in crust. Bake in 425° oven 10 minutes. Reduce heat to 375° for another ½ hour. Turn out onto a large round platter, and let each person serve himself, cutting as a piece of pie or cake. Serve extra meat sauce to those who desire it.

VERMICELLI ALLA PASTORA

Fine Noodles for the Shepherdess   *Calabria*

1 pound vermicelli	1 cup hot water
1 pound ricotta, well creamed	3 tablespoons olive oil
	salt and pepper to taste

While the noodles cook in rapidly boiling salt water, dilute the cheese in the hot water and olive oil, stirring constantly. Strain the noodles, and mix them thoroughly with the cheese sauce.

VERMICELLI ATTERRATI

Noodles, "Dead" Style
>   *Served on All Souls' Day, November 2, and in*
>   *Naples when a neighbor visits a bereaved family*

 1 **pound vermicelli**
 1 **cup pignon nuts or chopped walnuts**
 ½ **cup butter**
 ½ **cup grated bitter chocolate**

Boil the noodles in rapidly boiling salt water; strain, and mix
thoroughly with the nuts and melted butter. Sprinkle grated bitter
chocolate over the top.

VICISGRAS

Feast-Day Noodles of Ancona   *Le Marche*
>   *There is no feast day in Ancona without Vicisgras*
>   *(dialect name for baked lasagne).*

Prepare **Salsa alle Rigaglie di Ancona** (Chap. VI).
Prepare **Pasta Asciutta,** roll out thin, and cut noodles 3 inches
wide.

Filling

 1 **pound ricotta**
 2 **eggs**
 ½ **cup minced parsley**
 ½ **cup grated Parmesan cheese**
 1 **teaspoon crushed rosemary**
   salt and pepper

Parboil the cut noodles, and drain them. In a butter-lined casserole place in turn layers of parboiled noodles, filling, grated
Parmesan cheese, and giblet sauce. Salt and pepper to taste. Repeat
the layers till all is used. Pour remaining sauce over all, and top with
grated Parmesan cheese. Bake, uncovered, in 375° oven ½ hour.

CHAPTER IV

RISOTTI
Rice Dishes

ARANCINI

Little Oranges of Rice   *Sicilia*

Boil 1 pound of **rice** in 2 quarts of salted water till it reaches the *al dente* (chewy) stage. Drain off all water, and allow to cool. Add 3 **eggs,** ½ cup melted **butter,** and 1 cup grated **Romano cheese.** Mix thoroughly.

Filling
- ½ **pound chopped veal, beef, or pork**
- ½ **pound fresh shelled peas**
- ¼ **cup minced parsley**
- ¼ **cup chopped leek or green onion**
- 3 **tablespoons olive oil**
- ½ **cup mushrooms, chopped**
- 2 **tomatoes, peeled and diced**
  salt and pepper

Fry meat, peas, parsley, and leek together in the olive oil. When brown, add the mushrooms and tomato and fry together till thick. Add salt and pepper to taste. Wet your hands with water. Fill one palm with rice, place a tablespoon of filling in center, and cover with more rice to form an orangelike ball. Pass it through well-beaten **egg white,** and deep-fry in hot oil or lard.

CROCCHETTE DI RISO

Rice Croquettes   *Calabria*

Cook 1 pound of **rice** in 2 quarts salt water until half done (15 minutes). Drain in colander for 2 hours. Place in a large bowl, and add

4 well-beaten eggs   1 cup grated Romano cheese
salt and pepper to taste

Mix thoroughly, but carefully. With wet hands roll ¼ cupful of rice mixture at a time into little croquettes. Pass them through fine **bread crumbs,** and fry in ½ inch of hot **oil** or lard, turning occasionally till golden-brown.

RISI E BISI
(*Bisi is a dialect word for* piselli.)

Rice and Peas   *Venezia*
Favorite dish of Pope St. Pius X

½ cup minced leek or onion	1 quart boiling water
¼ cup minced parsley	1 quart cooked buttered peas
¼ cup butter	salt and pepper
1 cup rice	1 cup grated Parmesan cheese

Sauté the leek or onion and parsley in the butter till golden-brown. Add the rice, and stir constantly so that it will brown evenly. Add boiling water, 1 cup at a time, stirring constantly, until all water is absorbed and rice has reached the *al dente* (chewy) stage. Add the buttered peas, and salt and pepper to taste. Stir carefully. Serve topped with grated Parmesan cheese and melted butter

RISI E PEOCI
(*Peoci is a dialect word for* pesci in conchiglia.)

Rice and Shellfish   *Venezia*

   ¼ cup chopped leek or green onion
   ½ cup butter

        1 cup rice
    1½ quarts boiling water
        salt and pepper
        2 cups precooked fish (oysters, clams, shrimp, crab)

Sauté the chopped leek or onion in the butter. When delicately brown add the rice, and stir constantly so that it will brown evenly. Add the boiling water, 1 cup at a time, stirring constantly but carefully until all the water is absorbed and the rice reaches the *al dente* (chewy) stage. Add a lump of butter, salt and pepper to taste; add the prepared shellfish and stir well, but carefully.

RISO CON COSTOLETTE DI MAIALE

Rice with Pork Chops Calabria

Prepare **Salsa Parmigiana** (Chap. VI).
Cook 1 pound **rice** in salt water till half done; drain.
Fry 6 or 8 **pork chops** till golden-brown.
Line the bottom of a large casserole or roasting pan with the tomato sauce, a layer of rice, pork chops, grated **Romano cheese, salt** and **pepper** to taste. Repeat procedure till all is used. Place, uncovered, in 375° oven for ½ hour.

RISO CON FAGIOLI

Rice with Beans Calabria

½ cup chopped onion	2 cups water
1 clove minced garlic	salt and pepper to taste
¼ cup minced parsley	2 cups cooked kidney beans or
4 tablespoons olive oil	French-cut green beans
2 small cans tomato paste	1 cup rice
½ cup grated Romano cheese	

Sauté the onion, garlic, and parsley in the oil till delicately brown. Add the tomato paste, water, salt, and pepper, and let simmer for ½ hour. Add the kidney beans or green beans; stir well, and let cook another 10 minutes. In the meantime cook the rice in salt water to the *al dente* (chewy) stage. Drain the rice, and add it to the bean sauce. Stir well, and serve topped with grated Romano cheese.

RISO CON PATATE

Rice with Potatoes   *Puglia*
            Also known as La Casseruola (The Casserole)

In a butter-lined casserole place layers of

   ½ cup uncooked rice
   round slices of raw potato
   Salsa Parmigiana (Chap. VI)
   grated Romano cheese
   salt and pepper to taste

repeating till it is filled. Place a few dabs of butter on top, cover
with water, and place lid over casserole. Bake in 375° oven 1½ hours,
till done.

RISO DI SVIZZERA

Swiss Rice   *Alto Adige*

   ½ cup minced onion   1 quart chicken or beef broth
   ¼ cup butter   salt and pepper
   1 cup rice   ½ pound grated Swiss cheese

Sauté the onion in the butter. When golden-brown add the rice,
and stir constantly so that it will brown evenly. Add the broth, 1 cup
at a time, stirring constantly, until all is absorbed and rice reaches
the *al dente* (chewy) texture. Salt and pepper to taste; add cheese,
and stir carefully. Serve immediately.

RISO IN CAPPOTTO

Rice in a Cloak   *Puglia*

   Salsa Parmigiana (Chap. VI)
   1 large head cabbage (Savoy preferred)
   1½ cups rice (half cooked and drained)
   1 pound ground pork
   ½ cup chopped onion
   ¼ cup chopped parsley
   ½ cup grated Romano cheese
   salt and pepper

Parboil the cabbage. Mix the rice, pork, onion, parsley, and grated cheese; salt and pepper thoroughly. Place a scoop on each wilted cabbage leaf, and pin together with toothpick. Place in a butter-lined casserole or Dutch oven. Pour tomato sauce over all. Cover and bake in 375° oven about an hour. Serve with cooked potatoes.

RISOTTO ALLA MILANESE

Rice, Milanese Style   *Lombardia*
    Favorite of St. Frances Cabrini, first American Saint

- ½ **cup minced onion**
- ½ **cup butter**
- 1 **cup sliced mushrooms (optional)**
- 2 **cups rice (Italian preferred)**
- 2 **quarts chicken broth**
- ¼ **teaspoon powdered saffron dissolved in ½ cup broth**
  salt and pepper to taste
- 1 **cup grated Parmesan cheese**

In large frying pan slowly brown onion in butter. When delicately brown, add mushrooms, and cook slowly about 10 minutes. Add rice, and stir constantly for 15 minutes. Add broth 1 cup at a time, stirring well, until half is used. Add saffron, salt, and pepper, and continue to cook, adding broth as needed and stirring constantly but carefully. When rice reaches the *al dente* (chewy) stage, remove from fire, and stir in a lump of butter. Serve immediately, topped with grated **Parmesan cheese.**

RISOTTO ALLA MODA

Rice à la mode   *Abruzzi*

Prepare **Salsa con Polpettine** (Chap. VI). Cook 1 pound **rice** in 2 quarts salt water till half done; drain. Add ½ cup grated **Romano cheese** and ½ teaspoon **pepper.** Add 2 well-beaten **eggs** and mix thoroughly. Place half the rice mixture in a well-buttered casserole, forming a large nest. In the nest place all the **meat balls** and a little of the **sauce.** Add ½ pound **scamorza cheese,** cubed. Cover nest completely with remaining rice. Pour sauce over all. Cover, and bake in 375° oven 1 hour.

RISOTTO ALLA PIEMONTESE

Rice, Piedmont Style   *Piemonte*

- 1 large fryer or young stewing hen, disjointed
- 2 tablespoons olive oil
- ½ cup butter
- ½ cup minced onions
- ¼ cup minced parsley
- ¼ cup minced sweet basil
- 1 cup sliced mushrooms
- 1 small can tomato sauce
- 3 cups water
- salt and pepper
- 1½ cups rice
- 1 cup grated Parmesan cheese

In a large stew kettle or Dutch oven, brown the chicken in the oil and butter. When delicately brown, add the onions, parsley, and sweet basil. When onions are golden-brown add the mushrooms, tomato sauce, and water; salt and pepper to taste. Cover, and simmer for 1 hour, or until chicken is tender. Remove it to a platter. Add the rice to the sauce, and cook slowly, stirring constantly for ½ hour, until rice is cooked to the *al dente* (chewy) stage and sauce is well absorbed. Serve topped with grated **Parmesan cheese.**

RISOTTO CON FEGATINI DI POLLO

Rice with Giblets   *Toscana*

- ½ pound chicken giblets
- ¼ cup butter
- 1 cup sliced mushrooms
- ¼ cup tomato sauce
- 1 cup water
- salt and pepper
- 1 cup rice
- 1 quart strained chicken broth
- 1 cup grated Parmesan cheese

Chop and sauté the chicken giblets in butter; add mushrooms, and when all is golden-brown add the tomato sauce and 1 cup water. Salt and pepper to taste, and simmer ½ hour. Add rice, and stir continually so that it will not stick. Add broth, a cup at a time, until rice is completely cooked. Serve topped with abundant grated **Parmesan cheese.**

RISOTTO PRIMAVERA

Springtime Rice   *Toscana*

1 cup rice	2 or 3 fresh tomatoes
2 quarts water	¼ cup butter
½ cup grated Parmesan cheese	

Boil the rice in 2 quarts rapidly boiling salt water. Two minutes before it is done, toss in the fresh tomatoes, and let them cook; remove tomatoes, and peel. Strain the rice into a large bowl. Put the blanched tomatoes through a food mill, and pour over the rice; add the butter. Stir well, and serve topped with grated **Parmesan cheese.** This sauce can be used with cooked spaghetti.

STUFATO DI RISO E VERZE

Rice and Cabbage Stew   *Lucania*

- 2 cloves garlic, minced
- 1 teaspoon crushed chili pepper
- ¼ cup olive oil
- 1 cup tomato sauce and 2 cups water
- 1 or 2 ham hocks (optional)
- 1 large head cabbage (Savoy preferred) cut into bite-size pieces
- 1 cup rice
  salt and pepper
- ½ cup grated Romano cheese

Sauté garlic and hot pepper in the oil. When golden-brown add tomato sauce, water, and ham hocks. Let stew for 45 minutes. Add cabbage and rice and another cup of water. Salt and pepper to taste. Let cook until done, stirring frequently. Remove hocks, and serve rice and cabbage topped with grated **Romano cheese.**

SUPPLI AL TELEFONO

"Telephone-wire" Croquettes   *Lazio*
        *Wiry and stringy (though most delicious)—conse-
        quently the name*

rice croquettes around moz, cheese deep fry

2 cups rice	salt and pepper
2 quarts water	1 pound mozzarella cheese,
3 eggs	cubed
1 cup grated Parmesan	2 eggs, well beaten
cheese	2 cups fine bread crumbs
	2 cups lard

Cook rice in rapidly boiling salt water to the *al dente* (chewy)
stage. Drain in colander for an hour. Place in large bowl, and add
well-beaten eggs and grated Parmesan cheese, salt and pepper to
taste. Mix thoroughly. Wetting your hands, roll ¼ cup rice with cube
of mozzarella cheese in center, and form into thumb-size croquettes. Dip each croquette into well-beaten egg, then into fine
bread crumbs, and deep-fry in hot lard.

TIMBALLO DI RISO

Rice Timbale   *Emilia*

Line an angel-food pan or equivalent with abundant **butter** and
fine **bread crumbs**.

Filling

2 tablespoons minced onions	1 cup chopped mushrooms
1½ cups rice	1½ quarts rich broth
2 quarter-cups butter	½ cup grated Parmesan
¼ cup sweetbreads (parboiled,	cheese
veil removed), chopped	salt and pepper
½ cup brains (parboiled, veil	¼ cup chopped carrots
removed), chopped	½ cup fresh green peas
½ cup veal cutlet, chopped	½ cup Marsala wine

Sauté onions and dry rice in ¼ cup butter till delicately brown.
Add broth, a cup at a time, until rice is half cooked. Add cheese,
stir, and let rest. Salt and pepper to taste. Sauté sweetbreads, brains,
veal, and mushrooms in the other ¼ cup butter. Add carrots, peas,
and wine. Stir well. Add to the cooked rice, and mix thoroughly but
carefully. Pour into the butter-crumb-lined mold. Place in 375° oven
for 40 minutes. Turn out onto a round platter, and serve.

CHAPTER V

POLENTE
Glorified Corn-Meal Dishes

Farina gialla (fah ré na jáh la—Italian yellow corn meal) is made of extra-fine corn grits; regular grits are too coarse for true Italian dishes.

The northern mountaineers of Italy, particularly the Tirolese, eat polenta (corn-meal mush) almost as daily bread, preparing it as a firm round cake. In southern regions it has a softer consistency similar to that of firm mashed potatoes.

The gravy made from the following recipes, in other chapters in the book, may be served with polenta:

Anitra in Umido (Duck Stew)
Arrosto di Vitello (Veal Roast)
Baccalà alla Marinara (Codfish, Mariner Style)
Baccalà Stufato (Codfish Stew)
Coniglio in Umido di Bergamo (Rabbit Stew, Bergamo Style)
Golasch (Tirolese Stew)
Merluzzo (Codfish in White Sauce)
Pacco di Funghi (Mushroom Gravy)
Pollo alla Cacciatora (Chicken, Hunter Style)
Pollo in Bianco (Chicken in White)
Pollo in Umido (Chicken Stew)
Polpette con Verze (Meat Balls with Savoy Cabbage)

Polpettine di Palombo con Salsa (Halibut Balls with Sauce)
Ragù di Rognoni (Kidney Stew)
Spezzatino di Vitello alla Toscana (Veal Specialty, Tuscan Style)

POLENTA

Corn-Meal Mush   *Northern Regions*

In an open kettle on a stove (or outdoors over an open fire), mix:

2 quarts boiling water   3 teaspoons salt
4 cups yellow corn meal

In a 4-quart heavy-clad kettle, bring the salted water to a rapid boil. Slowly add corn meal, stirring constantly with a long wooden *bastone* (hickory stick) or spoon. Do not let the meal lump. Reduce the heat. With the hickory stick stir the polenta, slowly but constantly, as though you were folding egg whites into waffle batter. Cook about 45 minutes, until a thin crust begins to line the pan and the polenta is well congealed. Shake the kettle to loosen the corn-meal cake at the sides before turning it out onto a large round platter. Cut the pieces with a knife as you would slice bread, or by using a string held in a firm grip. Serve with a sauce.

Preparation in Bagnomaria (double boiler):

In top of double boiler place 1 part corn meal to 2 parts water, allowing ¾ teaspoon salt to each cup meal; stir well. Cover and cook at least 1 hour, stirring occasionally till well dissolved. Turn out onto a round platter, and serve with a sauce.

Preparation in Pentola a Pressione (pressure cooker):

4 cups boiling water with 2 teaspoons salt added
3 cups Italian corn meal thoroughly mixed with 2 cups
cold water

Mix together in oil-lined pressure cooker. When it comes to a boil, stir well, and close petcock for 3 minutes. Allow to cool, open petcock, and remove lid. Stir well. Close petcock, and cook for 12 minutes at 10-pound pressure. When ready to serve, open petcock, and remove lid. Shake pan so that corn-meal cake will readily turn out onto a large round platter. Serve with a sauce.

POLENTA ALLA CALABRESE

Corn-Meal Mush, Calabrian Style *Calabria*

Prepare a **Polenta;** however, use ¾ cup less of meal, to achieve the consistency of firm mashed potatoes, and serve on a platter.

Prepare **Salsa Parmigiana** (Chap. VI), adding 2 pounds **pork stew meat,** spareribs, ham hock, or sausage; cook slowly till meat is tender, adding more tomato sauce and water as desired. Line a large deep platter with sauce and grated **Romano cheese.** On top of the sauce place individual scoops of polenta and more layers of sauce and grated cheese, till all is arranged. Serve meat separately.

POLENTA ALLA ROMANA

Corn-Meal Mush, Roman Style *Lazio*

Prepare a **Polenta;** however, use ¾ cup less corn meal to achieve the consistency of firm mashed potatoes. Serve in a large bowl.

Stew

- ¼ **cup chopped salt pork**
- 3 **cloves garlic, minced**
- ½ **cup chopped parsley**
- ¼ **cup chopped sweet basil**
- 2 **small cans tomato paste and 5 cups water**
  salt and pepper to taste
- 2 **pounds cubed pork or beef**
- 2 **cups cooked green beans**
- 1 **cup diced potatoes**
- 1 **dozen cheese balls (1 cup grated Romano cheese, ½ cup cracker crumbs, 1 egg mixed together and formed into little marblelike balls)**

Sauté salt pork, garlic, parsley, and basil until all are delicately brown. Add tomato paste, water, salt and pepper, and cubed pork or beef. Cook slowly until meat is tender. Add green beans, potatoes, and cheese balls. Cook another 10 minutes. Place in large serving bowl; each person will serve himself polenta topped with a portion of stew.

POLENTA ALLA TOSCANA

Corn-Meal Mush, Tuscan Style   *Toscana*

Prepare a **Polenta.** To serve, slice with a string, firmly gripped. Arrange slices attractively on a platter, and top with the following sauce and meat:

- ½ cup minced onion
- ¼ cup minced parsley
- 1 tablespoon crushed rosemary leaves
- 2 pounds veal stew meat, cubed
- ¼ cup butter and 3 tablespoons olive oil
- 2 cups water
- 3 tablespoons tomato sauce, for color
  salt and pepper to taste
- 1 cup pitted black olives (Italian-treated preferred)

Sauté onion, parsley, rosemary leaves, and stew meat in butter and oil. When meat is well browned, add the water, tomato sauce, salt, and pepper, and let cook slowly about an hour. Add the olives, and let cook another 10 minutes. Serve grated **Parmesan cheese** to those who desire it.

POLENTA CON FAGIOLI

Corn-Meal Mush with Butter Beans   *Abruzzi*

Prepare a **Polenta;** however, use ¾ cup less corn meal; replace part of water with juice from 1 quart cooked **butter or lima beans.** When mush is cooked to a firm mashed-potato consistency, stir in the beans. Place in a butter-lined layer pan and bake in 325° oven for 15 minutes. Serve topped with **Salsa Parmigiana** (Chap. VI) or another sauce from the list at the beginning of the chapter.

POLENTA CON KRAUTI E LUGANIGHE

Corn-Meal Mush with Sauerkraut and Sausage   *Alto Adige*

- 1 quart sauerkraut   2 cloves garlic
- 2 pounds Tirolese sausage   2 cups water
            salt and pepper to taste

Place all in a kettle. Cover, and let simmer 2 hours. Discard garlic. Prepare a **Polenta.** Cut it into serving slices with a string, firmly gripped. The sauerkraut and sausage can also be served with boiled potatoes instead of polenta.

POLENTA CON LAPIN E BAGNA

Corn-Meal Mush with Rabbit Stew   *Piemonte*
   The French word lapin *is also an Italian dialect
   word for rabbit.*

  1 **rabbit, cleaned, disjointed, and soaked in salt water
     overnight**
  1 **cup chopped onion**
  ½ **cup butter and 3 tablespoons olive oil**
  2 **tablespoons crushed rosemary leaves**
  ¼ **cup chopped parsley**
  2 **bay leaves**
  3 **cups water**
  2 **cups milk**
  2 **cloves garlic (discard when all is cooked)
     salt and pepper to taste**
  ½ **cup red dry wine or 1 tablespoon vinegar**

Flour the pieces of rabbit, and slowly brown with the onions in the butter and oil. Add all the rest of the ingredients, except the wine. Cover and let simmer for 1½ to 2 hours. Add the wine or vinegar and let simmer another 5 minutes.

Prepare a **Polenta;** cut into serving slices with a firmly-gripped string. Place rabbit and sauce in a large bowl. Each person will serve himself.

POLENTA CON LARDO

Corn-Meal Mush with Salt Pork   *Liguria*

Prepare a **Polenta;** however, before adding the corn meal to the boiling water, add 1 pound *lean* **salt pork,** diced fine, preboiled 20 minutes, and drained. Cut into serving slices with a firmly-gripped string. Serve topped with a **sauce** from the list at the beginning of the chapter.

POLENTA CON SALSA DI UOVA

Corn-Meal Mush with Egg Sauce   *Piemonte*

> 1 polenta   6 eggs, well beaten
> 1 cup butter   1 quart tomatoes
>   salt and pepper

Melt the butter in a large heavy skillet. Add the tomatoes, and simmer 15 or 20 minutes. Add the eggs, and cook another 5 minutes, stirring constantly with a wooden spoon. Salt and pepper to taste. Cut the polenta with a firmly-gripped string. Serve topped with egg sauce and grated **Parmesan cheese.**

POLENTA CON SALSICCIA E RAPE

Corn-Meal Mush with Sausage and Turnips   *Piemonte*

> 2 pounds link sausage (Italian preferred)
> 8 turnips, peeled and sliced fine
> 1 cup water

Braise sausage in a large heavy skillet till golden-brown. Pour off half the grease. Remove sausage; add turnips and braise them till delicately brown. Place sausage on turnips, and add water. Cover, and simmer 45 minutes.

Prepare a **Polenta.** Cut into serving pieces with a firmly-gripped string. Top with sausage and turnip stew.

POLENTA CON STUFATO DI VITELLO

Corn-Meal Mush with Veal Stew   *Alto Adige*

> 1 polenta
> 1 large onion, chopped
> ¼ cup chopped parsley
> 2 sprigs sweet basil, chopped
> 1 tablespoon crushed rosemary leaves
> ½ cup butter
> 2 pounds veal stew meat

salt and pepper to taste
2 cups water
1 cup sliced mushrooms (optional)
½ cup white wine, Marsala preferred

Slowly brown onion, parsley, sweet basil, and rosemary in butter. Flour meat thoroughly, and add to herbs. When delicately brown add salt, pepper, and water. Cook slowly 45 minutes or until meat is tender. Add mushrooms and cook another 10 minutes. Add wine, stir, and cook 2 more minutes. Cut the polenta with a firmly-gripped string. Serve topped with stew.

POLENTA CON TONCO DI PORI

Corn-Meal Mush with Leek Gravy   *Alto Adige*

1 polenta	1 cup fine bread crumbs
1 cup finely-chopped leek	1 pound Italian sausage— preferably luganighe or salami
½ cup butter	
salt and pepper	3 cups water

Sauté leek in butter. Add salt, pepper, and bread crumbs; stir well. Add sausage, cut into inch slices. When all is delicately brown add water, and simmer 45 minutes. Cut the polenta with a firmly-gripped string. Serve topped with gravy.

POLENTA CON VERZA

Corn-Meal Mush with Savoy Cabbage   *Liguria*

Prepare a **Polenta;** however, before adding the corn meal to the boiling water, add 1 small head of **Savoy cabbage,** shredded. Serve topped with a sauce from the list at the beginning of the chapter.

POLENTA DI FORMENTONE

Buckwheat Mush   *Alto Adige*

Prepare a Polenta, using buckwheat flour instead of corn meal. In a well buttered casserole place a 1-inch layer of **buckwheat**

polenta and a layer of grated **Parmesan cheese,** repeating till all is used. On the top, poke holes here and there with a tablespoon. Pour abundant **melted butter** over all. Bake in 325° oven for 30 minutes. Serve with slices of Swiss cheese or fried sausage.

POLENTA E ZUCCA

Corn-Meal Mush and Pumpkin   *Piemonte*

    4 cups fresh pumpkin, cooked and mashed
    1 quart milk
    2 cups Italian corn meal
    1 tablespoon salt
    ¼ cup minced onion
    ½ cup butter
    1 tablespoon crushed rosemary leaves

Mix pumpkin, milk, corn meal, and salt thoroughly. Pour into butter-lined casserole. Sauté onion in butter till delicately brown; sprinkle over surface. Also sprinkle rosemary leaves over all. Bake in 300° oven 2 hours. Serve topped with a sauce from the list at the beginning of the chapter.

POLENTA E UCELLI DI BERGAMO

Corn-Meal Mush and Birds, Bergamo Style   *Lombardia*
        *Bergamo is known for this delicacy—a polenta
        centered on a huge round platter, with a garnish
        of roasted birds.*

Clean the little **birds** (quail, squab, Cornish hen, or grouse) thoroughly, removing entrails, beak, eyes, tongue, and feet; also head if desired. Stuff each bird full of chopped **lean side pork.** Place them all in a roaster with ½ cup melted **butter,** ½ cup minced **onion, salt** and **pepper** to taste. When well browned, add 1 cup **water** and ½ cup **wine** (Marsala preferred). Cover, and roast in 300° oven 45 minutes, until birds are cooked.

Prepare a **Polenta** and turn it out onto a large platter, placing the birds around it. Serve gravy in bowl.

CHAPTER VI

SALSE
Sauces

BAGNET'
(A dialect name familiar to the Piedmontese)

Parsley Sauce   *Piemonte*

- **2 cups finely-chopped fresh parsley florets**
- **3 cloves garlic, minced**
- **¼ cup finely-chopped sweet basil**
- **2 tablespoons wine vinegar**
- **¼ cup chopped anchovies (1 small can) and oil**
  black pepper to taste
- **3 tablespoons olive oil**
- **¼ cup pimentos, chopped fine**
- **3 tablespoons capers, chopped**

Mix thoroughly and allow to marinate at least 3 hours. The sauce will keep in refrigerator at least 2 weeks. Serve as edible garnish with fish, steak, boiled meats, cold meats, or even as a spread for sandwiches or snack crackers.

BATTUTO ALLA NAPOLETANA

Beaten Sauce, Neapolitan Style   *Campania*
> *Used as spread on lining of rolls of meat for roasting, or in sauces.*

¼ **pound salt pork**
½ **cup finely-chopped fresh parsley**
4 **cloves garlic, chopped**
½ **teaspoon pepper (freshly ground, preferred)**
¼ **cup chopped onion**
¼ **cup finely-chopped sweet basil**

Place all ingredients in mortar and, with pestle, pound and blend into a butterlike paste. The blending may also be done with a knife on a chopping board.

BESCIAMELLA

White Sauce   *Northern Regions*

¼ **cup butter (unsalted pre-   ½ cup flour**
      ferred)   ½ teaspoon salt
            3 **cups hot milk or cream**

Melt butter, and stir in the flour and salt, over low flame, to smooth paste. Slowly add milk or cream, stirring constantly to make smooth creamy sauce.

IL PESTO

Sweet Basil Sauce   *Liguria*
      A sauce peculiar to Liguria, served with taglierini

3 **cloves garlic   ¼ cup olive oil**
¼ **cup minced sweet basil   2 tablespoons grated Parmesan**
1 **tablespoon butter   cheese**
            ½ **cup hot water**

With mortar and pestle, or knife on chopping board, mash and blend garlic and sweet basil into a creamy paste. Add butter, oil, and grated cheese. Mix thoroughly. Just before serving, add boiling water. Stir well, and pour over cooked strained noodles. Sprinkle more grated cheese over top, and serve immediately.

MAIONESE

Italian Mayonnaise *Northern Regions*
> Served with fish or vegetables, or with Insalata
> Bandiera (Chap. VII, A)

2 egg yolks   **juice of 1 lemon**
4 tablespoons olive oil   **½ teaspoon salt**

Whip egg yolks till creamy. Add oil, 2 drops at a time, stirring constantly with wooden spoon until all is absorbed. Add lemon juice and salt, and continue beating until light and creamy.

PACCO DI FUNGHI

Mushroom Gravy *Alto Adige*

2 cloves garlic, minced
½ cup chopped parsley
¼ cup butter
2 tablespoons olive oil
2 cups sliced mushrooms and juice
     salt and pepper
2 tablespoons flour mixed with ½ cup water (or more)

Sauté the garlic and parsley in the butter and oil. When delicately brown add the mushrooms and juice. Salt and pepper to taste. Simmer 15 minutes. Add the flour and water, stirring constantly. Cook to the consistency of medium-thin gravy. Serve with cooked rice, potatoes, noodles, or Polenta (Chap. V).

POMAROLA

Meatless Tomato Sauce *Toscana*
> (For noodle-dough preparations)

¼ cup minced onion   **1 cup tomato sauce**
2 tablespoons olive oil   **½ cup water**
¼ cup minced basil   **1 cup chopped mushrooms**
2 tablespoons minced   **(optional)**
     parsley   **salt and pepper**
¼ cup butter

Sauté onion in oil. When delicately brown add basil, parsley, tomato sauce, water, and mushrooms. Salt and pepper to taste. Simmer ½ hour. Add butter, and stir well. Serve over cooked and strained pasta, preferably spaghetti. Top with grated Parmesan cheese, as desired.

RAGU ALLA BOLOGNESE

Tomato Sauce, Bologna Style   *Emilia*
(For noodle-dough preparations)

¼ **pound minced salt pork**	¼ **cup butter**
½ **cup minced onion**	**pepper to taste**
1 **cup minced celery**	2 **cups milk**
½ **cup minced carrot**	3 **tablespoons red or white**
2 **pounds ground beef**	**wine (optional)**

1½ **cups tomato purée or sauce**

Place salt pork in a kettle (a Dutch oven is ideal). When it begins to render its own lard, add onion, celery, and carrot. When onion is golden-brown add the meat. When meat is golden-brown add butter and pepper, and stir well. Add milk, stirring to mix. Cook over low heat until liquid is partially evaporated, about 15 minutes. Add wine and tomato purée, stir, cover and let simmer 1½ hours. Serve over cooked and strained pasta.

RAGU CON FEGATO DI POLLO

Tomato Sauce with Chicken Livers   *Emilia*
(For noodle-dough preparations)

To the ingredients of the preceding recipe **(Ragù alla Bolognese),** add a pinch of **nutmeg,** 3 whole **cloves,** and ½ pound sliced **chicken livers.** Follow the directions given there, adding cloves and nutmeg with the tomatoes and simmering 1 hour. Add chicken livers for the last ½ hour of cooking.

SALSA AGRODOLCE

Sour-Sweet Sauce   *Sicilia*
    Served with boiled meat or fish, particularly fish

½ cup minced onion	2 cups diced tomatoes
¼ cup minced parsley	salt and pepper to taste
¼ cup minced basil	1 small cinnamon stick
¼ cup olive oil	1 teaspoon sugar
1 tablespoon wine vinegar	

Sauté onion, parsley, and basil in the oil. When golden-brown add the tomatoes, salt and pepper, and cinnamon stick. Cook slowly till well blended and thick. Add sugar dissolved in vinegar; stir well, and simmer 2 minutes.

SALSA ALLA MARINARA

Mariner's Sauce   *Le Marche*
    (*For noodle-dough preparations*)

3 cloves garlic, minced	2 cups diced tomatoes
¼ cup minced parsley	1 teaspoon origano
½ cup olive oil	salt and pepper to taste

Sauté garlic and parsley in oil. When garlic is delicately brown add tomatoes, origano, salt, and pepper, and simmer ½ hour or longer, till well blended and thick.

SALSA ALLE RIGAGLIE DI ANCONA

Giblet Sauce, Ancona Style   *Le Marche*
    (*For noodle-dough preparations*)

- ¼ pound minced salt pork
- 3 tablespoons minced onion
- 2 tablespoons sweet marjoram
- 2 tablespoons minced carrot
- 1 cup chopped chicken liver, gizzard, and heart
- 1 small can tomato paste diluted in 3 times the quantity of water

Pound and chop the salt pork, onion, marjoram, and carrot; sauté a few minutes till delicately brown. Add giblets. When well browned add tomato paste, and let simmer about an hour, until sauce is thick.

SALSA CON CAPPERI

Caper Sauce   *All Regions*

> ½ **cup olive oil**   ½ **cup capers, drained**
>   **juice of 1 lemon**

Mix together and serve with fish, wild game, over a salad, or even with breaded veal cutlets.

SALSA CON POLPETTINE

Tomato Sauce with Tiny Meat Balls   *Abruzzi*
           (For baked lasagne, particularly)

> ¼ **cup minced onion or 2 cloves garlic, minced**
> ¼ **cup minced parsley**
> ¼ **cup minced basil**
> 3 **tablespoons olive oil**
> 1 **quart canned or fresh chopped tomatoes (or 4 small
>   cans tomato paste and 5 cans water)**
> 1 **tablespoon chili pepper (optional)**
>   **salt and pepper to taste**

In a large kettle, sauté the onion or garlic, parsley, and basil in the oil. When delicately brown add the other ingredients, stir well, and let cook slowly while preparing the meat balls:

> 1 **pound ground beef**   1 **clove garlic, minced**
> 1 **pound ground veal or**   ¼ **cup minced parsley**
>   **pork**   ¼ **cup minced basil**
> ½ **cup minced onion**   2 **eggs**
> ½ **cup grated Romano**   2 **cups bread crumbs**
>   **cheese**   1½ **cups water or broth**
>   **salt and pepper to taste**

Mix thoroughly. Occasionally wetting the palms of hands, roll marble-size balls. Carefully drop the balls into the cooking sauce, and continue cooking slowly for at least 2 hours, stirring occasionally.

SALSA CON UVETTE E PINOLI

Raisin and Pignon-Nut Sauce   *Sicilia*
    Served with boiled chicken or broiled fish

3 teaspoons sugar	¼ cup pignon nuts
½ cup water	½ cup tomato sauce
¼ cup small seedless raisins	½ cup wine vinegar

In a saucepan add the sugar and water. When melted and yellow (not burnt), add the raisins and pignons and heat 1 minute. Add the tomato sauce and simmer 10 minutes. Serve with boiled chicken or broiled fish.

SALSA DI LIMONE

Lemon Sauce   *Toscana*
    Served with roasts or boiled meat

2 tablespoons butter	¼ teaspoon salt
2 tablespoons flour	1 tablespoon minced capers
1 cup milk	1 teaspoon minced parsley
1 well-beaten egg yolk	juice of 1 large lemon

Melt butter, add flour, and mix thoroughly. Add milk, and stir into a cream sauce. Simmer about 5 minutes, stirring constantly. Remove from fire, and add egg yolk and salt. Return to fire; add capers, parsley, and lemon juice. Stir, and simmer to desired consistency. Serve cold.

SALSA DI MENTA

Mint Sauce   *Lucania*

½ cup minced fresh mint leaves	1 clove garlic, minced
	½ cup olive oil
2 teaspoons vinegar	salt and pepper to taste

Mix together, and allow to marinate for ½ hour before using. Serve over cooked strained zucchini, cauliflower, or green beans.

SALSA DI UOVA E AGRO DI LIMONE

Egg and Lemon Sauce *Toscana*

3 egg yolks	**¼ cup minced parsley**
juice of 2 lemons	**2 cloves garlic**
2 tablespoons olive oil	

Beat egg yolks and lemon juice until thick and creamy. In a saucepan, sauté parsley and garlic in oil until garlic is delicately brown. Discard garlic. Slowly add the creamed egg and lemon mixture and cook slowly, stirring constantly with wooden spoon until thick and creamy. Serve over beef or veal.

SALSA PARMIGIANA

Basic Tomato Sauce *Emilia*
Used in many casserole dishes

- **¼ cup minced onion**
- **1 clove garlic, minced (optional)**
- **¼ cup olive oil**
- **¼ cup minced carrot**
- **1 cup minced celery**
- **¼ cup minced sweet basil**
  salt and pepper to taste
- **3 cups tomato sauce, or 2 small cans tomato paste diluted in 3 cans water**

Sauté onion and garlic (if used) in oil till golden-brown. Add carrot, celery, sweet basil, salt, and pepper, and continue cooking till vegetables are wilted. Add tomato sauce, and simmer 45 minutes, till tasty and thick. Serve over your favorite cooked pasta.

SALSA PER L'INSALATA

Salad Dressing *All Regions*

3 parts olive oil	**1 part wine vinegar**
1 clove garlic, cracked	

Mix in a jar, and shake well. Let marinate at least 3 hours before using. Salt and pepper the salad to taste before adding the desired amount of dressing.

SALSA PICCANTE

Piquant Sauce   *Campania*
Served with fish

- 3 tablespoons melted butter
- 1 tablespoon wine vinegar
- ½ teaspoon sugar
- 1 teaspoon prepared mustard
- 3 hard-boiled egg yolks, mashed
- 2 raw egg yolks, well beaten
- 1 cup tomato sauce
  salt and pepper to taste

Over a very low flame, melt the butter; add the vinegar, sugar, mustard, and the mashed boiled egg yolks. Stir well, and slowly add the 2 well-beaten raw yolks. Add the tomato sauce, salt, and pepper, and cook rapidly for 2 minutes, stirring constantly with a wooden spoon. Serve cold.

SALSA SENAPE

Mustard Sauce   *Toscana*
Served with broiled or fried fish

¼ cup butter	1 tablespoon water
2 egg yolks, well beaten	1 tablespoon dry mustard
juice of 1 lemon	salt and pepper to taste

In the top of a double boiler melt the butter. Add the well-beaten egg yolks, lemon juice, and water. Stirring constantly with a wooden spoon, let cook until well blended. Add the powdered mustard, salt, and pepper. Stir, and cook until creamy and blended.

SALSA VERDE

Green Sauce   *Northern Regions*
Served with boiled meats

    3 hard-boiled eggs, minced
    1 cup parsley florets, chopped
    ¼ cup capers, chopped
    ¼ cup olive oil
      juice of 2 lemons
      salt and pepper to taste
    1 clove garlic, minced, or 2 teaspoons minced onion

Mix thoroughly. Allow to marinate at least 1 hour before using.

SALSA VERDE PICCANTE

Piquant Green Sauce   *Campania*
Served with fish

    ½ cup parsley florets, minced
    ¼ cup chopped pignon nuts
    2 tablespoons capers, chopped
    ½ cup fine bread crumbs
    6 pitted black olives, minced
    3 tablespoons olive oil
    1 tablespoon wine vinegar or lemon juice
      salt and pepper to taste
    1 teaspoon crushed chili pepper
    1 teaspoon minced chives, onion, or garlic

Mix all ingredients thoroughly.

CHAPTER VII

PRIMI PIATTI
Main-Course Recipes

A. CARNE (*Meat*)

ABBACCHIO ALLA ROMANA

Roast Lamb, Roman Style   *Lazio*

> *The very special specialty of Rome. This roast is
> of a matured lamb, and yet not quite mutton. The
> meat is white and delicate—just matured enough
> to roast to perfection. The cut may be either the
> leg or the loin.*

Wash and dry the **roast.** Rub it all over with **salt** and **pepper.**
Brown well on all sides in **lard.** Then wash well with white dry
wine; again with a little **wine vinegar** and **water,** blended. Finally
rub the whole with a minced blend of

1 tablespoon rosemary leaves, crushed	2 chopped filets of anchovies
	2 cloves of garlic, minced

Cover roaster, and place it in 325° oven, allowing 30 minutes to
the pound.

AGNELLO CON PISELLI

Lamb Stew with Peas   *Sicilia*

½ cup chopped onion or 2   2 cups water
   cloves garlic, minced   salt and pepper to taste
2 pounds lamb stew meat   1 pound fresh peas
      ½ cup olive oil

In a large kettle (a Dutch oven is fine), brown onion or garlic
and meat in oil. When golden-brown add 2 cups water, salt, and
pepper; cover, and simmer ½ hour. Add peas, and stir well. Let cook
another 15 minutes. Thicken with a little flour. Serve with boiled
potatoes.

ANIMELLE ALLA TOSCANA

Sweetbreads, Tuscan Style   *Toscana*

Soak the **sweetbreads** in cold salt water for ½ hour. Drain them,
and remove all the skin. Cut each sweetbread into 3 pieces. Boil in
salt water 15 minutes. Drain and dry. Dip in **flour** and well-beaten
egg yolk, and deep-fry in **olive oil. Salt,** and serve.

ANIMELLE FRITTE

Sweetbreads, Fried   *Lombardia*

Parboil the **sweetbreads,** and remove the skin. Lay them on a
cloth and pat them gently, without mashing—they are very delicate.
Cut in uniform size; dip in well-beaten **egg** that has been seasoned
with **salt,** and then in fine **bread crumbs.** Fry in deep **butter** very
slowly, so that the butter will not burn.

ARISTA

Roast Pork   *Toscana*
          Specialty of Tuscany

1 roast of pork loin   2 tablespoons crushed rosemary
4 cloves garlic   8 whole cloves
     salt and pepper to taste

Sprinkle salt and pepper over top of pork loin (fat side up). Cut 4 small slits—one on each side and each end. Poke ½ tablespoon rosemary into each slit, and then insert a clove of garlic. Stud the loin with cloves. Roast uncovered in a 350° oven, allowing 25 minutes to the pound. Remove it from the oven, and slip out the garlic, cloves, and bones. Let it cool a bit before slicing.

ARROSTO ALLA MODA

Roast à la mode   *Emilia*

Obtain a 3-pound **beef roast** without bone, and tied well. Rub the whole well with **garlic** and **flour.** Sprinkle with **salt** and **pepper** to taste. Place in a Dutch oven lined with melted **butter** and **olive oil.** Around the roast place

1 diced carrot	**½ teaspoon sage**
¼ cup minced onion	**2 cloves garlic**

Cover, and place in 400° oven for 20 minutes. Turn the meat over, cover, and cook another 20 minutes. Add a cup of water, and cook 20 minutes more. Add another cup of water, and cook ½ hour longer. Remove roast. Pass gravy and vegetables through a sieve. Slice the meat, and place on a platter. Garnish with the gravy.

ARROSTO DI AGNELLO

Roast Lamb   *Emilia*

> *Lamb (prepared with a blend of herbs that varies with the region) is a particular Easter delicacy throughout Italy, as is turkey on Thanksgiving in America.*

Taking a **leg of lamb** or an entire baby lamb, rub it well with **garlic** and **rosemary** leaves, **salt,** and **pepper.** Pour ½ cup **olive oil** into the roaster. Set lamb in it and roast, uncovered, in 350° oven (turning occasionally) until practically done, allowing 30 minutes to the pound. Place tiny peeled new spring **potatoes** around meat, and continue roasting until they are tender.

ARROSTO DI CAPRETTO

Roast Baby Goat   *Southern Regions*

Easter specialty

Clean the **goat** thoroughly, and remove all fat. Rub the entire goat or the disjointed pieces well with **garlic, salt, pepper, olive oil,** and **sweet marjoram.** Cover, and place in 400° oven for ½ hour. Add 1 cup water, cover, and roast another ½ hour. If fresh sweet basil is available, a sprig of it may be used to sprinkle the roast with wine vinegar occasionally. Add small white **potatoes,** and reduce heat to 350°; continue roasting till done.

ARROSTO DI MAIALE AL LATTE

Roast Pork with Milk   *Emilia*

Rub a 4-pound tenderloin of **pork roast** with **garlic, salt, pepper,** and **rosemary.** Brown thoroughly in **butter** and **oil,** and discard grease. Cover meat completely with **milk.** Add 1 cup pitted **black olives.** Cover, and cook 3 hours over a slow fire, stirring olives occasionally. To serve, slice the meat, and arrange it attractively on a platter. Pass gravy through food mill, and serve it in a gravy boat.

ARROSTO DI MANZO ALLA MILANESE

Roast Beef, Milanese Style   *Lombardia*

Cut occasional gashes on top of **beef,** and insert in each a clove of **garlic** and a floret of **parsley.** Brown the meat well in **butter.** Crush a few **sweet basil** leaves over the top. **Salt** and **pepper** to taste. Roast, uncovered, in 350° oven, adding a little water occasionally, and allowing 30 minutes to the pound. Discard garlic before serving.

ARROSTO DI MANZO BRASATO

Braised Beef Roast *Venezia*

3–pound beef pot roast	**1 cup hot broth**
salt and pepper to taste	**½ cup minced onion**
¼ cup butter	**½ cup minced carrot**
1 tablespoon flour	**½ cup minced celery**
½ cup white wine	**4 whole cloves**

Rub the meat well with salt and pepper, and brown both sides in butter. Remove from pan. To the juice add the flour, wine, and broth. While this simmers, add minced vegetables and cloves. Place roast back in the pan; cover it, and cook slowly until tender. Pass gravy and vegetables through a sieve. Serve meat in thin slices topped with gravy.

ARROSTO DI PORCHETTINO

Roast Suckling Pig *Sardegna*
Feast specialty, roasted on a spit

1 suckling pig	**1 teaspoon powdered sage,**
1 cup minced onion	**or 2 fresh leaves**
½ cup olive oil	**salt and pepper to taste**
3 cups bread crumbs	**3 hard-boiled eggs, chopped**
1 teaspoon rosemary	**1½ cups milk**

Wash the pig thoroughly inside and out.

Brown onion in oil. Add bread crumbs, rosemary, sage, salt, and pepper, and mix thoroughly. When crumbs are golden-brown, remove from fire; add chopped eggs and milk, and mix thoroughly. Stuff the pig, and sew up opening.

Prepare a garnish sauce of ½ cup **olive oil** mixed with 1 teaspoon **rosemary** leaves, 1 teaspoon **salt,** and ½ teaspoon **pepper,** and rub the stuffed pig well with it. Truss the forelegs forward. Truss the hind feet forward and under the body. Place an **apple** in the mouth. Set in open roaster in 350° oven, basting occasionally. Allow 25 minutes to the pound.

ARROSTO DI ROGNONE DI VITELLO

Roast Veal and Kidney   *Lombardia*

This roast is one complete **veal kidney** and its surrounding **meat.**
Cut two slits, one at each end. Into each slit insert ½ teaspoon **salt,**
¼ teaspoon **pepper,** and a clove of **garlic.** Sprinkle the whole with
salt and pepper to taste. Scatter ½ cup chopped **parsley,** 1 teaspoon
crushed **rosemary,** and 1 teaspoon crushed **origano** over top. Cover,
and roast in 325° oven, allowing 25 minutes per pound. When meat
is well seared (½ hour), add ½ cup water. When just about cooked,
remove lid and let it brown well. Slice the kidney so that each person
may have a serving along with the chop.

ARROSTO DI VITELLO

Veal Roast   *Venezia*

3–pound veal roast	½ cup white wine
salt and pepper	1 tablespoon flour
½ cup butter	1 cup sliced mushrooms
½ cup minced onion	1 tablespoon rosemary leaves

Salt and pepper meat to taste. Sear it on both sides in butter till
golden-brown. Remove it from the pan. Brown onion, add wine and
flour; stir well, and add mushrooms and rosemary. Set the roast
back in the pan. Cover in 350° oven, and allow 25 minutes to the
pound. Serve sauce with polenta or mashed potatoes.

ARROSTO DI VITELLO CON TASCA

Veal Roast with Pocket   *Lazio*

        1 good-sized veal roast with pocket
        3 cups bread crumbs, and enough water to dampen them
        1 dozen roasted or boiled chestnuts, chopped *
        1 cup chopped celery

    * See Castagne Arrostite, Castagne Imbiancate, Chapter IX.

½ **cup chopped parsley**
1 **teaspoon rosemary leaves**
2 **eggs**
½ **cup chopped onions (browned in butter)**
2 **tablespoons grated Romano cheese**
   salt and pepper to taste

Soak bread crumbs in water for a few minutes; squeeze and place in a bowl. Add the seasonings, and mix thoroughly. Stuff into the pocket of the veal, and set it with twine. Brown the meat well in olive oil. Add finely-crushed rosemary leaves and ½ cup water. Cover and roast in 325° oven, allowing 30 minutes to the pound. When almost done, place potatoes around it and continue roasting till they are tender.

ARROSTO MORTO

Marinated ("Dead") Roast   *Toscana*

"Dead Roast," whatever the kind of meat, is a roast that has been rubbed well with herbs and marinated overnight before cooking.

For veal, lamb, or pork, use salt, pepper, garlic, rosemary leaves, and olive oil.

For beef, use salt, pepper, garlic, and sweet basil.

Wild meat is to be stripped of all fat and soaked in salt water at least 3 hours, then drained, washed, and dried. Brush it then with red dry wine, rub it with garlic, oil, salt, pepper, rosemary leaves (¼ cup to a 3-pound roast), and let it marinate overnight.

Place any one of these roasts in a pan lined with olive oil. Bake covered in 350° oven 25 minutes per pound, except the wild meat, which usually needs to cook a bit longer.

ARROTOLATO DI VITELLO

Roll of Veal   *Toscana*

6 **thin slices prosciutto or boiled ham**
1 **large round steak of veal, ½ inch thick**
   salt and pepper to taste

½ teaspoon powdered sage or 1 teaspoon chopped fresh
    leaves
¼ cup chopped parsley
4 hard-boiled eggs, peeled

Lay the ham slices over steak. Sprinkle salt, pepper, sage, and
parsley over entire area. Place eggs across center of steak. Roll up,
and tie well with twine. Place roll in a roaster lined with ½ cup olive
oil and ¼ cup melted butter, and surround it with peeled medium-
sized potatoes. Cover, and bake in 350° oven approximately 45 minutes. To serve, slice and arrange attractively on platter, garnished
with the roasted potatoes and florets of parsley.

AVVOLTO

Entwined Roll   *Campania*
    Served on Ascension Thursday, forty days after Easter

¼ pound baby lamb casings, split open and cleaned well
    (soak and wash in salt water)
1 lamb kidney in ¼-inch slices
1 lamb liver in ¼-inch slices

Filling

¼ pound salt pork, chopped
½ cup chopped parsley
4 cloves chopped garlic
½ teaspoon black pepper
¼ cup chopped onion
¼ cup chopped sweet basil

Pound all ingredients for filling in a mortar, and blend into a
butterlike paste. Spread some of the paste between slices of kidney
and liver, making a sandwich, and wrap casings around this four
times; repeat until you have a roll of four sandwiches. Place this
with similar rolls in a casserole well greased with olive oil. Cover,
and roast in 325° oven about an hour. To serve, slice as meat loaf.

BISTECCA AI FERRI

Broiled Steak   *Campania*

Rub a **steak** 1 inch thick with **salt** and **pepper** to taste. Broil one side, and turn over. Then baste often with a **sauce** composed of

½ **cup olive oil**	¼ **cup chopped parsley**
¼ **cup wine vinegar**	¼ **cup chopped sweet basil**

Serve immediately.

BISTECCA ALLA FIORENTINA

Broiled T-Bone Steak   *Toscana*

Rub the **steak** with **olive oil, salt,** and **pepper.** Broil to desired consistency (preferably outdoors over charcoal). Place on serving plate. To the sizzling steak, add immediately 1 tablespoon **butter.** Serve at once, garnished with a **lemon slice.** For a garnish of mushrooms, slice these and sauté them in butter (adding 2 cloves garlic which are removed when light brown). Serve them around the hot steak.

BISTECCA CON PATATE

Beefsteak with Potatoes   *Lucania*

Place **beefsteak** in a well-oiled casserole. Sprinkle abundantly with **salt, pepper,** grated **Romano cheese,** and add a bit of chopped **onion** to the surface. Then cover it with a layer of medium-sized **potatoes.** Sprinkle more salt, pepper, grated cheese, and some chopped **parsley** florets over potatoes. Dot with a bit of **lard.** Bake, uncovered, in a 375° oven. When gravy begins to form, add ½ cup water, and baste occasionally. Bake a medium cut of steak 45 minutes. Swiss cut needs a few minutes more.

BOCCONE DEL VESCOVO

Bishop's Morsel   *Piemonte*

> 6 choice veal chops   1½ cups fine bread crumbs
>   salt and pepper   2 eggs, well beaten
>   ½ cup butter

With a boning knife, slide the meat from the rib joint of each
veal chop, and shape it into a round medallion toward the lower
end. Salt and pepper to taste. Dip into well-beaten egg, then into
finely-ground bread crumbs. Sauté the chops in butter, without
letting the butter burn. Serve each chop with a paper frill on the
end, so that it may be held neatly in the fingers for eating.

BOCCONE DEL CARDINALE

Cardinal's Morsel   *Abruzzi*

> 6 choice lamb chops   salt and pepper
>   ½ cup olive oil

Use a boning knife to slide the meat of each chop from the rib
joint and form a small medallion of meat with a bone handle that
the fingers can hold for eating. Fry in oil till golden-brown. Salt and
pepper to taste. Serve with a garnish of lemon.

BRACIOLA CON PELLE DI MAIALE

Roll of Pork Rind   *Lucania*

Wash and clean thoroughly 1 large **pork rind** (about 10 by 12
inches). Scrape off the excess fat. Over entire surface sprinkle

> 1 cup bread crumbs
> ½ cup grated Romano cheese
> ½ cup chopped parsley
>   salt and pepper to taste
> ¼ cup dots of chopped salt pork
> 2 tablespoons raisins
> 2 eggs, beaten, poured over all

Roll up the rind and tie it with twine. Brown in a little lard or oil. Add 1 pint of **tomato sauce,** and stew at least an hour till tender. Serve sauce over cooked pasta. Slice the rolled pork rind and serve on a platter.

BRACIOLA ALLA CALABRESE

Meat Roll, Calabrian Style   *Calabria*

Spread the following mixture over a 3-pound slice of **round steak** of veal or beef:

- ¼ **pound salt pork, chopped very fine**
- ½ **cup finely chopped parsley**
- 2 **cloves garlic, minced**
- 1 **cup fine bread crumbs**
- ½ **cup grated Romano cheese**
- 3 **hard-boiled eggs, crumbled**
- ¼ **cup raisins**
  salt and pepper to taste
- ½ **cup chopped pignon nuts or walnuts**

Roll it up, and tie with string. In a Dutch oven, with ½ cup **olive oil,** brown the meat roll, and reduce the heat. Add 1 large can **tomatoes,** 1 pint **water,** and 2 small cans **tomato paste.** Cover, and simmer at least 2 hours, until meat is tender and sauce is thick. Serve meat in slices on a platter, and sauce over cooked spaghetti, topped with grated Romano cheese.

BRACIOLA ALLA SICILIANA

Meat Roll, Sicilian Style   *Sicilia*

Spread the following mixture over a 3-pound piece of **round steak** of veal or beef:

- 2 **cups chopped livers and gizzards**
- ½ **cup olive oil**
- 4 **hard-boiled eggs, sliced**
- ½ **cup raisins**

¼ **pound salami, chopped**
2 **cups bread crumbs**
salt and pepper to taste
4 **cloves garlic, chopped**
¼ **cup chopped sweet basil**
½ **cup chopped parsley**
1 **tablespoon crushed chili pepper (optional)**

Roll meat up carefully, and tie with string. Place it in a large kettle with the olive oil, and brown well. Add 1 quart **tomatoes,** 1 small can **tomato paste,** and 2 cups **water.** Cover and stew slowly for 3 hours, stirring occasionally. Serve sauce over cooked pasta, topped with grated Romano cheese.

BRACIOLINE RIPIENE

Stuffed Veal Cutlets   *Emilia*

12 **thin veal cutlets**
6 **slices Gruyère cheese (or equivalent)**
6 **slices prosciutto or boiled ham**

Prepare sandwiches of 2 cutlets with 1 slice each of ham and cheese in center, and place them in a casserole lined with abundant butter. Cover, and bake in 375° oven 20 minutes. Turn sandwiches over, cover, and continue baking 20 minutes.

BROSTINCIANA

Broiled Spareribs   *Toscana*

Rub **spareribs** with **garlic, salt,** and **pepper,** and place them 5 inches below broiling unit for 15 minutes. Turn them over, and continue broiling another 15 minutes. If possible, broil outdoors over charcoal.

CARNE LESSA

Boiled Roast   *Lombardia*
             Very special main-course delicacy

For this boiled dinner, cut an occasional gash on top of a choice **roast** (beef or veal), and insert a clove of **garlic** and a floret of

parsley in each gash. Cover with boiling water, and boil until tender. For seasoning, add a bit of **onion, parsley, celery, salt,** and **pepper.** Do not cook the roast too long. It will become tender quickly and will slice like butter. For a superb broth, boil a stewing hen along with the beef roast. Let the broth determine your choice of minestra (see Chapter II). Slice the meat, and arrange it attractively on a platter. Garnish it with a **sauce**—perhaps Salsa Verde or Salsa con Uvette e Pinoli (Chap. VI).

CERVELLO FRITTO

Fried Brains   *Puglia*

Parboil and peel the veil from the **brains** (lamb or veal), and place them in a flat bowl of **olive oil, lemon juice,** and minced **parsley** to marinate for 15 minutes. Dip in **flour,** then in well-beaten **egg.** Fry in olive oil. **Salt** to taste.

CERVELLO FRITTO MILANESE

Fried Brains, Milanese Style   *Lombardia*

Parboil and peel the veil from the **brains,** and drop them into boiling salted water for a few minutes to sear. Remove and let cool. Cut them into small pieces. Dip these in well-beaten **eggs,** then in fine **bread crumbs,** and fry in **butter.**

COSTOLA

Sparerib Stew   *Piemonte*

2 pounds spareribs	2 cups water
1 cup diced carrots	salt and pepper to taste
1 cup diced celery	1 cabbage head (Savoy preferred)
2 cloves garlic	

In a Dutch oven, braise the spareribs until some fat is rendered. Add the carrots, celery, and garlic, and sauté 5 minutes. Remove the garlic, and add the water, salt and pepper. Cover, and cook slowly 1 hour. Add the broken cabbage leaves, and continue cooking 10 minutes. Do not let the cabbage overcook. Serve with boiled potatoes.

COSTOLE CON FAGIOLINI

Spareribs with String Beans   *Sicilia*

2 pounds cut spareribs	**1 pound green beans**
½ cup chopped onion	**1 cup tomato paste**
salt and pepper	**2 cups water**

In a Dutch oven or large stewing kettle, braise spareribs until some fat is rendered. Add onion; when golden-brown add beans, tomato sauce and water, salt, and pepper. Cover, and cook slowly 1 hour. Serve with boiled potatoes.

COSTOLETTE DI VITELLO ALLA MILANESE

Veal Cutlets, Milanese Style   *Lombardia*

Pound each **cutlet** with a mallet to tenderize. Dip it into well-beaten **egg** (seasoned with **salt** and **pepper**) and then into fine **bread crumbs.** Pat cutlets firmly to be sure crumbs will stay on the meat. Fry in abundant **butter,** over a medium-low flame until golden-brown. Serve with garnish of **lemon** and, if desired, **Salsa con Capperi** (Chap. VI).

COSTOLETTE DI VITELLO ALLA PARMIGIANA

Veal Cutlets with Parmesan Cheese   *Emilia*

> 1 **preparation of Basic Tomato Sauce (page 68)**
> 6 **choice veal cutlets, ⅜ inch thick**
> 1 **cup flour**
> 2 **eggs, well beaten and seasoned with salt and pepper**
> 2 **cups fine bread crumbs**
> ¾ **cup olive oil**
> 1 **cup grated Parmesan cheese**

Dip each cutlet into flour, then into egg and bread crumbs, patting firmly to be sure coatings will adhere. Pan-fry the cutlets in

olive oil over a medium flame until golden-brown. Place side by
side on a broiling sheet or in a shallow casserole. Cover each cutlet
with ⅛ inch of tomato sauce, and sprinkle grated cheese over all.
Place the cutlets 4 inches under the broiler for 2 minutes, or until
the cheese melts. Serve immediately with Contorno (Chap. VIII).

COSTOLETTE DI VITELLO CON RENE

Veal Cutlet with Kidney Attached   *Calabria*

> **2 eggs**   **¼ cup minced parsley**
> **2 cloves garlic, minced**   **¼ cup grated Romano cheese**
> **¼ cup minced sweet basil**   **salt and pepper to taste**
>   **6 veal loin chops with slice of kidney attached**

Beat eggs until well blended, then add other ingredients and mix
thoroughly into a batter. Place chops in batter, and let them marinate 2 hours. Then dip them one at a time in a cup of flour, and
pan-fry them in olive oil. Garnish each cutlet with a lemon slice.

CUORE DI VITELLO FRITTO

Veal Heart, Fried   *Lombardia*

Cut the **veal heart** into serving slices, ¼ inch thick. Sauté slowly
in abundant **butter,** without letting the butter burn. **Salt** to taste,
and serve with garnish of **lemon.**

CUORE IN UMIDO

Heart Stew   *Abruzzi*

Cut the **heart** down the center, and lay it open, washing it well in
salt water. Over center area distribute

> **1 teaspoon black pepper**   **¼ cup minced parsley**
> **½ cup salt pork, minced**   **2 cloves garlic, minced**
>   **¼ cup grated Romano cheese**

Roll it up, and tie with string. Brown it well in ¼ cup **oil** to which
¼ cup chopped **onion** has been added. Add 1 large can strained

tomatoes. Cover, and simmer till tender, 1½ to 2 hours. Slice the meat, and serve it on a platter. Serve the sauce over cooked spaghetti or other pasta.

FEGATO FRITTO ALLA BOLOGNESE

Fried Liver, Bologna Style   *Emilia*

On each slice of **liver** sprinkle finely-chopped **onion, parsley, salt** and **pepper,** and a dash of **sage** and **lemon juice.** Pat each slice well, and place it on an oiled paper to marinate ½ hour. Dip each successively into **flour,** well-beaten **eggs,** and fine **bread crumbs.** Sauté all slices carefully in **butter** until golden-brown on both sides. Garnish with parsley and lemon.

FEGATO FRITTO D'ANCONA

Fried Liver, Ancona Style   *Le Marche*

1½ **pounds thinly-sliced liver**	2 **cloves garlic, minced**
½ **cup olive oil**	4 **fresh tomatoes, peeled and quartered**
1 **teaspoon sweet basil**	**salt and pepper**

Place the liver cutlets evenly in a well-oiled frying pan. Sprinkle the sweet basil and garlic over all, and toss the tomato on top. Salt and pepper to taste. Sauté over medium heat, carefully turning when necessary. Cook about 25 minutes, or until tender and well blended.

FILETTO AL SUGO SIGNORE

Tenderloin of Beef with "Gentleman Sauce"   *Toscana*

2–**pound roast of tenderloin**	¼ **cup minced onion**
salt and pepper to taste	¼ **cup olive oil**
	3 **tablespoons wine vinegar**
2 **cups cream or milk**	

Rub roast well on all sides with salt and pepper. In a small roaster, sauté the minced onion in the oil. Brown roast well on all sides. Add vinegar, and cook a few minutes to let vinegar evaporate. Add the cream or milk, cover, and place in 350° oven for 1 hour. Serve in 1-inch slices topped with sauce.

FRITTO MISTO DI CARNE

Fried Mixed Meats   *Lazio*

> *Each region boasts of its own particular Fritto Misto. See also section B (Fish) and Chapter VIII, section D (Vegetables).*

Choice of Meats	Batter
brains, parboiled, veil removed	2 tablepsoons olive oil
sweetbreads, parboiled and veil removed	2 tablespoons flour
calf or chicken livers	3 eggs, well beaten
lamb cutlets	½ teaspoon crushed rosemary leaves
breast of chicken	salt and pepper to taste
veal cutlets	
pork tenderloin	

Cut the chosen meat into 1-inch pieces. Whip the olive oil, flour, and seasoning into a smooth, creamy batter. Dip each little piece of meat into the batter, and deep-fry all in olive oil. Drain them, and arrange attractively on a platter. Garnish with lemon slices and parsley florets.

GOLASCH

(The Hungarian word gulyáshús, or gulyás, has been transmuted through the German Gulasch into the Tirolese dialect.)

Tirolese Stew   *Alto Adige*

1 cup diced onion	3 tablespoons flour
1 teaspoon paprika	2 pounds pork and beef stew meat (no bone)
¼ cup butter or bacon drippings	4 cups beef or chicken broth or 2 cups water
salt and pepper to taste	

Brown onion and paprika in butter or bacon drippings. Add salt, pepper, and flour, and stir. Add meat, and brown well, taking care not to burn the onions. Add the broth or water, and cook slowly until meat is tender. Serve with polenta, potatoes, or cooked rigatoni.

OSSO BUCO ALLA MILANESE

Veal Shanks, Milanese Style   *Lombardia*

½ **cup butter**	¼ **cup chopped onion**
4 **veal shanks (cut in thirds,**	¼ **cup chopped celery**
with marrow in center	¼ **cup chopped carrot**
of each round-bone	¼ **cup minced parsley**
piece)	2 **tablespoons tomato paste**
1 **cup flour**	1 **cup water**
salt and pepper to taste	

In a large casserole or Dutch oven, melt butter. Dip each piece of meat in flour, and slowly brown in the butter. Push all the pieces to one side of pan, and sauté vegetables in it. Add tomato paste and water, salt, and pepper, and stir all together. Cover, and simmer 1 hour or until tender.

POLPETTE ALLA TOSCANA

Meat Balls, Tuscan Style   *Toscana*

2 **pounds ground beef**	½ **cup chopped prosciutto or**
½ **teaspoon nutmeg**	**boiled ham**
¼ **cup minced parsley**	1 **egg**
salt and pepper to taste	¼ **cup grated Parmesan cheese**

Mix thoroughly, and form into balls of the size and shape of eggs. Flatten a little, roll in fine bread crumbs, and pan-fry in olive oil.

POLPETTE ALLA ROMANA

Meat Balls, Roman Style   *Lazio*

2–**pound beef roast**	1 **cup chopped carrot**
1 **cup chopped celery**	1 **cup blanched diced tomatoes**
1 **cup chopped onion**	**salt and pepper to taste**
2 quarts water	

Bring the water to a rapid boil in a large kettle. Place the other ingredients in it, and cook until meat is tender. Save the broth as a base for soup. Grind the meat, and mix it thoroughly with

1 cup chopped parsley	2 tablespoons grated Romano
2 cloves garlic, minced	cheese
¼ cup minced onion	2 eggs
1 cup broth	1 cup bread crumbs
salt and pepper to taste	

Form into long rolls, like croquettes. Dip into well-beaten eggs and then into fine bread crumbs. Deep-fry in olive oil.

POLPETTE ALLA SICILIANA

Meat Balls, Sicilian Style   *Sicilia*

2 pounds ground beef	1 cup pignon nuts
1 cup chopped Italian	3 slices bread soaked in a
sausage	little milk
½ cup grated Romano	1 egg
cheese	½ cup seedless raisins
salt and pepper to taste	

Mix thoroughly, and form balls of the size and shape of eggs. Flatten a little, and pan-fry in oil or lard. Top with Salsa di Uova e Agro di Limone (Chap. VI).

POLPETTE CON SPAGHETTI

Meat Balls and Spaghetti   *Lucania*

> *Many Italian émigrés say that in Italy one never finds meat balls cooked in a sauce and served with spaghetti. However, old-timers from Lucania, like my husband's grandparents, made them in Italy. "Gramma" LaSasso always used homemade spaghetti.*

1½ pounds ground beef
1½ pounds ground pork

    2 eggs
    5 slices hard bread, soaked in water and squeezed
    ½ cup chopped parsley
    1 clove garlic, minced
    1 teaspoon crushed basil
    ½ cup grated Romano cheese
       salt and pepper to taste

Mix thoroughly and form into balls the size of a golf ball. Brown well in just enough olive oil or lard to cover the bottom of the kettle. Remove the drippings and add

1 clove garlic (optional)	1 pint mashed tomatoes
½ cup minced onion	1 teaspoon crushed chili pepper
½ cup minced parsley	(optional)
2 small cans tomato paste	2 cups water or broth
3 cups water	salt and pepper to taste

Let the meat balls cook slowly, at least 2 hours, until they are tender and the sauce is medium-thick. Fifteen minutes before eating, cook the **spaghetti**. Strain it, and put it on a deep platter. Pour the sauce and sprinkle the grated cheese over all, with extra sauce in a gravy boat for those who desire it. Serve the meat balls separately.

POLPETTE CON VERZE

Meat Balls with Savoy Cabbage   *Alto Adige*

    ¼ cup minced onion
    ½ cup butter
    1 teaspoon crushed rosemary
    ¼ cup chopped parsley
       salt and pepper to taste
    ¼ teaspoon allspice
    1 pound ground veal or beef
    1½ pounds ground pork
    1 cup broken dry bread, soaked in 1 cup broth or water

1 head Savoy cabbage, parboiled
¼ teaspoon cinnamon

Sauté onion in half the butter. When it is delicately brown, add rosemary, parsley, salt, pepper, allspice, and cinnamon, and add the whole to the ground meat and soaked bread. Mix thoroughly and form balls the size and shape of eggs. Wrap each one in a wilted cabbage leaf, and truss it with a toothpick. Place balls in a casserole lined with the other half of the butter (melted). Add ½ cup water, cover, and let cook slowly about an hour. Serve with boiled potatoes or polenta.

POLPETTE DI TRIPPA

Tripe Patties   *Toscana*

4 cups boiled, ground tripe	1 egg
	½ cup grated Parmesan cheese
1 cup bread crumbs	½ teaspoon powdered sage
salt and pepper to taste	

Mix thoroughly, and form into small patties like hamburgers. Dip these in fine bread crumbs, and pan-fry in olive oil.

POLPETTONE ALLA FIORENTINA

Meat Loaf, Florentine Style   *Toscana*

3 pounds ground veal and pork	1 egg
	2 cups bread crumbs
½ teaspoon nutmeg	1 teaspoon powdered sage or
salt and pepper to taste	1 tablespoon fresh minced
¼ cup minced parsley	sage
1 clove garlic, minced	2 cups water

Mix thoroughly, and form into a huge meat loaf. With a spatula, place loaf in a large kettle of boiling salt water and cook 2 hours. Serve hot with vegetables or cold with sandwiches. The broth may be used as the base for a soup.

POLPETTONE ALLA LOMBARDA

Meat Loaf, Lombard Style   *Lombardia*

2 pounds ground beef	2 cups bread crumbs
½ pound ground pork	1 clove garlic, minced
½ pound ground veal	¼ cup minced onion
1 teaspoon minced basil	¼ cup minced parsley
1 tablespoon salt	1 teaspoon crushed rosemary
½ cup grated Parmesan cheese	1 teaspoon pepper
	3 eggs
2 cups water	

Mix all thoroughly (the more the mixing and kneading, the better seasoned and smoother the meat loaf). Form the mixture into a large loaf, and place it in a butter-lined roaster in a 425° oven for ½ hour, turning occasionally with a spatula so that it will brown evenly. Add 1 cup water, cover, and reduce heat to 350°. Check occasionally, adding broth or water if necessary. Serve the gravy with cooked pasta or potatoes.

RAGU DI ROGNONI

Kidney Stew   *Sardegna*

2 cups chopped onion	1 tablespoon caraway seeds
1 cup olive oil	3 bay leaves
2 pounds kidneys, diced into 2½-inch cubes and soaked in salt water overnight	¼ cup minced parsley
	salt and pepper to taste
	¼ cup flour
	juice of 1 lemon
2 cloves garlic	1 cup sour cream

Brown onion in oil; drain kidneys, and fry with onion until well browned. Add enough water to cover kidneys. Add garlic, caraway seeds, bay leaves, parsley, salt, and pepper. Cook slowly 2 hours. Thicken gravy with flour, and add lemon juice. Stir well, add sour cream, and stir again. Serve with boiled potatoes or Polenta (Chap. V).

SALTIMBOCCA ALLA ROMANA

Roman Veal Medallions   *Lazio*

> *Saltimbocca ("jump in the mouth") was the favorite delicacy of the Prince in the movie* Three Coins in a Fountain.

On each tenderized midget **veal cutlet,** place

salt and pepper	**1 thin slice prosciutto or boiled**
½ fresh sage leaf	**ham**

Truss the medallions thus formed with toothpicks, and sauté them in butter, turning over carefully when necessary. Serve three on a plate, bordered with contorno of vegetables (mashed potatoes, fresh young peas, and a salad).

SCALOPPINE DI VITELLO AL LIMONE

Veal Slices with Lemon Sauce   *Emilia*

Slice 1 pound of **tenderloin tip** into filets, and pound them into flat medallions. **Flour** lightly, and fry in ¼ cup melted **butter.** When golden-brown, add ¼ cup **white wine** and juice of 1 **lemon.** Sprinkle ¼ cup minced **parsley, salt,** and **pepper** over all. Cover, and simmer 10 minutes. Remove meat. Drop into pan the yolk of 1 **egg,** and stir rapidly. Return meat to the sauce, and serve immediately.

SCALOPPINE DI VITELLO ALLA MARSALA

Veal Slices with Wine Sauce   *Lombardia*

Slice 1 pound of tenderloin of **veal** into filets and pound them into flat medallions. **Flour** lightly, and sauté in **butter.** Add 2 cups sliced **mushrooms,** and sauté with the meat. When dark brown, add ¼ cup **Marsala** or **sherry** wine, and simmer 3 minutes. Sprinkle with finely-chopped **parsley** florets, **salt** and **pepper** to taste, and border with chosen **contorno** (mashed potatoes, buttered peas, asparagus, or the like; see Chap. VIII).

SPEZZATINO DI VITELLO ALLA NAPOLETANA

Veal Specialty of Naples   *Campania*

Cut 1 pound of **veal steak** into small strips, and brown them in **olive oil**. Remove, and sauté ¼ cup shredded **onion** till golden-brown. Add 1 cup finely sliced **green peppers** and 1 cup sliced **mushrooms,** and cook 10 minutes. Add the browned veal strips and 2 cups strained **tomatoes.** Add **salt** and **pepper** to taste, and cook another 20 minutes.

SPEZZATINO DI VITELLO ALLA ROMANA

Veal Specialty, Roman Style   *Lazio*

Cut 1 pound of **veal steak** into small strips, and fry them golden-brown in **bacon fat, olive oil,** or **lard.** Transfer to absorbent paper. Beat 2 **eggs** in a saucepan, and add juice of 1 **lemon.** Place over low heat to warm, without cooking. Add the fried meat, and mix thoroughly. Serve immediately.

SPEZZATINO DI VITELLO ALLA TOSCANA

Veal Specialty, Tuscan Style   *Toscana*

2 pounds veal steak, cubed	**salt and pepper to taste**
1 teaspoon rosemary	**½ cup olive oil**
leaves	**½ cup pitted sliced black olives**
1 clove garlic	**2 tablespoons tomato paste**
1 cup water	

Sauté meat, rosemary leaves, and garlic in oil. When garlic is delicately brown remove it. Add olives, salt, pepper, water and tomato sauce. Cover, and let cook ½ hour. Serve with cubed boiled potatoes or Polenta (Chap. V).

SPIEDINI DI CARNE ALLA CALABRESE

Skewers of Meat, Calabrian Style   *Calabria*

1 **pound round steak of veal**	**salt and pepper to taste**
1 **pound pork**	1 **tablespoon minced basil**
6 **skewers**	1 **teaspoon crushed origano**
¼ **cup olive oil**	½ **teaspoon crushed chili pepper (optional)**
	½ **cup water**

Cut meat into medallions, silver-dollar size. Alternate pork and veal medallions on skewers. Pour oil into small roasting pan, and brown skewered meat. Sprinkle all seasoning over top; add ½ cup water, cover, and roast 45 minutes in a 325° oven.

SPIEDINI DI CARNE ALLA SICILIANA

Skewers of Meat, Sicilian Style   *Sicilia*

- 1 **pound ground beef or pork**
  salt and pepper
- ¼ **cup chopped parsley**
- 1 **tablespoon minced sweet basil**
- 1 **pound sliced mozzarella or scamorza cheese**
- 1 **loaf sliced bread (crust removed)**
- 12 **skewers**
- 3 **eggs, well beaten (in flat bowl for dipping)**
- 2 **cups fine bread crumbs**
  oil or lard

Salt and pepper the meat, add parsley and sweet basil. Mix well, and form silver-dollar-size patties. Cut cheese and bread into medallions of the same size. On each skewer, place in turn a medallion of bread, one of cheese, and a meat patty, repeating until it is full, with bread at the end. Pass skewers into eggs, then into bread crumbs, and deep-fry in oil or lard. Slide contents of skewers off onto large platter for serving.

TRIPPA ALLA ROMANA

Tripe, Roman Style   *Lazio*

Parboil 2 pounds honeycomb **tripe,** drain, and free of all excess fat. Wash thoroughly and boil in fresh water until tender. Drain, and dry well with clean cloth. Cut into strips, and place in a skillet with 1 cup slivered **onions** and 1 cup **olive oil.** Cook slowly, stirring often with a spatula. Add **salt** and **pepper** to taste. In a large bowl, beat 2 **egg** yolks and juice of 1 **lemon.** Add to the cooked tripe, stir well, and serve immediately.

TRIPPA FARCITA

Stuffed Tripe   *Lucania*

Soak 1 complete **pork tripe** 1 hour in cold salt water, then wash thoroughly. Turn inside out, and scrape off all excess globules of fat. Parboil.

Stuffing
- 8 **whole eggs, boiled**
- 1 **cup grated Romano cheese**
- 2 **pounds Italian sausage cut in 2-inch pieces**
- 1 **cup diced scamorza cheese**
- 1 **teaspoon pepper**
- 1 **teaspoon crushed chili pepper (optional)**
- 1 **tablespoon salt**

Mix ingredients well, and stuff into parboiled clean tripe. Sew tripe together with twine, and place it in a large kettle with enough water to cover. Cook slowly 2 hours, or until a fork piercing the tripe will come out clean. Remove to a platter to cool, laying a heavy press on it to strain all the broth. Slice it as lunch meat. Use broth as a base for soup.

TRIPPA IN UMIDO ALLA TOSCANA

Tripe in Sauce, Tuscan Style   *Toscana*

Parboil 2 pounds of honeycomb **tripe,** drain it, and free it of all excess fat. Wash thoroughly and boil in fresh water until tender. Drain, and slice in long fine strips like spaghetti.

Sauce

- 1 **cup diced onions**
- ¼ **cup butter and ¼ cup olive oil**
  salt and pepper to taste
- 2 **tablespoons tomato paste mixed with 1 cup water**
- ½ **cup minced parsley**
- ¼ **teaspoon powdered sage**

Sauté onions in oil and butter till golden-brown. Add salt, pepper, tomato paste, parsley, and sage. Cook slowly 45 minutes. Serve over cooked tripe, topped with abundant grated **Parmesan** cheese.

TESTA DI AGNELLO AL FORNO

Baked Lamb Head   *Sicilia*

Clean **lamb head** thoroughly, and remove everything from eyes and ears. Place in boiling water for about 10 minutes, then scrape off any remaining hair and clean thoroughly. Wash again, and prepare a stuffing of

4 **cups bread crumbs**	½ **cup chopped onion (green**
3 **tablespoons grated Ro-**	**preferred)**
mano cheese	**salt and pepper to taste**
1 **cup chopped parsley**	1 **teaspoon crushed chili pepper**
3 **cloves garlic, minced**	2 **tablespoons dried currants**
1 **cup olive oil**	

Stuff head, and place in well-oiled roasting pan. Add ½ cup water, cover, and roast in 350° oven 2 hours, occasionally adding water if necessary. Remove lid for the last ½ hour of roasting.

VITELLO A FETTINE

Dainty Veal Steaks, Ancona Style   *Le Marche*

1½ pounds thinly-cut veal	2 tablespoons rosemary leaves
steaks	2 cloves garlic, chopped
½ cup olive oil	salt and pepper to taste

Arrange steaks evenly in a large frying pan. Fry them in olive oil
over a medium flame until delicately brown on both sides. Sprinkle
rosemary leaves, garlic, salt, and pepper over all. Cover the pan,
and simmer 5 minutes.

B. PESCE (*Fish*)

AGONI FRITTI

Fried Young Trout   *Lombardia*

> *Many Coloradans remember Dora Peduzzi, a
> native of Lombardy renowned for her cooking,
> who told me about the agoni of Lake Como—a
> wonderful delicacy similar to our young trout. I
> suggest that our trout be cooked in the same man-
> ner as the agoni.*

Dip the **trout** in **corn meal,** then in **flour,** and fry in sweet **butter**
till golden-brown. Season with **salt,** and serve with a garnish of
lemon.

ANGUILLA AL FORNO

Baked Small Eels   *Abruzzi*
                     Christmas Eve delicacy

First step in cleaning an **eel** is to remove the skin. With a pair
of pointed scissors, poke it loose at the tip of the tail. Grasp the
loosened skin with a cloth, and pull it off. Cut stomach open and

remove entrails. Wash well, and twist up like a cinnamon roll. Lay prepared eels in roasting pan lined with **olive oil**. Sprinkle with **salt** and **pepper,** chopped **garlic,** and a dash of **lemon juice.** Pour a little olive oil over each one. Bake, uncovered, in 425° oven about ½ hour.

ANGUILLA FRITTA

Fried Small Eels *Lucania*
Christmas Eve delicacy

Clean the **eels** as in preceding recipe (Anguilla al Forno). Cut into three parts, dip into well-beaten **egg** and then into **bread crumbs** or flour. Deep-fry in **olive oil** or leaf lard. Drain, and sprinkle with **salt.**

ARAGOSTA ALLA GRIGLIA

Broiled Lobster *Campania*

1 **live lobster**	2 **cloves garlic, minced**
1 **cup bread crumbs**	1 **teaspoon paprika**
¼ **cup chopped parsley**	½ **cup water**
¼ **cup grated Romano**	**salt and pepper to taste**
cheese	**olive oil**

Kill lobster by cutting spinal cord between body and tail shells. Clean and remove the craw. Mix the other ingredients thoroughly into a stuffing, and fill the cleaned craw with this. Rub well with olive oil. Broil till tender.

ARAGOSTA ALLA MARSALA

Lobster in Wine *Campania*

Prepare **Besciamella** (Chap. VI), adding 1 ounce of Marsala or sherry **wine.** Boil **lobster** till tender. Remove meat from the shells, cut into small pieces, and stir them into the cream sauce. Serve over diced, boiled potatoes or in patty shells.

ARAGOSTA LESSATA

Boiled Lobster   *Sardegna*

Kill **lobster** by cutting spinal cord between body and tail shells. Clean, and remove the craw. Drop lobster immediately into boiling water to which have been added

2 cups diced carrots	½ cup chopped celery
juice of 1 lemon	¼ cup chopped onion
2 bay leaves	salt and pepper
	olive oil

Boil ½ hour or until tender. Drain and remove meat. Sprinkle minced onion over top. Sprinkle a little olive oil over all, and then a dash of lemon juice. Salt and pepper to taste.

ARSELLE

Clam Soup   *Toscana*

Specialty of Livorno

12 fresh clams in shell	1 tablespoon salt
¼ cup minced parsley	¼ cup olive oil
¼ cup minced leek or chives	1 teaspoon pepper

Wash clam shells well to free of all sand. Using a large skillet, sauté parsley and leek or chives in oil with salt and pepper. When delicately crisp add clams in shell, simmer 5 minutes, or until shells open and liquor is expelled. Remove shells, and cook another 5 minutes. Serve over Crostini (Chap. X) in soup bowls.

BACCALA

Dried Codfish   *All Regions*

Dried codfish can be used in many appetizing ways and is much tastier than fresh cod, but it requires considerable work to prepare it for cooking. Here are two ways of freshening it:

1. Saw the dried fish in half, and soak the pieces 5 days in plenty of cold water, changing the water twice daily. It is well to do this

outside the house, because of the odor. On the last day soak it in limewater (1 tablespoon powdered lime to 1 gallon water). Before using, wash the fish thoroughly, and remove all bones.

2. Soak the dried fish 1 day in a large vessel of cold water containing 1 tablespoon lye to each 2 gallons water. Replace the lye solution with fresh water, and soak 3 more days, changing the water twice daily. Wash the fish thoroughly, and remove all bones.

BACCALA AL FORNO

Baked Codfish   *Venezia*

> **tail half of a prepared dried cod * (or 2 pounds fresh cod)**
> **2 cloves garlic, minced**
> **¼ cup minced parsley**
> **½ cup minced onion**
> **1 teaspoon salt**
> **1 tablespoon pepper**
> **½ cup olive oil**

Split open tail half of a dried codfish, and lay it in an oiled roasting pan. (Fresh codfish may be substituted.) Sprinkle all the seasoning and the olive oil over the fish. Cover, and bake in 375° oven till tender—about 1 hour. Serve over boiled potatoes.

BACCALA ALLA MARINARA

Codfish, Mariner Style   *Liguria*

> **¼ cup chopped green onion**
> **3 tablespoons minced parsley**
> **3 tablespoons minced basil**
> **¼ cup sliced mushrooms (optional)**
> **¼ cup olive oil**
> **1 cup tomato sauce**
> **2 cups codfish,** shredded**
> **salt and pepper**

* See directions preceding.
** See Baccalà, p. 100, for the initial preparation.

Sauté onion, parsley, sweet basil, and mushrooms in olive oil until delicately brown. Add tomato sauce and shredded fish, and simmer ½ hour. Salt and pepper to taste. Serve with polenta or cooked spaghettini.

BACCALA ARROSTITO

Roasted Codfish   *Lazio*

In an oiled roasting pan place bite-size pieces of **codfish**. Sprinkle **bread crumbs, pepper** to taste (no salt), minced **parsley**, minced **sweet basil**, and grated **Romano cheese** over the fish. Place 1 whole clove of **garlic** on it at each end and 1 in the center. Dot it over all with **butter**. Cover, and roast it in a 375° oven 10 minutes. Uncover, and continue roasting ½ hour. Do not turn the fish. If desired, add a little **white wine** 5 minutes before taking it from the oven. Remove garlic before serving.

BACCALA ARROSTITO CON PIGNOLI

Roma

Roasted Codfish with Pignon Nuts   *Lazio*

Place half a prepared **fish,*** cut open, in a Dutch oven lined with a little **olive oil.** On it place

½ **pound parboiled celery root, in slices**	1 **handful pignon nuts**
½ **cup butter, cut into bits**	1 **handful white raisins**
	pepper to taste (no salt)

Cover, and place in 375° oven for 10 minutes. Uncover, and roast ½ hour more. Add ½ cup **white wine,** and roast another 10 minutes.

BACCALA FRITTO

Fried Codfish   *Abruzzi*

2 **pounds codfish ***	½ **cup water**
¼ **cup flour**	1 **teaspoon baking powder**
	½ **teaspoon salt**

* See Baccalà, page 100, for the initial preparation.

Cut fish into bite-size pieces. Blend other ingredients into smooth batter. Dip pieces of fish separately into batter, and deep-fry in oil or lard.

BACCALA STUFATO

Codfish Stew   *Alto Adige*

2 pounds boned codfish	2 cloves garlic, chopped
2 cups bread crumbs	1 teaspoon pepper
1 teaspoon cinnamon	dash of thyme
¼ cup chopped parsley	3 tablespoons olive oil
4 chopped anchovies	¼ cup melted butter

cold water

Cut fish into bite-size pieces. Mix together bread crumbs and cinnamon. Roll pieces in crumbs, and lay in oil-lined Dutch oven. Sprinkle with parsley, anchovies, garlic, pepper, thyme, and olive oil. Pour melted butter over all, and add enough cold water to reach 1½ inches above the fish. Cover, and simmer 2 hours, until most of the liquid is absorbed (do not stir). Serve with boiled potatoes or polenta.

CALAMAIO AL FORNO

Baked Squid   *Puglia*

8 squid 4 inches long	2 tablespoons small raisins
1 cup bread crumbs	½ cup grated Romano cheese
2 eggs	¼ cup chopped parsley

salt and pepper to taste

Remove head and entrails of each squid, including complete ink sac. Wash squid well, inside and out. Mix remaining ingredients thoroughly into stuffing. Stuff each squid, and place them in a casserole lined with ½ cup olive oil. Bake, uncovered, in a 375° oven ½ hour, or until tender.

CAPITONE AL FORNO

Large Eel, Baked   *Sardegna*

The **eel** is very slick, and the skin must be removed for cooking. With a sharp boning knife, poke and loosen the skin at the tip of the tail. Nail the tail to a board, and pull skin back over body until you can cut it off along with the head. Cut stomach open, and remove entrails. Wash the eel thoroughly. Rub inside and out with **salt, pepper, garlic, olive oil,** and **thyme.** Pour a little oil into a roasting pan, and roll eel in it. Sprinkle chopped **parsley** and **onion** over surface. Bake, uncovered, in 375° oven until tender. Serve with Salsa Agrodolce (Chap. VI).

EPERLANI FRITTI

Silver Smelts, Fried   *Southern Regions*
             Christmas Eve specialty

Smelts are truly a delicacy, similar to baby trout if properly prepared. To clean, remove the little heads and fins, then open the fish completely and remove entrails and bones. Dip into **flour,** and deep-fry in **oil** or lard. **Salt** to taste.

FRITTO MISTO DI PESCE *

Fried Mixed Fish   *Lazio*
             Christmas Eve delicacy in Rome

Choice of Fish

smelts	whitefish
codfish	salmon
tuna	baby eel
oysters	small fish balls
shrimp	filet of sole
scallops	halibut

* See Fritto Misto di Vegetali, Chapter VIII, D. They can be served with the Fried Mixed Fish.

Batter

3 tablespoons flour	1 teaspoon crushed rosemary
3 tablespoons olive oil	salt and pepper to taste
3 well-beaten eggs	1 teaspoon crushed basil

Cut fish into bite-size pieces. Whip other ingredients into a smooth batter. Dip pieces into batter and deep-fry in oil. Drain, and arrange attractively on large platter. Serve with Salsa Verde, Maionese, or another sauce as desired. (See Chapter VI, Sauces.)

GRANCHIO ALLA GRIGLIA

Broiled Soft-shell Crab　　　　　　　　　　　　　　　*Le Marche*

Lift the wings of the upper shell of a live **soft-shell crab** and remove the soft fins from under the sides of the back shell; also remove the flap on the under shell. Wash, and place the crab in a large kettle of boiling water; boil for just 5 minutes. Brush it completely with **oil, salt,** and **pepper,** and broil it 10 minutes on each side (preferably outdoors over charcoal). Serve it with your favorite sauce or with melted butter.

LUMACHE CON SALSA

Snails with Sauce　　　　　　　　　　　　　　　　*Lazio*
> *Snails are the special Roman delicacy, and this is the traditional dish of the Feast of St. John the Baptist, June 24.*

Snails, as soon as they have been taken from the ground, must be placed in a covered pan for three days to digest their food and evacuate all. Then, hold them one at a time under running cold water; when a snail shows itself drop it immediately into a pot of boiling water. With a fork, pull it out of the shell. Wash all in strong **vinegar water** in order to remove the greasy film, and rinse them in cold water. In a skillet, sauté chopped **onion** and a clove of **garlic** in melted **lard** or **oil** until golden-brown. Add the snails and, when they are browned, **tomato sauce.** Simmer about ½ hour. Add a pinch of **black pepper** and **chili pepper.** Serve with cooked spaghettini.

MERLUZZO

Codfish in White Sauce   *Piemonte*

2 pounds boned codfish *	**½ cup butter**
3 cups sliced onions	**2 tablespoons olive oil**
1 tablespoon pepper	**2 cups water**

Soak codfish in cold water long enough to remove the excess salt, and chop it. Brown onions in butter and oil. Add codfish and pepper. Brown slowly; add water, and simmer till tender (about 45 minutes), stirring often to prevent sticking. If desired, add ½ cup white wine, and cook 2 more minutes. Serve with polenta or boiled potatoes.

OSTRICHE AL FORNO

Baked Oysters   *Campania*

12 oysters on the half-shell	**1 cup bread crumbs**
	1 teaspoon minced thyme
2 cloves minced garlic	**salt and pepper to taste**
¼ cup minced parsley	**¼ cup minced celery**
½ cup olive oil	

Remove oysters from their shells, and arrange on a baking sheet. Mix remaining ingredients thoroughly, and place 1 teaspoonful of sauce on each oyster. Set under the broiler until delicately brown. Serve 3 to a person.

OSTRICHE CRUDE

Raw Oysters   *Puglia*

A snack delicacy, a wonderful appetizer, a perfect energy-builder

Hold **oysters,** in the shell, one at a time under cold running water. When the shell begins to open, pry it open all the way with a dull

° See Baccalà, page 100, for the initial preparation.

knife. Drop the oyster into a sauce dish, give it a dash of **lemon juice,** and devour.

OSTRICHE FRITTE

Fried Oysters *Puglia*

Dip shelled and cleaned **oysters** into well-beaten **eggs** (3 eggs for 2 dozen oysters), then into fine **bread crumbs,** and pan-fry them in **olive oil** or **butter** (or a combination of the two). **Salt** to taste. Serve with garnish of **lemon.**

OSTRICHE IN UMIDO

Oyster Stew *Puglia*

12 oysters in shell, or 1 pint oysters with juice	**3 cups rich milk**
	1 teaspoon salt
	½ teaspoon pepper
¼ cup butter	**1 crushed chili pepper**
2 tablespoons chopped parsley	

Hold oysters, in the shell, one at a time under cold running water. When the shell begins to open, pry it open all the way with a dull knife and drop the oyster and its juice into a bowl until all are shelled. Melt butter in top of a double boiler, and add oysters and juice, milk, salt, pepper, and chili pepper. Stir carefully, blending all together, and cook until oysters rise to surface. Stir in the chopped parsley florets, and serve.

PALOMBO AL FORNO

Baked Halibut *Liguria*

4 halibut steaks	**½ cup fine bread crumbs**
¼ cup olive oil	**2 tablespoons minced parsley**
salt and pepper	**2 cloves garlic, minced**
¼ cup grated Parmesan cheese	

Place steaks in oil-lined baking pan. Salt and pepper to taste. Sprinkle bread crumbs, parsley, garlic, and cheese over top of the steaks. Sprinkle a little oil over each one. Bake in 375° oven ½ hour. Serve immediately with garnish of **lemon**.

PALOMBO CON POMODORO

Halibut with Tomato   *Liguria*

Before putting **Palombo al Forno** (the preceding recipe) into the oven, prepare **Salsa Parmigiana** (Chap. VI). Pour it over the fish. Bake in 375° oven ½ hour, basting occasionally. Serve with boiled potatoes.

PESCE FARCITO

Stuffed Fish   *Sardegna*

Obtain a large fat **fish** (carp, bass, salmon, swordfish, trout) weighing 5 to 7 pounds. Skin and scale it if necessary. Cut it open, and remove entrails. Wash and dry well. Remove head and fins. With sharp boning knife, carefully sever each bone tip from flesh. Loosen spine in tail area, and slip point of knife along backbone from tail to neck, separating bones from meat. Rub inside and out with **garlic** and **olive oil, salt** and **pepper**.

Stuffing

¼ cup minced salt pork or bacon	½ cup chopped parsley
	salt and pepper to taste
¼ cup chopped green onion	2 crushed chili peppers
1 cup chopped celery	¼ cup white wine or juice of 1
2 cups bread crumbs soaked in 1 cup milk	lemon

Render the pork or bacon in a frying pan. Add the onion and celery, and sauté about 10 minutes. Remove from fire, and add to the bread, milk and parsley. Season with salt and pepper and chili peppers. Mix all thoroughly, and stuff the fish. Place it in an oil-lined roasting pan. Pour wine or lemon juice over all, and bake in 375° oven till delicately brown and tender.

PESCE SPADA CON SALSA AGRODOLCE

Swordfish with Sour-Sweet Sauce   *Sicilia*

Pan-fry 6 floured **swordfish steaks** in **olive oil** and drain on absorbent paper. Place in casserole, and pour **Salsa Agrodolce** (Chap. VI) over them, adding **salt** and **pepper** to taste; also a dash of grated **Romano cheese**, if desired. Place in 375° oven for 10 minutes.

POLPETTINE DI TONNO CON SALSA

Tuna Balls with Tomato Sauce   *Campania*

1 cup tuna	½ cup fine bread crumbs
1 egg	1 tablespoon minced parsley
salt and pepper to taste	

Blend all together, and form marble-size balls. Brown these in **olive oil,** and then remove them. To the oil add 1 cup **tomato paste** and 2 cups **water.** Simmer ½ hour. Return fish balls to sauce, to simmer another 20 minutes. Serve over cooked vermicelli or spaghettini.

POLPETTINE DI PALOMBO CON SALSA

Halibut Balls with Sauce   *Liguria*

2 cups halibut, shredded	½ cup bread crumbs
1 egg	1 tablespoon minced parsley
salt and pepper to taste	1 tablespoon minced basil

Blend all together, and form tiny balls. Dip these in **flour,** and fry them in ¼ cup **olive oil.** When delicately brown, add 1 cup **tomato sauce** and 1 cup **water** and simmer ½ hour. Serve with polenta or spaghettini.

RANE CON RISO

Frog Legs with Rice   *Venezia*

½ cup minced green onion	¼ cup butter
¼ cup minced celery	8 frog legs (hind legs)
¼ cup minced carrot	¼ cup Marsala wine
salt and pepper to taste	1 cup water
1 cup rice	

Parboil the (skinned) frog legs 3 minutes. Wash in cold water, and dry. Sauté onion, celery, carrot, salt, and pepper in butter. When delicately brown add frog legs, and fry these until delicately brown. Add wine and water, and simmer till meat falls off bones (about 20 minutes). Remove bones. Pass meat and sauce through a food mill. Cook rice in salt water till it reaches *al dente* (chewy) stage. Strain, and add to the frog sauce. Serve topped with grated **Parmesan cheese.**

RANE FRITTE

Fried Frog Legs   *Venezia*

Only the hind legs of the **frog** are used for cooking. Remove the skin, and parboil the legs 3 minutes. Dip them into well-beaten **eggs,** then into fine **bread crumbs.** Deep-fry in **olive oil** till delicately brown. Serve with **Maionese** (Chap. VI).

SCHIACCIATINA DI BACCALA

Codfish Pancakes   *Liguria*

2 cups codfish, boned and shredded *	1 egg
	½ cup flour
2 tablespoons minced green onion	2 cups water
	pepper to taste (no salt)

Beat together all ingredients except the fish, making a smooth thin batter. Add the fish, and mix thoroughly. Drop a tablespoonful

* See Baccalà, page 100, for the initial preparation.

at a time into a skillet containing about ½ inch of olive oil and fry
as pancakes.

SGOMBRO AL FORNO

Baked Mackerel *Campania*

Clean and bone the **mackerel** (see directions for Pesce Farcito).
Open it, and lay it flat in oiled baking pan. Cover it with **bread
crumbs** and 2 cloves **garlic**, minced. Season with **salt, pepper,** and
a dash of **thyme.** On half the fish place sliced fresh **tomatoes.** On
the other half place sliced rings of **onion.** Coat all with **olive oil.**
Bake, uncovered, in 375° oven 45 minutes, or until delicately brown
and tender.

SCAMPI FRITTI

Fried Scallops *Venezia*

> 1 dozen scallops 1 cup fine bread crumbs
> 2 eggs, well beaten olive oil

Dip scallops into eggs, then into bread crumbs, and deep-fry in
olive oil. Serve with **Maionese** (Chap. VI).

SOGLIOLA ALLA CASSERUOLA

Filet of Sole in Casserole *Venezia*
> *Served on the Feast of the Redemption, July 19.*
> *Mediterranean sole are equivalent in size to Amer-*
> *ican trout. American "filet of sole" is usually*
> *flounder.*

> ¼ cup minced parsley ½ cup melted butter
> ½ cup minced onion salt and pepper to taste
> 1 cup sliced mushrooms ¼ teaspoon thyme
> 2 pounds filet of sole

Sauté parsley, onion, and mushrooms in butter, in a casserole,
stirring often. Add salt, pepper, and thyme, and stir well. Add the
fish, cover, and simmer 10 minutes. Turn filet, and simmer another
10 minutes.

SOGLIOLA ALLA MARINARA

Sole, Mariner Style   *Venezia*
  Served on the Feast of the Redemption, July 19

1 two-pound sole	salt and pepper to taste
¼ cup minced parsley	1 cup white wine
1 tablespoon minced basil	1 cup fine bread crumbs
olive oil	

Cover sole, in a flat bowl, with parsley, sweet basil, salt and pepper, and wine. Let marinate ½ hour. Drain (saving the sauce), roll in bread crumbs and pat well. Deep-fry in hot oil. Drain, and place in casserole. Pour the remaining sauce over fish, and bake 6 minutes in moderate oven.

SOGLIOLE FRITTE

Fried Sole   *Venezia*
  Served on the Feast of the Redemption, July 19

4 medium-sized sole	¼ cup flour
2 well-beaten eggs	½ cup olive oil

Roll fish in eggs and then in flour. Pan-fry in oil, turning when necessary, till delicately browned. Drain on absorbent paper, and serve immediately with Salsa di Uova e Agre di Limone (Chap. VI).

TONNO CON PISELLI

Tuna with Peas   *Venezia*
  Popular Lenten dish

1 cup tuna in oil	2 cups shelled peas

Cook together in a skillet until well blended, adding **pepper** to taste.

TOTANO AL FORNO

Baked Red Snapper   *Sicilia*

> Served on the Feast of St. Joseph, March 19. Any
> large fish can be prepared in this manner; trout is
> delicious.

1 three- or four-pound red snapper	¼ cup chopped parsley
2 cups bread crumbs	2 cloves garlic, minced
2 tablespoons grated Romano cheese	¼ cup chopped green onion
	salt and pepper to taste
	2 tablespoons dried currants

½ cup olive oil

Remove entrails of fish, but not head or tail. Wash well, and dry.
Mix remaining ingredients together and stuff fish. Place on rack in
large roasting pan (if without rack, cut a large onion into three
pieces, and place one at each end of pan and one in center). Place
thin slices of **onion, lemon,** and **fresh tomato** over fish. Sprinkle
chopped parsley and garlic over all. Salt and pepper to taste. Bake,
uncovered, in 350° oven 1½ hours, adding water occasionally if the
fish appears too dry.

VONGOLE AL FORNO

Baked Clams   *Toscana*

**1 dozen clams in shell   6 teaspoons fine bread crumbs
3 tablespoons melted butter**

Scrub clams thoroughly to free of sand; dry, and arrange in baking pan. Place in 375° oven for 5 minutes, until clams open. Remove
upper shells. Sprinkle ½ teaspoon bread crumbs and ½ teaspoon
melted butter over each clam, without spilling the juice from lower
shells. Place pan under broiler for 2 minutes. Serve clams in lower
shells with lemon slice.

VONGOLE IN UMIDO

Clams in Sauce   *Campania*

Scrub 1 dozen **clams** thoroughly to free of sand. Hold each clam in cold running water. When shell begins to open pry it wide with a dull knife, letting clam and juice fall into a bowl. In a medium-sized skillet, sauté 1 cup minced **parsley** in ½ cup **butter** and ¼ cup **olive oil.** Add clam juice, and heat thoroughly. Add clams, and cook 5 minutes. Serve over cooked noodles.

C. POLLAME *(Poultry)*

CAPPONE ARROSTITO ALLA GENOVESE

Roasted Capon, Genoa Style   *Liguria*

Rub a 10-pound **capon** inside and out with **garlic, olive oil, salt,** and **pepper.** Boil **giblets** (liver, heart, and gizzard) and **neck** in 3 cups salted water till tender. Cut ¼ pound of **salt pork** into 1-inch cubes.

Dressing
cooked giblets and meat from neck, ground
½ **cup chopped onion (green preferred)**
½ **cup butter**
½ **cup chopped celery**
½ **cup chopped parsley**
2 **sage leaves, minced, or** ½ **teaspoon powdered**
2 **cups broth**
5 **cups toasted bread, broken into small pieces**
salt and pepper to taste
2 **eggs**

Sauté ground giblets and neck meat with onion in butter. Add celery, parsley, and sage, and simmer about 5 minutes. In large bowl, pour broth over pieces of toast, and add giblet mixture, salt, and pepper. Add eggs and stir well. Stuff capon, and sew with twine. Using toothpicks, stud it all over with cubes of pork. Set it in open roaster, in 375° oven, allowing 30 minutes per pound.

CAPPONE ARROSTITO ALLA ROMANA

Roasted Capon, Roman Style   *Lazio*

- 1 **ten-pound capon**
- 5 **cups coarsely-ground hard bread**
- 3 **cups water to dampen the bread**
- 1 **dozen peeled and chopped chestnuts (parboiled chestnuts peel easily)**
- 1 **cup chopped celery**
- ½ **cup chopped parsley**
- 4 **eggs**
- ½ **cup melted butter and 3 tablespoons olive oil**
- ½ **cup chopped onion**
- 3 **tablespoons grated Romano cheese**
   salt and pepper to taste

Rub capon inside and out with garlic, olive oil, salt, and pepper. Soak bread in water 10 minutes; squeeze, and put into large bowl. Add the seasonings, and mix all thoroughly. Stuff capon where craw was removed, and sew slit in neck. Stuff rest of body and sew opening with twine. With butter and oil, grease roasting pan well. Set capon in it and roast, uncovered, ½ hour in 450° oven. Add ½ cup water, cover pan, and lower temperature to 350°, allowing 25 minutes per pound.

CAPPONE ARROSTITO ALLA TIROLESE

Roasted Capon, Tirolese Style   *Alto Adige*

- 1 **ten-pound capon**
- 1 **large loaf Italian bread, several days old**
- 5 **large apples, peeled and diced**
- ½ **cup minced parsley**
- 1 **teaspoon minced sage**
- 2 **sprigs sweet basil, or 1 tablespoon dried basil flakes**

    4 eggs
    salt and pepper to taste
    5 or 6 link sausages, cut fine
    1 small onion, minced
    1 cup finely-chopped celery
    ½ cup butter
    4 thin slices bacon
    2 cups broth or bouillon

Break loaf into small pieces, soak in water, and squeeze. Mix with apples, parsley, sage, eggs, salt, and pepper. Sauté sausages, onion, and celery in butter until delicately brown, and combine thoroughly with the bread mixture. Rub capon inside and out with salt, pepper, garlic, and butter. Stuff capon, and sew with twine. Grease a roasting pan well with butter and oil, and set capon in it. Arrange bacon slices and sweet basil on top. Roast uncovered in 375° oven, basting occasionally with bouillon or broth, allowing 25 minutes per pound.

INTESTINI DI POLLO CON RIGAGLIE

Chicken Casings with Gizzards   *Puglia*
> *Truly a delicacy—please don't shudder! After all,*
> *in eating sausages of all descriptions, we certainly*
> *eat casings.*

Fresh chicken **casings** cannot be bought. They must be taken from a young fryer when it is killed and dressed. Slit full length of intestines with a knife and hold them in running water to remove all mucus. After spraying all the waste away, rub them with **salt** and let them stand in water an hour. Wash again, and boil in salt water 5 minutes. Drain, and rinse. Wrap and fasten casings around **gizzards,** and fry slowly in **olive oil. Salt** and **pepper** to taste.

INTESTINI FRITTI

Fried Casings   *Piemonte*

Cut fresh chicken **casings,** as prepared in the preceding recipe, into inch lengths. Sauté with chopped **onions** (green preferred) in **butter** till delicately brown and a bit crisp.

The Piedmontese use the casings from freshly butchered young **veal** in the same manner, adding minced **parsley,** a few sliced **mushrooms,** and scrambling the mixture with **eggs**—which suggests that, by the use of a little ingenuity, this delicacy can be prepared with herbs to satisfy individual tastes.

METODO PER DISOSSARE IL POLLO

Method for Boning a Young Hen　　　　　　　*Northern Regions*

In killing a chicken, turkey, or capon, hold it by the legs and neck. By stabbing the fowl in the jugular vein below the ear, one can catch the blood in a pan and save it for use as part of the liquid in the dressing.

A turkey or chicken that is to be boned should not weigh more than 8 pounds. When you pull feathers, take care not to tear the skin. Place bird breast down on table. Remove (cut) oil sac at base of tail, and cut off head. Carefully, with a sharp boning knife:

1. Cut off tip of each wing at second joint.
2. Cut off legs at knee joint, loosening skin and flesh.
3. Cut along backbone from neck to tail, making a V cut at tail joint.
4. Loosen flesh from backbone and ribs, to hip joint. Sever tendons at joint, and the leg bone will pull right out.
5. Slide out bone from shoulder-part of one wing. Carefully sever flesh from breast, and slide bone out of shoulder-part of the other wing.
6. Remove bone from other leg. Carefully cut around tail without puncturing colon, and remove carcass with entrails enclosed.
7. Remove entrails from carcass, salvaging the giblets (liver, heart, and gizzard). The carcass and pieces of the wings may be used for broth or gelatin.

Follow the same procedure with a dressed and drawn bird; however you may have to do a bit of mending with needle and twine if the skin was severed in the drawing.

Spread the completely boned bird out on a table, skin down. It is ready to be dressed, according to the recipe for Pollo in Galantina.

PETTO DI TACCHINO ALLA CARDINALE *

Breast of Turkey for the Cardinal   *Emilia*

Slice breast of **turkey** into filets, and pound them lightly. Sauté filets in **butter** till delicately brown, then remove from fire. Place on each a thin slice of **Parmesan cheese,** thin slices of **truffles** (or white mushrooms), and a thin slice of salt-cured **tongue.** Return filets to pan, over a very low flame, until cheese is completely melted. Serve on blankets of **mashed potatoes.**

POLLO ALLA CACCIATORA

Chicken, Hunter Style   *All Regions*

I. Northern Region Style

Sauce

1 cup chopped onion	¼ cup minced sweet basil
½ cup chopped parsley	1 tablespoon crushed rosemary
½ cup butter	leaves
1 cup water	2 bay leaves
1 cup sliced mushrooms	salt and pepper
(optional)	⅓ cup wine (Marsala preferred)

Cut a chicken into small serving pieces. Brown onion and parsley in butter. Add the pieces of chicken, and brown delicately. Add water, mushrooms, basil, rosemary, and bay leaves; salt and pepper to taste. Simmer about 2 hours, adding water if necessary. When meat is tender, add wine. Serve with boiled potatoes or polenta.

II. Southern Region Style

Sauce

½ cup chopped onion	½ cup olive oil
¼ cup chopped parsley	1 cup chopped green
2 cloves garlic,	pepper
minced	salt and pepper to taste

* I am deeply grateful to the Zurla brothers of Bologna, proprietors of the Ristorante "Al Pappagallo," for this elegant recipe.

1 pint tomatoes and 1 pint water

¼ cup diced, pitted black olives

¼ cup chopped sweet basil

½ cup chopped celery

2 crushed chili peppers (optional)

Cut a chicken into small serving pieces. Brown onion, parsley, and garlic in olive oil. Add the pieces of chicken, and brown. Add the rest of the ingredients and simmer 2 hours, or until tender, adding water if necessary. Serve with boiled potatoes.

POLLO ARROSTITO ALLA POTENZESE

Roast Chicken, Potenza Style   *Lucania*

1 or two young fryers *

½ cup lard

salt and pepper to taste (more than usual)

4 cloves garlic, minced, or ½ cup minced onion

1 cup grated Romano cheese

½ cup chopped parsley

4 large potatoes, peeled and halved

1 cup cold water

Cut the chicken into serving pieces, rub with lard, and place in well-greased roasting pan. Sprinkle with salt, pepper, garlic or onion, cheese, and parsley. Rub potatoes with lard, and sprinkle with salt, pepper, garlic or onion, cheese, and parsley, and intersperse among pieces of chicken. Set uncovered pan in 375° oven for 20 minutes. Add water, lower heat to 325°, and roast another 30 minutes, or until tender, basting occasionally.

POLLO ALLA TETRAZZINI

Chicken Tetrazzini   *Toscana*

3 cups slivered chicken **

1 cup mushrooms

1 cup grated Parmesan cheese

1 pound capellini or spaghettini, parboiled till wilted

* If you use stewing hens, boil them until they are half cooked, and save the broth for soup making.

** From a stewing hen that has been cooked in just enough salted water with onion flavor to make the rich broth used for the sauce below.

Sauce

½ cup butter	¼ cup flour
½ cup chicken broth	

Fry mushrooms in 2 tablespoons butter till golden-brown. Slowly brown flour in ½ cup butter. Gradually add broth, stirring constantly, until the sauce is smooth and creamy. Add the browned mushrooms, and stir well.

In a well-buttered casserole place layers of wilted capellini or spaghettini, chicken slices, sauce with mushrooms, grated cheese; repeat until all is used, topping with sauce and grated cheese. Place, uncovered, in 375° oven for 20 minutes.

POLLO FRITTO

Fried Chicken   *All Regions*

Cut the **fryers** into serving pieces, and place these in a large bowl with several cloves of **garlic** for 1 hour, turning the chicken often. Remove garlic.

Batter

2 tablespoons flour	½ cup milk
½ cup grated cheese	1 teaspoon minced parsley
1 teaspoon minced basil, rosemary, or origano	salt and pepper to taste

Whip ingredients into a smooth, creamy batter. Dip pieces of chicken into well-beaten **egg** and then into the batter. Fry slowly in lard.

POLLO IN BIANCO

Chicken in White   *Campania*

- 1 or 2 fryers
- ½ cup olive oil
- ½ cup rendered fat (suet, leaf lard, bacon, or salt pork)
- 2 cups minced onion

8 slices toasted or dried bread, coarse-ground
salt and pepper to taste
½ cup grated Parmesan cheese
½ cup pignon nuts (optional)
3 eggs
½ cup chopped parsley
¼ cup minced sweet basil **or 1 tablespoon rosemary**
2 sage leaves, minced (or 1 teaspoon dried)
2 cups broth or bouillon
8 cubes salt pork or bacon

Bone roasting hen (8 pounds or less), as described under *Metodo per Disossare il Pollo* earlier in this chapter.

Sauté ground meat, giblets, onion, and celery in butter and oil till delicately brown. Add the remaining ingredients, except salt pork or bacon. Mix thoroughly, and stuff bird. Sew neatly with needle and twine, beginning at the posterior. When you reach the neck area, fold the skin back, envelope style, for sewing. Set bird in greased roasting pan, and attach cubes of salt pork or bacon here and there over top with toothpicks. Place in 400° oven for 15 minutes. Reduce heat to 350° and cook 1¾ hours (2 hours in all), basting occasionally. Before serving, remove salt pork, toothpicks, and twine.

SPEZZATINO DI POLLO

Bits of Chicken *Campania*

Cut 1 or 2 **fryers** into small pieces, the breast in 4 pieces. Even the thighs and legs are cut in two with a cleaver. The **giblets** are also used. Pan-fry the pieces in **olive oil,** or rendered **salt pork** or **bacon.** When delicately brown, remove from pan. Sauté 1 cup chopped **green pepper,** ½ cup sliced **mushrooms,** and ½ cup chopped **onion.** When all is brown and tender add 1 cup **tomato sauce** and 1 cup **water;** stir well, and add chicken. **Salt** and **pepper** to taste. Simmer ½ hour. Serve chicken on a platter. Serve sauce with Crostini (Chap. X) or cooked spaghettini, topped with grated **Romano cheese.**

D. SELVAGGINA (*Wild Game*)

ANITRA ARROSTITA

Roast Duck   *Sicilia*

½ cup minced onion	1 teaspoon crushed rosemary
¼ cup chopped salt pork	leaves
1 pound ground pork	1 cup hard bread, diced
pepper to taste	½ cup orange juice or Marsala
2 crushed chili peppers	wine

6 black olives, pitted and chopped

Rub the duck inside and out with garlic and salt pork.

Sauté onion in salt pork; when golden-brown add the rest of the
ingredients, and mix thoroughly. Stuff duck, and sew with twine or
fasten together with small skewers. Place in well-greased roasting
pan, in a 350° oven, allowing 25 minutes per pound. Baste often
with a little orange juice diluted with water.

ANITRA IN SALMI

Marinated Duck   *Umbria*

1 cup red wine	2 anchovies, chopped
½ cup minced onion	1 clove garlic, minced
1 tablespoon rosemary	1 tablespoon basil

pepper to taste

Clean the **duck** and cut it into small serving pieces.

Mix other ingredients into a marinade and pour it over the pieces
in a shallow bowl, to marinate 2 hours. Baste them often. Drain off
the marinade and save it. Brown the duck in 3 tablespoons **butter**
and 2 tablespoons **olive oil.** When it turns a dark amber color, add
the marinade again and simmer till tender.

ANITRA IN UMIDO

Duck Stew Piemonte

1 duck	¼ cup olive oil
1 cup chopped onion	¼ cup butter
¼ cup chopped parsley	2 cups water
3 tablespoons minced	salt and pepper to taste
basil	½ cup red wine

Clean the duck, cut it into small serving pieces, and roll these in flour.

Sauté onion, parsley, and basil in oil and butter. When delicately brown, add floured pieces of duck. When the duck is browned add 2 cups water, salt and pepper to taste, and simmer till tender. Add wine, and continue simmering 5 minutes. Serve the meat on a platter, and the sauce with polenta.

ARROSTO DI SELVAGGINA

Roast of Wild Game Sardegna

Remove all fat from wild **game** (venison, elk, antelope, buffalo). Cut occasional slits and insert cloves of **garlic**. Rub well with plenty of **salt** and **pepper**. Sear in **olive oil** and rendered **salt pork** or **bacon**. Add 1 cup minced **onion,** and let brown. Pour ½ cup **water** around the meat and sprinkle top with **parsley, sweet basil, marjoram, myrtle, origano,** or **rosemary,** or a combination of all. Roast in 350° oven till tender, at least 30 minutes per pound, basting occasionally.

CONIGLIO FRITTO ALLA LOMBARDA

Fried Rabbit, Lombard Style Lombardia

1 rabbit, cut into serving	2 teaspoons minced sweet
pieces	basil
2 eggs, well beaten	1 teaspoon crushed rosemary
salt and pepper to taste	1 teaspoon minced parsley
¼ cup butter	1 cup fine bread crumbs
3 tablespoons olive oil or bacon fat	

Blend eggs with salt and pepper, basil, rosemary, and parsley. Dip each piece of rabbit into egg mixture and then into bread crumbs; pat well. Fry all the pieces slowly in melted butter and oil or bacon fat. When golden-brown and tender, remove immediately to serving plate.

CONIGLIO IN UMIDO DI BERGAMO

Rabbit Stew, Bergamo Style   *Lombardia*

Cut 1 **rabbit** into serving pieces, and soak in salt water at least 1 hour. Drain off the water, and roll pieces in **flour**. In a large kettle sauté ½ cup minced **onion**, ¼ cup minced **parsley**, and 2 tablespoons minced **sweet basil** in ½ cup **butter**. When they are delicately brown, add the floured rabbit and continue to cook. Add 1 cup **water, salt** and **pepper** to taste. Cover, and simmer 45 minutes. Add 1 cup **Marsala wine** or **vermouth,** cover, and simmer another 30 minutes, or until meat is tender. Serve rabbit on a platter and sauce with polenta, cooked spaghettini, or Casunsei (Chap. III).

FAGIANO ALLA DIAVOLA

Broiled Pheasant   *Umbria*

Clean the **pheasant,** and cut it in two longitudinally. Brush the halves with **salt** and **lemon** to taste, and with **olive oil.** Broil 15 minutes. Turn over, and broil another 15 minutes or until golden-brown. Serve with Patate Fritte (Chap. VIII, D).

FAGIANO IN SALMI

Marinated Pheasant   *Umbria*

Clean the **pheasant,** and cut it into small serving pieces. Prepare a marinade of

2 **anchovies, chopped**	6 **black olives, pitted and**
2 **cloves garlic, minced**	**chopped**
3 **tablespoons capers**	1 **tablespoon chopped sage**
4 **green olives, pitted and**	¼ **cup chopped prosciutto or**
chopped	**bacon**

Fry the pieces of pheasant in **olive oil** until golden-brown. Add the marinade, and let the pheasant stew till it is tender and the liquid is of a rich consistency. Serve over Crostini (Chap. X).

LEPRE DOLCE E FORTE

Hare in Sour-Sweet Sauce   *Alto Adige*

Clean the **hare,** and cut it into small serving pieces. Brown well in **olive oil,** chopped **onion, parsley,** and **sweet basil** to taste. Add 2 cups **water,** 3 tablespoons **tomato sauce, salt** and **pepper** to taste. Stir well, cover, and simmer 1½ hours, or until tender. Mix thoroughly

- 1 **cup vinegar**
- 1 **cup water**
- 2 **tablespoons grated bitter chocolate**
- 2 **tablespoons sugar**
- ½ **cup pignon nuts**
- ⅓ **cup white raisins**
- 2 **tablespoons chopped candied fruit**

making a sauce, and add to the cooked hare. Stir well, cover, and let simmer another 10 minutes.

OCA ARROSTITA

Roast Goose   *Emilia*

Clean the **goose** well, and pass it over fire to be sure all hair is removed. Remove leaf fat, and save it.

Stuffing
- ½ **pound Italian sausage, chopped, or ground pork**
- 3 **tablespoons chopped parsley**
- ½ **cup chopped onion**
- 1 **goose liver, chopped fine**
- 1 **tablespoon chopped shallots or chives**
  salt and pepper to taste
- ½ **cup butter**
- 2 **cups bread crumbs**

        1 cup finely-chopped roasted chestnuts *
        2 well-beaten eggs
        1 cup water

Sauté sausage or pork, parsley, onion, liver, shallots or chives, and salt and pepper in butter, and add bread crumbs, nuts, eggs, and water. Mix all these together well, and stuff goose; sew it with twine. Chop the saved leaf fat fine, and lay it in roasting pan with goose. Cover in 425° oven for 15 minutes. Reduce heat to 350° and roast till tender, basting often.

PICCIONE ARROSTITO

Roast Pigeon or Dove   *Toscana*

Clean each **bird** thoroughly, and stuff it with a slice of **prosciutto** or **bacon**. Rub with **salt, pepper, origano, parsley,** and **butter** to taste. Place in a covered roaster, in a 350° oven about 15 minutes (until heated thoroughly). Remove cover, and continue roasting till tender.

PICCIONI IN SALMI

Marinated Pigeons or Doves   *Umbria*

Clean the **birds** thoroughly, cut them into serving pieces, and place these in a large shallow bowl. Prepare a marinade of

2 anchovies, chopped	4 black olives, pitted and chopped
2 cloves garlic, minced	
¼ cup minced parsley	4 green olives, pitted and chopped
2 tablespoons capers	
3 whole cloves	½ teaspoon pepper
½ teaspoon sage	2 crushed chili peppers
¼ cup vinegar	1 cup water

Pour marinade over all, and stir well; allow to marinate 2 hours, stirring occasionally. Then drain. In a kettle sauté:

½ cup minced onion	½ cup chopped prosciutto or bacon
½ cup olive oil	

* See Castagne Arrostite, Chapter IX.

When golden-brown add pieces of bird, and brown them. Add the marinade, and simmer ½ hour. Add juice of 1 **lemon**. Stir, and simmer until tender.

TACCULA

Thrushes °   *Sardegna*

6 thrushes
2 cloves garlic, minced
1 cup minced bacon
1 tablespoon myrtle or
    rosemary leaves

½ cup olive oil
¼ cup butter
½ cup Marsala wine
    salt and pepper to taste

Mix garlic, bacon, myrtle or rosemary leaves, and salt and pepper. Stuff the birds. Sauté in the oil and butter. When golden-brown add wine, cover, and simmer ½ hour.

UCCELLI CON FAGIOLI

Birds with Beans °   *Toscana*

2 tablespoons minced onion
1 tablespoon minced, or 1 teaspoon dried sage
½ cup olive oil
6 small wild birds
1 cup tomato sauce mixed with ½ cup water
    salt and pepper to taste
4 cups cooked beans (navy or Windsor)

Sauté onion and sage in oil; add birds and sauté until golden-brown. Add tomato sauce, salt, and pepper, and simmer 15 minutes. Add beans, and simmer another 15 minutes.

° In the United States, where the taking of small wild birds is illegal, baby chickens, squabs, or Cornish hens may be used instead.

CHAPTER VIII

CONTORNO
Accompaniment to Main Course

A. INSALATE (Salads)

INSALATA BANDIERA

Flag Salad   *Emilia*

A salad of many colors to be offered in individual servings in a large lazy susan, with Italian mayonnaise in a center dish. In preparing it, choose:

> **fresh tomatoes, sliced or diced**
> **green beans, boiled, drained, and cooled**
> **chopped carrots, fresh or boiled and cooled**
> **florets of cauliflower, boiled, drained, and cooled**
> **potatoes, boiled, peeled, and diced, with a bit of chopped green onion added**
> **red beets, boiled, peeled, and sliced or diced**
> **finely-cut endive or other greens**

Prepare **Maionese** for the center dish and **Salsa per l'Insalata** for the individual servings (see Chap. VI).

In preparing the Flag Salad, make your own choice among the vegetables, parboiling, straining, and cooling each vegetable separately (drop it into rapidly boiling salt water, and leave it just a few minutes, till cooked but firm). Do not cook the tomatoes or members of the lettuce family (romaine, endive, chicory, escarole, dandelion). When each vegetable is cooled, sprinkle it with salt and pepper and salad dressing to taste; toss well and place in one or another of the individual dishes on the lazy susan, so that each dish is different from the others. For instance, place tomatoes in one dish, endive in the next, carrots in the third, creating a patterned effect.

INSALATA COTTA

Cooked Salad   *All Regions*

Choice of Vegetables

Swiss chard	dandelion greens
spinach	broccoli
endive	chicory

Place the washed greens in a large kettle with as little water as possible. Cover, and simmer until wilted. Stir carefully, and cook in the natural juice until tender but firm. Remove to a bowl; **salt** and **pepper** to taste. With a fork and a sharp knife, cut (do not chop) through greens several times just for serving convenience. Top with 1 or 2 tablespoons **olive oil** and a dash or two of **lemon juice.** Carefully stir to serve.

INSALATA DI ARANCI

Orange Salad   *Southern Regions*
*Known in Abruzzi as Christmas Salad, it is always
served on Christmas Eve.*

Arrange round thin slices of peeled **oranges** on a platter. Sprinkle abundantly with **black pepper.** Thinly pour **olive oil** over all, and let marinate ½ hour before serving.

INSALATA DI ASPARAGI LESSATI

Boiled Asparagus Salad   *Lombardia*

Boil **asparagus** tips in salt water till tender but firm. Drain and cool. Sprinkle with **salt** and **pepper** to taste, a little **olive oil,** and a dash or so of **wine vinegar** or **lemon juice.**

INSALATA DI BARBABIETOLE

Red Beet Salad   *Lucania*

Cover **beets** (young ones preferred) in double boiler, and cook over boiling water 30 minutes or until tender. Peel and chill. Slice onto a deep platter. Sprinkle chopped **parsley, mint,** and **onion** to taste over all, then a little **olive oil, salt, pepper,** and **wine vinegar.** Allow to marinate at least ½ hour before serving.

INSALATA DI CAVOLFIORE

Cauliflower Salad   *Campania*

Boil **cauliflower** florets in salt water till tender but firm; drain and cool. Sprinkle with **salt** and **pepper** then with chopped **parsley** and **onion** over all. Add a little **olive oil** and a dash or so of **wine vinegar** or **lemon juice.** Stir carefully and serve.

INSALATA DI CAVOLFIORE E FAGIOLINI

Cauliflower and Green Bean Salad   *Abruzzi*

Boil **cauliflower** florets and **green beans** in separate pots of salt water till tender but firm; drain, and cool. Arrange the florets and the beans attractively in a deep platter. **Salt** and **pepper** to taste. Sprinkle a little chopped **mint** and **garlic** over all. Pour a little **olive oil** and a dash or so of **lemon juice** over all. Stir salad carefully, and let marinate ½ hour before using.

INSALATA DI CICORIA

Chicory Salad *All Regions*

When you are cleaning young heads of **chicory,** preserve the hearts. Place these whole in a salad bowl, add chopped **garlic** or **onion** as desired and **salt** and **pepper** to taste. Pour in a little **olive oil,** sprinkle on a dash or so of **wine vinegar** or **lemon juice.** Mix all thoroughly, and serve the salad immediately.

INSALATA DI CIPOLLE

Onion Salad *Alto Adige*

Boil **Bermuda onions** till tender but firm. Drain and cool, then slice or dice into a deep platter. Pour a little **olive oil** over them, and **salt** and **pepper** to taste. Add a dash or so of **wine vinegar.** Allow the salad to marinate 15 minutes before using.

INSALATA DI CRESCIONE

Water Cress Salad *Piemonte*

To a bowlful of freshly washed and crisped **water cress,** in bite-size pieces, add 2 or 3 hard-boiled **eggs,** peeled and sliced. Add 2 or 3 chopped fresh **green onions,** and **salt** and **pepper** to taste. Top with 1 or 2 tablespoons **olive oil** to taste. Add a dash or so of **wine vinegar,** and mix as a tossed salad.

INSALATA DI ENDIVIA MARINATA

Marinated Endive Salad *Lombardia*

Clean and chop **endive,** and place it in a salad bowl which has been rubbed with **garlic.** In a small skillet, render ½ cup finely-chopped **lean bacon,** then add 1 tablespoon **wine vinegar,** and stir. Pour over the endive to marinate. Add **salt** and **pepper** to taste.

INSALATA DI FAGIOLI

Kidney Bean Salad   *Alto Adige*

Boil **kidney beans** in salt water till tender. Drain off water for a soup base, and chill the beans. Place them in a salad bowl, and add chopped **onion** and **garlic** and **salt** and **pepper** to taste. Pour a little **olive oil** over them, and a dash or so of **wine vinegar.** Stir well.

INSALATA DI FAGIOLINI E PATATE

Green Bean and Potato Salad   *Piemonte*

- **4 large potatoes**
- **1 pound fresh green beans (Italian preferred)**
- **2 medium-sized onions, chopped**
  olive oil and wine vinegar
  salt and pepper

Wash potatoes and boil until tender; drain, peel, and cool. Boil beans in salt water till tender but firm; drain, and cool. Slice or dice potatoes into a large bowl, add beans, onions, salt and pepper to taste, and mix all carefully. Thinly pour in about 3 tablespoons olive oil and 1 tablespoon wine vinegar (according to taste). Stir the salad carefully, and let it marinate at least 2 hours before serving.

INSALATA DI GAMBERI

Shrimp Salad   *Campania*

- **3 large potatoes, boiled, peeled, cooled, diced**
- **¼ cup capers**
- **1 dozen cooked shrimp**
- **2 cups green beans, boiled, drained, cooled, diced**
- **2 tablespoons minced onion (fresh green preferred)**
  salt and pepper
  olive oil and vinegar

Arrange the potatoes, capers, beans, and onion attractively on a platter. Salt and pepper to taste. Thinly pour a little olive oil over the salad, and add a dash or so of wine vinegar. Let marinate at least ½ hour before serving.

INSALATA DI POMODORO

Tomato Salad *Lucania*

5 tomatoes, sliced or cubed	¼ teaspoon wine vinegar
1 teaspoon crushed	2 cloves garlic, chopped
origano	3 tablespoons olive oil

salt and pepper to taste

Mix all together thoroughly, and let marinate ½ hour before serving. Serve with crusty Italian bread.

INSALATA DI POMODORI RIPIENI

Stuffed Tomato Salad *Calabria*

6 large firm tomatoes	2 hard-boiled eggs, peeled and
½ cup capers	minced
2 cloves garlic, minced	1 teaspoon crushed origano
3 tablespoons olive oil	¼ teaspoon wine vinegar

salt and pepper to taste

Carefully hollow out tomatoes, discarding core. Chop the center pulp, mix it thoroughly with the other ingredients, and stuff the shells.

INSALATA DI RAVANELLI D'INVERNO

Winter Radish Salad *Alto Adige*

Scrape **winter radishes** clean, and slice them very thin. **Salt** and **pepper** to taste, cover thinly with **olive oil,** and add a dash or so of **wine vinegar.** Let marinate 15 minutes before using.

INSALATA DI SALMONE

Salmon Salad *Toscana*

> 2 cups red salmon, broken into cubes
> ¼ cup chopped onion (fresh green preferred)
>   salt and pepper to taste
> 2 tablespoons olive oil
> ¼ teaspoon wine vinegar or lemon juice

Carefully mix all together thoroughly. Let the salad marinate ½ hour before serving.

INSALATA DI TONNO

Tuna Salad *Toscana*

> 2 cups tuna, broken into cubes
> ¼ cup chopped onion (fresh green preferred)
>   salt and pepper to taste
> 2 tomatoes, cubed (optional)
> 1 cup cooked, strained, cooled pinto beans (optional)
> 3 tablespoons olive oil
> 1 teaspoon wine vinegar or lemon juice

Carefully mix all the ingredients thoroughly, and let them marinate ½ hour before serving.

INSALATA PRIMAVERA

Springtime Salad *Umbria*

> 1 head crispy endive, dandelion shoots, or other desired
>   green, broken into bite-size pieces
> 2 fresh tomatoes, diced
> 1 clove garlic, minced
> 2 tablespoons capers
> 5 or 6 radishes, thinly sliced
> 2 sprigs of parsley, minced
>   salt and pepper to taste

½ teaspoon crushed origano
olive oil and wine vinegar

Place all in a salad bowl. Pour a little olive oil over all, and add a dash or so of vinegar. Mix thoroughly as a tossed salad.

INSALATA RICCIOLINA

Curly Salad *Toscana*

Prepare **Salsa per l'insalata** (Chap. VI). In a large salad bowl rubbed with **garlic,** place chopped crisp curly **lettuce** (or endive, or dandelion shoots). **Salt** and **pepper** to taste. Add salad dressing to taste, mix thoroughly, and serve immediately.

INSALATA SUPERBA

Superb Salad *Puglia*

Maionese (Chap. VI)
6 large potatoes, boiled, peeled, cooled, diced
2 tablespoons minced onion (green preferred)
2 hard-boiled eggs, peeled and minced
6 or 8 green olives, pitted and sliced
salt and pepper to taste
1 tablespoon olive oil
1 tablespoon milk

Pour the milk over the potatoes and stir carefully. Add the rest of the ingredients, and mix all thoroughly. Let the salad marinate ½ hour before serving.

B. UOVA (*Egg Dishes*)

Papa was a master at flipping an omelet into the air and inverting it for browning the underside. A large plate may be used in turning an omelet over for underside browning; however the oven method, suggested in the following recipes, is very satisfactory.

FRITTATA CON CIPOLLE

Onion Omelet   *Piemonte*

- ¼ cup butter
- 1 tablespoon olive oil
- salt and pepper to taste
- 1 pound onions, peeled and sliced
- 6 eggs, well beaten

Blend butter and oil in 12-inch skillet. Add onions, cover the skillet, and simmer about 15 minutes, until they are thoroughly wilted. Remove lid, increase heat, and sauté onions till delicately brown. Add eggs, salt, and pepper. Distribute onions evenly, and when omelet has formed, place under broiler until golden-brown. Cut as a pie to serve.

FRITTATA CON CIPOLLE E FUNGHI

Onion and Mushroom Omelet   *Piemonte*

Follow the preceding recipe until the **onions** are wilted. Add 2 cups sliced **mushrooms,** increase the heat, and sauté them with the onions, stirring occasionally, until both are delicately brown. Add the **eggs** as directed, and continue.

FRITTATA CON PEPERONI

Pepper Omelet   *Sicilia*

- 1 dozen green or red peppers, or 8 or 10 chili peppers, or a mixture of all kinds
- ½ cup olive oil
- 6 eggs, well beaten
- salt and pepper to taste

Remove hearts and seeds from peppers, and slice into ½-inch strips. Place in skillet with olive oil. Cover and cook slowly until thoroughly

pepper to taste. Sauté all together till golden-brown. Add eggs, and mix thoroughly. Bake the omelet in 350° oven ½ hour, or until golden-brown. Cut as pie to serve.

FRITTATINE TRITATE

Small Omelets in Full Dress *Piemonte*

5 eggs, well beaten	½ cup minced parsley
1 tablespoon flour	1 tablespoon milk

2 tablespoons grated Parmesan cheese

Mix all into a creamy batter. Drop it a teaspoonful at a time into a buttered skillet. When the little omelets are delicately brown on both sides, remove them to a platter.

Sauce

¼ cup butter	2 teaspoons chopped mint
2 tomatoes, blanched and cubed	leaves
	salt and pepper to taste

Melt butter in a saucepan. Add tomatoes, mint leaves, salt, and pepper. Simmer till tomatoes liquefy. Add little omelets, heat all thoroughly, and serve.

UOVA IN PURGATORIO

Eggs in Purgatory *Campania*

eggs, desired number	¼ cup chopped onion
1 tablespoon olive oil	¼ cup minced parsley
salt and pepper to taste	2 cups cubed, blanched tomatoes (or canned)

Sauté onion and parsley with salt and pepper in oil 10 minutes. Add tomatoes, and simmer ½ hour, stirring often. Bring to a boil, then carefully drop in the eggs, one at a time, to poach. Serve on buttered toast.

C. SFORMATI (*Molds*)

*Molds are most effective as edible garnishes and,
with ingenuity, can contribute to an artistic and
appetizing table.*

SFORMATINI DI GELATINA

Small Molds of Gelatin   *Northern Regions*

Stewing hen, veal shanks, pork or beef knuckles make the best
gelatin. The connective tissue in the cords leading to the feet really
is the best gluten, and a thrifty cook will use chicken feet as a
gelatin base.

Chicken gelatin: Dip **chicken feet** into boiling water to soften
the tough outer skin, which can readily be pulled off along with the
toenails. Wash the feet well, and place them in a large kettle with
the disjointed chicken. Add 2 teaspoons **salt,** 1 teaspoon **pepper,**
1 cup chopped **celery,** ½ cup chopped **parsley,** and 1 cup minced
carrot for seasoning, and completely cover with cold water. Gradually bring to boiling point, and simmer 3 or 4 hours. Remove chicken,
and strain stock through a cloth. While it cools, stir it occasionally
for even cooling. Pour the cool stock into miniature molds, and set
in cool room or refrigerator for jelling. *For a fancier garnish,* place
½ hard-boiled **egg** in each miniature mold before the cool stock is
poured in. When jelling is complete, set molds for a second in a
shallow pan containing a little hot water, and invert them on
platter to be garnished. The yellow and white egg is very effective
centered in the gelatin.

Veal shanks, pork knuckles, and beef knuckles are treated in the
same manner.

SFORMATO DI UOVA

Mold of Egg   *Emilia*

Prepare **Besciamella** (Chap. VI). Butter and let cool an angel-
food pan, or mold with a hole in center, and brush it with fine

bread crumbs. To the cold Besciamella add 3 well-beaten **egg yolks** and 1 cup chopped **Swiss cheese.** Mix well, and slowly fold in 3 stiffly-beaten **egg whites.** If desired, add ½ cup chopped **prosciutto.** Place filled mold in larger pan of boiling water; put both in 325° oven for 1 hour. Remove from oven, turn out onto a platter, and serve immediately. In the center buttered peas, green beans, mushrooms, or carrots may be added.

SFORMATO DI VEGETALI

Mold of Vegetables   *Toscana*

> 2 **cups of Besciamella (Chap. VI)**
> 4 **eggs**
> ½ **cup grated Parmesan cheese**
> 2 **cups parboiled and chopped spinach, Swiss chard, cauliflower, green beans, broccoli, zucchini squash, or asparagus**

Beat eggs well with ½ cup cheese. Add these and vegetables to the cold Besciamella. Stir well, and pour into an angel-food pan (or mold with a hole in the center) which has been buttered and has been brushed with fine bread crumbs. Set pan in a larger pan of boiling water in 325° oven, for a hot-water bath of 1 hour. Remove from oven, empty onto a platter, and serve immediately. In the center, you may place buttered mushrooms, Scaloppine di Vitello al Limone (Chap. VII, A), or whatever you care to serve.

D. VEGETALI (*Vegetables*)

For a *colorful* vegetable, leave cover off kettle while cooking. However, for preservation of vitamins, use as little water as possible, cover the kettle, and steam the vegetable just long enough to cook it.

ASPARAGI ALLA PANNA

Asparagus with Cream   *Emilia*

Boil 1 pint rich **milk,** and let it cool. Drop 1 pound **asparagus** tips into boiling salt water, and cook till tender but firm; drain. Take thick creamy **skim** from milk, and stir it into the cooked tips. **Salt** and **pepper** to taste. (The skimmed milk should be saved for another purpose.)

ASPARAGI CON BURRO E FORMAGGIO

Asparagus with Butter and Cheese   *Piemonte*

**2 dozen asparagus spears   ½ cup grated Parmesan cheese
½ cup melted butter**

Boil asparagus spears in salt water till tender but firm. Drain, and arrange attractively on platter, with tips in center (as a sunburst). Sprinkle tips with cheese and salt and pepper, and cover spears with hot, delicately brown butter. Pass the platter around the table immediately, for the diners to transfer spears with their fingertips to their own plates. Each spear is then picked up with the fingertips and nibbled from tip to white portion, which is discarded on the side of the plate.

CARCIOFI DI BOLOGNA

Artichokes of Bologna   *Emilia*

Cut young tender **artichoke buds** in two lengthwise. Sauté a bit of minced **onion** in a little **olive oil.** When delicately brown add **artichoke halves** (exterior leaves down). Sprinkle each heart with **salt, pepper,** and a dab of **butter.** Add ½ cup water, cover, and simmer 20 minutes. Baste with juice before serving.

CARCIOFI FRITTI

Fried Artichokes   *Lazio*
*For the spring of the year, when artichokes are
beautiful fresh buds with tender leaves*

Parboil **artichokes** in salt water. Drain, and dry with soft towel. Dip in **flour,** then in well-beaten **egg,** and deep-fry in hot **olive oil.**

CARCIOFI RIPIENI ALLA ROMANA

Stuffed Artichokes, Roman Style *Lazio*

- 4 young crisp artichokes
- 1 cup bread crumbs dampened with a little water
- 1 tablespoon minced mint leaves
- 2 cloves garlic, minced
  salt and pepper to taste
- ½ cup olive oil

Holding artichokes firmly, strike them one at a time hard against the table. The leaves will now open readily. With a knife handle, poke center of each artichoke, and remove prickly choke at head of heart. Remove any thorns from leaves. Remove stems evenly so that artichokes will stand well in pan. Mix remaining ingredients, and stuff artichokes. Set in roaster, in 1 inch of water to which a lemon slice and a teaspoonful of salt have been added. Cover, and bake in 350° oven for 1 hour.

CARCIOFI RIPIENI ALLA SICILIANA

Stuffed Artichokes, Sicilian Style *Sicilia*

- 6 artichokes
- 2 cups bread crumbs
- ¼ cup chopped parsley
- 3 cloves garlic, minced
- 1 small can anchovies in oil, chopped
- ½ cup olive oil
  pepper to taste

Follow directions for preceding recipe, Carciofi Ripieni alla Romana.

CAVOLFIORE ALLA PIEMONTESE

Cauliflower, Piedmont Style *Piemonte*

Drop **cauliflower** florets into boiling salt water, and cook until tender but firm. Drain, and place in a bowl. Sprinkle with abundant grated **Parmesan cheese,** and top with hot melted **butter.** Serve immediately.

CAVOLFIORE INDORATO

Cauliflower Dressed in Egg   *Abruzzi*

Drop **cauliflower** florets into boiling salt water and cook till tender but firm. Drain, and dry with soft towel. Roll them separately in **flour**, then in well-beaten **egg**, and deep-fry in hot **oil**. Let them drain on absorbent paper. **Salt** and serve.

CIPOLLE RIPIENE

Stuffed Onions   *Alto Adige*

> 6 **fairly large onions**
> ½ **cup butter**
> 1 **large tomato, parboiled, peeled, and chopped**
> 1½ **cups milk**
> ½ **teaspoon salt**
> 4 **slices dry bread, broken into small pieces**
> 1 **tablespoon sugar**
> ¼ **cup seedless raisins**
> 2 **eggs**
> 1 **tablespoon grated Parmesan cheese**

Peel and parboil onions. Cut 1 inch off top of each onion and, with a fork, pull out heart and surrounding rings, until only a thin shell remains. Chop the pulled-out rings well, and sauté in butter. Add remaining ingredients, and thoroughly mix. Stuff onion shells with the mixture, and place upside-down in casserole that has been thinly coated with olive oil. Bake, uncovered, in 350° oven till golden-brown.

FAGIOLI ALL'UCCELLETTO SCAPPATO

Beans with the Bird That Flew Away   *Toscana*
> *The name refers to the somewhat similar main-*
> *course dish Uccelli con Fagioli (Chap. VII, D).*

> 2 **sage leaves, chopped**
> 3 **cloves garlic**

    2 tablespoons olive oil
    ½ cup tomato sauce or 2 fresh tomatoes, blanched and
        chopped
      salt and pepper to taste
    1 cup water
    2 cups cooked beans (navy, Windsor, or pinto)

Sauté the sage and garlic in the oil. When the garlic is golden-brown discard it. Add the tomato sauce, salt and pepper, and water. Let them simmer 15 minutes. Add the cooked beans, and let them simmer another 15 minutes.

FAGIOLI RIFATTI

Cooked Dry Beans   *Toscana*
    *The Tuscans, who like beans, cook a pot of dried
    beans so that they can be recooked in many ways.
    Therefore the name* Rifatti *(literally, remade) for
    basic beans.*

I. Wash 1 pound dried **beans,** and soak overnight in 3 quarts water. In the morning, cook in the same water till tender (3 to 6 hours), adding **salt** to taste and stirring occasionally.

II. Wash 1 pound dried **beans,** and soak them in 1½ quarts water. Add 1 teaspoon **salt** and ¼ teaspoon **soda,** and cook till tender (2 to 3 hours), stirring occasionally.

FAGIOLINI AL BURRO

Green Beans in Butter   *Alto Adige*
    ¼ cup butter   1 pound green beans (Italian
    4 tablespoons cold water   preferred)
              salt and pepper to taste

Wash and cut beans. Place butter and water in saucepan over fire. When butter melts add beans, salt and pepper. Cover, and steam slowly till tender, stirring occasionally.

FAGIOLINI ALLA VENEZIANA

Green Beans, Venetian Style   *Venezia*

- 2 pounds green beans
     (Italian preferred)
- 2 cloves garlic
- ¼ cup butter

- 2 tablespoons lard or bacon
     drippings
- salt and pepper to taste
- pinch of clove

Boil beans in salt water till tender; drain. In a skillet, sauté garlic in butter and lard. Discard garlic when delicately brown, and add the beans. Season with salt, pepper, and cloves. Cover, and simmer about 15 minutes. If desired, add 2 tablespoons grated Parmesan cheese; stir well, and simmer 3 more minutes.

FAVE CON CIPOLLE

Windsor Beans with Onions   *Abruzzi*

- 1 cup chopped onion
- 1 clove garlic, minced
- ¼ cup olive oil
- 2 pounds shelled fresh
     Windsor beans

- ½ cup chopped parsley
- 2 tablespoons grated Romano
     cheese
- 1 cup tomato sauce
- 2 cups water

Sauté onions and garlic in oil till golden-brown. Add remaining ingredients, and stir well. Cover, and simmer 45 minutes.

FINOCCHI FRITTI

Fried Sweet Fennel   *Sicilia*
       *Sweet (Florence) fennel is similar to celery but
       has a faint licorice taste.*

Cut **fennel** stems into 3-inch lengths, and parboil in **salt water.** Dry them with soft towel, and roll them in well-beaten **egg** and in fine **bread crumbs.** Deep-fry in **olive oil** or lard.

FIORI DI ZUCCHINI

Squash Flowers *Venezia*

From squash plants as they grow, pick **blossoms** of suckers that will not mature. Wash carefully, and shake dry. Remove stamen and green nodule around outside of each flower. Dip all the flowers into a batter of 1 **egg,** 1 tablespoon **milk,** and 1 tablespoon **flour,** and deep-fry them in **oil.** Sprinkle with **salt** and **pepper.**

FRITTO MISTO DI VEGETALI *

Fried Mixed Vegetables *Abruzzi*

Specialty for Christmas Eve

Choice of Vegetables

artichoke hearts	fennel stems
asparagus tips	mushrooms
broccoli buds	potatoes
cauliflower florets	Swiss chard stems
celery stems	zucchini
eggplant	zucchini blossoms

Batter

½ **cake yeast**	1 **teaspoon salt**
2 **eggs, well beaten**	½ **cup lukewarm water**

4 or 5 **tablespoons flour**

Cut chosen vegetable into bite-size pieces. Unless choice is zucchini blossoms, parboil, drain, and dry thoroughly with soft towel. Mix other ingredients into a smooth and creamy batter. With a fork, dip each piece of vegetable into the batter, and deep-fry all the pieces in hot oil or pure lard. Or, as they do in Milan, without any batter, dip pieces into well-beaten **egg** and then into fine **bread crumbs,** and deep-fry them in **oil** or lard.

° See Fritto Misto di Pesce and Fritto Misto di Carne, in Chapter VII, Sections A and B. Either can be served with this recipe. Of course meat is not served on Christmas Eve in Italy.

FUNGHI ALLA GRATICOLA

Broiled Mushrooms   *Toscana*

For broiling, use large fresh **mushrooms,** not the button size nor the canned. Wash them well, and remove the stems. Place the mushrooms in an oil-lined broiling pan, stem side up, and cover them with a film of **olive oil, salt, pepper,** and **garlic** to taste. Add a dash of **butter** to each. Broil them till they are tender, basting occasionally. Remove the garlic before serving.

FUNGHI ALLA MARSALA

Mushrooms with Wine   *Emilia*

    1 pint mushrooms, drained and dried with a soft towel
    1 cup flour
    ¼ cup butter
      salt and pepper
    ¼ cup water
    3 tablespoons white wine (Marsala preferred)

Fresh mushrooms should be sliced and boiled in salt water till tender but firm, then drained and dried well with a soft towel. Dip them in flour, and fry them slowly in the butter till delicately brown. Salt and pepper to taste. Add water, cover, and then simmer 15 minutes. Add wine, stir, and cover again. Simmer 2 more minutes.

FUNGHI RIPIENI

Stuffed Mushrooms   *Lombardia*

Clean and wash fresh **mushrooms** well; remove stems. Place tops, hollow side up, in a saucepan lined with **butter.** Chop stems, and mix them with half the quantity of fine **bread crumbs** and a little melted butter. Then thoroughly mix in 2 well-beaten **eggs,** 1 tablespoon **cream,** and 1 tablespoon grated **Parmesan cheese.** Fill hollows of mushroom tops, then pour over them a little melted butter and add a few bread crumbs, salt, and pepper. Bake in 350° oven ½ hour, or until delicately brown.

MELANZANE ALLA PARMIGIANA

Eggplant in Cheese Sauce   *Campania*

> 1 preparation of Salsa Parmigiana (Chap. VI)
> 2 medium-sized eggplants
> 3 eggs, well beaten with ½ cup grated Romano cheese,
>   salt and pepper to taste
> ½ cup flour (in a shallow bowl)
> ¼ cup olive oil
> 1 cup crumbled ricotta or chopped mozzarella

Cut eggplants into ½-inch slices, and parboil in water to remove bitterness. Drain, and squeeze; dry with soft towel. Dip one by one into egg mixture and flour, and fry in oil till golden-brown on both sides. Place in a casserole successive layers of tomato sauce, fried eggplant, ricotta or mozzarella, till all is used. Cover with remaining tomato sauce, and set the casserole, uncovered, in 350° oven for 20 minutes.

MELANZANE FRITTE

Fried Eggplant   *Abruzzi*

> 2 medium-sized eggplants
> 2 eggs, well beaten, with salt and pepper to taste
> 2 cups fine bread crumbs
> ¼ cup butter and ¼ cup olive oil

Cut eggplants into ½-inch slices. Parboil in water to remove bitterness; drain and squeeze. Dry with soft towel. Dip slices one by one into egg, then into bread crumbs. Fry in butter and oil till golden-brown on both sides.

For **Melanzane Indorate,** follow directions as for **Zucchini Indorati** (page 160).

MELANZANE RIPIENE ALLA CALABRESE

Stuffed Eggplant, Calabrian Style   *Calabria*

3 medium-sized eggplants	½ pound ground beef
3 tablespoons minced onion	½ pound ground pork
	2 eggs
¼ cup minced parsley	¼ cup grated Romano cheese
2 tablespoons minced basil	2 cups cooked rice or fine bread crumbs
¼ cup olive oil	

salt and pepper

Have freshly prepared **Salsa Parmigiana** (Chap. VI) in readiness.
Cut eggplants in two, and boil in salt water 5 minutes. Drain,
squeeze, and dry with soft towel. With sharp knife, remove pulp,
leaving ½-inch-thick shells. Chop pulp, and sauté it with onion,
parsley, and sweet basil in a little olive oil. Add meat, and fry till
golden-brown. Let cool, then add eggs, grated cheese, rice or bread
crumbs, and salt and pepper to taste. Mix all thoroughly with 1 cup
of the tomato sauce, and fill shells. Top with sauce and a little
grated cheese. Place in oil-lined casserole, and top with remaining
sauce. Bake, uncovered, in 350° oven 45 minutes.

MELANZANE RIPIENE ALLA SICILIANA

Stuffed Eggplant, Sicilian Style   *Sicilia*

3 eggplants
1 cup ricotta
2 eggs
6 fresh sardines, cleaned and diced (or canned, with oil)
¼ cup capers
½ cup grated Romano cheese
¼ cup chopped parsley
salt and pepper to taste

Have freshly prepared **Salsa Parmigiana** (Chap. VI) in readiness.
Cut the eggplants in two, and boil them in salt water 5 minutes.
Drain, squeeze, and dry with a soft towel. Remove centers, leaving

½-inch shells. Chop the pulp, and mix with the ricotta, eggs, sardines, capers, parsley, and half of the grated cheese. Add salt and pepper and ½ of the tomato sauce. Stir well, and stuff shells. Place these in oil-lined roasting pan, and pour tomato sauce over all topping it with the remaining cheese. Cover, and bake in 350° oven 45 minutes.

PANZEROTTI

Vegetable Puffs   *Emilia*
> *These delicious miniature puff balls with filling can also be used as a cocktail snack.*

1 cup milk	1 teaspoon salt
½ cup butter	1 cup flour

4 eggs

Heat milk, butter, and salt in a saucepan over a slow fire until butter has melted. With wooden spoon, stir in flour, and make a smooth paste. When it forms a smooth ball, remove pan from fire. Add 1 egg at a time, stirring well. When all 4 eggs are in, drop a scant teaspoonful of batter at a time onto a greased cooky sheet. Bake in 350° oven ½ hour.

With a pastry tube, insert the desired vegetable into the little puff balls. Place them in 300° oven for 3 minutes before serving. The **filling** may be any desired cooked vegetable with a little gravy or white sauce or butter—such as finely-minced buttered broccoli, spinach, peas, or cauliflower. Creamed ricotta or minced mozzarella cheese with a bit of minced parsley, so used, is also very appetizing.

PASTINACA

Parsnips   *Abruzzi*
Served on Christmas Eve

Clean young, tender **parsnips,** and boil whole in salt water till tender. Drain, dry with soft towel, and slice. Dip the slices one at a time into **flour,** then into well-beaten **egg,** and deep-fry them in **olive oil** till golden-brown. **Salt** to taste.

PATATE ALLA TOSCANA

Potatoes, Tuscan Style   *Toscana*

> 1½ **pounds potatoes**   2 **cups cream**
> ½ **cup melted butter**   **salt and pepper to taste**
> 1 **tablespoon flour**   3 **tablespoons minced parsley**
> ¼ **teaspoon nutmeg**

Peel and dice potatoes. Cream melted butter and flour in a saucepan, and add cream, salt, pepper, parsley, and nutmeg. When the mixture is about to boil, add the potatoes. Stirring carefully, simmer about 35 minutes.

PATATE CON BURRO E PREZZEMOLO

Potatoes with Butter and Parsley   *Toscana*

> ½ **cup butter**   **salt and pepper to taste**
> **enough water to cover**   1 **cup chopped parsley**
> 4 **large potatoes, peeled and diced**

Place butter and water in a deep skillet. When butter is melted add potatoes, salt, pepper, and parsley, and stir well. Cook over medium heat, stirring occasionally, till water is absorbed. Serve immediately.

PATATE CON FAGIOLINI

Potatoes with Green Beans   *Abruzzi*

> ¼ **cup minced onion**   ½ **cup tomato paste**
> 1 **clove garlic, minced**   2 **cups water**
> 3 **tablespoons minced**   **salt and pepper to taste**
>   **parsley**   2 **pounds green beans (Italian**
> 2 **tablespoons chopped**   **preferred)**
>   **basil**   4 **medium-sized potatoes**
> ½ **cup olive oil**   **peeled and quartered**

Sauté onion, garlic, parsley, and sweet basil in oil. When delicately brown add tomato paste, water, salt and pepper. Add the beans and potatoes, stirring well. Cover, and simmer ½ hour or longer, till done.

PATATE FRITTE ALLA BOLOGNESE

Fried Potatoes, Bologna Style   *Emilia*

Peel and cut 4 large **potatoes** in fourths, lengthwise, making triangles, and slice these to ½-inch thickness. Shake them in a paper bag with ½ cup **flour**. Dip the little triangles into 2 well-beaten **eggs** with **salt** added, and deep-fry them in a large skillet in just enough **olive oil** to cover them. Strain, and serve immediately.

PATATE RIPIENE ALLA TOSCANA

Stuffed Potatoes, Tuscan Style   *Toscana*

6 large potatoes	¼ pound prosciutto, chopped
1 cup sliced mushrooms	3 eggs
2 tablespoons chopped parsley	¼ teaspoon nutmeg
¼ cup butter	1 teaspoon salt
¼ pound chicken livers, chopped	½ teaspoon pepper
	Parmesan cheese

Boil potatoes, and remove the jackets. Carefully remove (and mash) the inside, leaving ½-inch-thick shells. In a small pan, sauté mushrooms and parsley in half the butter. In another pan, sauté chicken livers in rest of butter. Put them together, add all the rest of the ingredients, including the mashed potato, and mix. Fill the shells, and sprinkle with grated Parmesan cheese. Place in greased casserole and bake, uncovered, in 350° oven 20 minutes.

PISELLI AL PROSCIUTTO

Green Peas with Ham   *Emilia*

1 teaspoon minced onion	2 tablespoons butter
1 cup prosciutto, or lean boiled ham, minced	2 cups fresh-shelled peas
1 tablespoon olive oil	2 tablespoons water
	salt and pepper to taste

Sauté the onion and ham in the oil and butter. When the onion is delicately brown, cover the pan and let it simmer 10 minutes. Add the peas and water, salt and pepper, and let simmer 10 minutes.

PEPERONI E POMODORI FRESCHI

Green Peppers and Fresh Tomatoes   *Puglia*

Render ½ cup chopped **salt pork,** and add 5 **green peppers** (from which core and seeds have been removed), cut in slices. Cover, and cook till they are wilted and a bit browned. Add 2 or 3 blanched and sliced **tomatoes,** and **pepper** to taste. Cover, and simmer ½ hour.

PEPERONI RIPIENI ABRUZZESI

Stuffed Peppers, Abruzzi Style   *Abruzzi*

6 green peppers	¼ cup chopped anchovies
2 cups bread crumbs or	pepper to taste
ground raw potato	2 cloves garlic, minced
½ cup minced parsley	⅓ cup olive oil
¼ cup grated Romano cheese	

Carefully remove stems and hearts of peppers, discard seeds and stems. Chop hearts, and mix them thoroughly with the other ingredients, except the cheese. Fill the pepper shells, and place them in an oil-lined casserole, sprinkling the top of each pepper with cheese. Cover, and bake in 350° oven 45 minutes. Uncover, and bake another 10 minutes.

PEPERONI RIPIENI ALLA TOSCANA

Stuffed Peppers, Tuscan Style   *Toscana*

6 green peppers	2 cups leftover roast, ground
¼ cup minced parsley	3 tablespoons minced onion
2 eggs	3 tablespoons grated Parmesan
¼ cup melted butter	cheese
salt and pepper to taste	

Carefully remove stems and cores of peppers, discarding seeds and stems. Chop the pulpy hearts, and mix them thoroughly with the other ingredients. Fill pepper shells, and place them in oil-lined casserole, adding a few bread crumbs and a dash of olive oil to each pepper. Cover, and bake in 350° oven ½ hour. Uncover, and bake another 20 minutes.

POMODORI RIPIENI AL FORNO

Baked Stuffed Tomatoes   *Lazio*

6 large firm tomatoes	3 tablespoons olive oil, or ¼
1 cup rice	cup minced salt pork
2 cloves garlic, minced	½ cup grated Romano cheese
¼ cup minced parsley	salt and pepper

Carefully hollow out tomatoes, and discard cores. Chop the center pulp. Cook rice in 1 quart boiling salt water till half done. Drain, and cool. Sauté garlic and parsley in oil or salt pork till delicately brown. Add tomato pulp and half-cooked rice. Add cheese, salt and pepper to taste. Mix thoroughly, and stuff the tomatoes. Place in oil-lined casserole, and bake, uncovered, in 350° oven ½ hour or a little longer.

SCHIACCIATINE DI PATATE

Potato Pancakes   *Abruzzi*

3 cups grated, peeled potatoes	1 teaspoon baking powder
	1 teaspoon salt
1 egg	3 tablespoons flour

Mix the ingredients together into a thick batter. Over medium-high flame, in a large skillet, melt about ¼ inch bacon grease or lard. With a tablespoon, drop batter into hot grease, frying cakes of desired size. When golden-brown on both sides, drain and serve.

SEDANI E FAGIOLI

Celery and Beans   *Lucania*

    1 **cup chopped salt pork**
    2 **tablespoons butter or olive oil**
    3 **cups celery, cut into 1-inch lengths**
    2 **cloves garlic, minced**
    2 **cups cooked butter beans**
    4 **large tomatoes, blanched and diced, or 1 quart canned**
        tomatoes
      salt and pepper

Fry out the salt pork until crisp, and drain off excess fat. Add the butter or oil, celery, and garlic. When delicately brown, add the beans and tomatoes. Stir, cover, and let simmer ½ hour. Salt and pepper to taste.

SPINACI COL PROSCIUTTO

Spinach with Ham   *Emilia*

    1 **cup chopped prosciutto or boiled ham**
    ¼ **cup butter**
      salt and pepper
    3 **eggs blended with 3 tablespoons cream**
    2 **cups cooked strained spinach or other greens**
      bread crumbs

Sauté chopped ham in butter. Salt and pepper to taste. Add eggs and cream, and stir well. Fold in the warm spinach. Place in casserole lined with butter and bread crumbs, and sprinkle buttered crumbs on top. Bake, uncovered, in 350° oven 15 minutes.

VERZE FRITTE

Savoy Cabbage, Fried   *Alto Adige*

    1 **head cabbage (Savoy   2 cloves garlic**
        preferred)   ¼ cup butter (or more)
                       salt and pepper

Wash cabbage, and remove heart and core. Place broken cabbage leaves and garlic in skillet. Cover, and simmer till well wilted. Discard garlic. Place slices of butter over all, cover, and simmer 10 minutes more. Remove lid, stir well, and continue to cook till delicately brown. Salt and pepper to taste.

ZUCCHINI AL BURRO

Squash with Butter   *Venezia*

If **squash** is young, slice it whole. If tough, peel it before slicing. When all slices are in the skillet add a large piece of **butter, salt** and **pepper** to taste, and a dash of **cinnamon.** Cover, and simmer till done, stirring when necessary.

ZUCCHINI ALLA MONTANARA

Mountaineer Squash   *Piemonte*

In a large skillet place sliced **squash** and a big lump of **butter,** and **salt** and **pepper** to taste. Cover, and let stew till tender. Just before serving, soak pulp of **bread** in rich **milk,** and add it to the squash, stirring well. Serve topped with grated **Parmesan cheese.**

ZUCCHINI ALLA PARMIGIANA

Squash in Cheese Sauce   *Campania*

Have **Salsa Parmigiana** (Chap. VI) in readiness. Clean 6 young **zucchini,** and slice them lengthwise. Dip each slice in turn into well-beaten **egg salted** and **peppered** to taste, into **flour,** and back into egg. Fry in ¼ inch **olive oil** till golden-brown on both sides. In an oil-lined casserole place successive layers of tomato sauce, fried squash, sauce and grated **Romano cheese,** till all is used. Cover with remaining sauce, and top with grated cheese. Place, uncovered, in 350° oven for 20 minutes.

ZUCCHINI ALLA TOSCANA

Squash, Tuscan Style *Toscana*

½ cup minced salt pork
¼ cup minced parsley
½ cup minced onion

6 small zucchini, cut in fourths
2 tomatoes, blanched and diced
salt and pepper

On a chopping board, or with mortar and pestle, blend salt pork and parsley into a paste. Simmer it in skillet until it melts. Add onion; when golden-brown add zucchini. When all is golden-brown, add tomatoes and salt and pepper to taste. Cover, and simmer ½ hour. Serve topped with grated **Parmesan cheese.**

ZUCCHINI INDORATI

Squash Dressed in Egg *Campania*

2 medium-sized zucchini
½ cup flour

2 eggs
½ cup olive oil

Romano cheese

Beat the eggs well, add salt and pepper to taste, and then 2 tablespoons grated Romano cheese. Cut zucchini into ⅛-inch slices, and parboil them in water to remove bitterness; drain, and squeeze dry with soft towel. Dip slices in turn into flour, then into egg mixture. Fry in oil till golden-brown on both sides. Drain, and serve.

Eggplant may be similarly prepared.

ZUCCHINI RIPIENI ALLA NAPOLETANA

Stuffed Squash, Neapolitan Style *Campania*

Prepare **Salsa Parmigiana** (Chap. VI).

6 medium-sized zucchini
1 cup ground beef or leftover roast
½ cup chopped prosciutto, boiled ham, or Italian sausage

½ **cup chopped onion**
3 **tablespoons chopped parsley**
   salt and pepper to taste
3 **tablespoons olive oil**
1 **egg**
¼ **cup grated Romano cheese**

Hollow out center pulp of zucchini lengthwise with a sharp boning knife, without breaking them. Parboil shells, and lay on a towel to dry. Chop the pulp. Sauté meat, onions, parsley, salt, and pepper in oil. Remove from fire. Add pulp, egg, and cheese, and mix all thoroughly. Stuff shells, and place them in a casserole. Pour tomato sauce over all, and sprinkle with grated cheese. Bake 40 minutes, uncovered, in 350° oven.

ZUCCHINI RIPIENI ALLA SICILIANA

Stuffed Squash, Sicilian Style   *Sicilia*

6 **medium-sized zucchini**   ¼ **cup minced parsley**
1 **small can tuna and oil**   1 **small can anchovies**
2 **cloves garlic, minced**   **pepper to taste**
1 **egg**   1 **cup bread crumbs**

Use a boning knife or apple corer to hollow out inner pulp of zucchini lengthwise, without breaking squash. Parboil shells, and lay them on a towel to dry. Chop center pulp, and mix it thoroughly with remaining ingredients. Stuff shells, and place them in oil-lined casserole. Cover and bake in 350° oven ½ hour. Uncover, and continue baking 20 minutes.

CHAPTER IX

I DOLCI
Sweets

A. CANDITI (*Nuts and Candies*)

CASTAGNE ALLA FIAMMA

Chestnuts Aflame   *Abruzzi*
> *A delicious snack for Yuletide*

Place roasted and peeled chestnuts on a platter, and sprinkle them with sugar. Pour rum over all and light with a match. After 1 minute, blow out the flame.

CASTAGNE ARROSTITE

Roasted Chestnuts   *Lombardia*

With pointed knife or fork, prick shell of each nut (fresh) at both ends, to prevent it from exploding. Put the nuts into a baking pan in 300° oven for 35 minutes, stirring occasionally. Take pan from oven, and cover nuts with a dish towel to steam. They can soon be peeled very easily.

CASTAGNE IMBIANCATE

Blanched Chestnuts *Piemonte*

Cover dried chestnuts in saucepan with water, cover, and boil 10 minutes; drain, and peel. Cover with fresh water, and boil until tender (½ hour or longer). Then boil fast, reducing the liquid to about ½ cup. Drain when cool.

CASTAGNE LUSTRATE

Glazed Chestnuts *Lombardia*

2 cups very fine granulated   **1 cup hot water**
    sugar   **⅛ teaspoon cream of tartar**

Place all ingredients in saucepan over slow fire. Stir constantly with wooden spoon until sugar is well dissolved. Cook *quickly without* stirring, until syrup turns pale yellow. Test a drop in cold water; if it cracks, set pan immediately in cold water to check boiling. If desired, place 4 drops oil of cinnamon or lemon or other flavoring on the surface and rock pan back and forth (do not stir) to equalize the flavor. Place pan in hot water to keep syrup from hardening. Use strainer to dip blanched **chestnuts** into hot syrup and drop them onto a cooky sheet to dry.

CILIEGE LUSTRATE

Glazed Cherries *Lombardia*

The cherries (Black Marranze preferred) must have no blemishes, and each one should have a stem. Wash them, and dry them. Dip into syrup used in the preceding recipe for Glazed Chestnuts.

CROCETTE

Little Crosses *Calabria*
Calabrian Christmas specialty

Each cross consists of 4 fresh **figs** and 8 **walnut** halves. Cut a fig lengthwise from the bottom *almost* to the stem. Lay it open, and place a half-walnut on each part. Treat a second fig in the same way, and lay it on crosswise. Now prepare a third fig similarly, and invert it over the two, parallel with the first. A fourth fig, with the same treatment, is inverted and placed over all, parallel with the second. Press all together firmly. With a spatula, slide all the crosses onto a cooky sheet, and leave in 325° oven 5 minutes. Sprinkle with **powdered sugar.**

MARRONI LUSTRATI

Glazed Chestnut Balls   *Toscana*

Cover blanched **chestnuts** with fresh water, and bring to the boiling point. Cook until tender (½ hour or more). Cook rapidly so that the water evaporates to about ½ cup. Mash chestnuts well. For each cup of mashed chestnuts provide:

1 **cup powdered sugar**	1 **tablespoon cherry brandy, or**
1 **tablespoon cocoa (op-**	**substitute**
tional)	½ **cup finely-chopped nuts**

Mix all ingredients except the chopped nuts together, and roll into balls smaller than walnuts. Roll the balls into the chopped nuts, and arrange on a platter.

OSSI DI MORTO

Bones of the Dead—Nougat Candy   *Campania*
Delicacy of All Souls' Day, November 2

1 **cup honey**	½ **cup blanched filberts**
1 **cup sugar and ¼ cup**	1 **cup blanched almonds**
cold water	½ **cup pignon nuts**
3 **egg whites (beaten stiff)**	1 **teaspoon vanilla**

Have **Glassatura alla Cioccolata** (Chap. IX, D) in readiness.

Heat honey in double boiler, and at the same time warm sugar and water *slowly* in a saucepan, stirring with wooden spoon, until it reaches the burnt-sugar stage. Just as honey starts to bubble, stir in egg whites. Add burnt sugar as the bubbling continues, stirring constantly until it begins to caramelize. Add nuts and vanilla; mix thoroughly. When cool enough to handle, roll into shape of fore-fingers. Roll in the glazed chocolate frosting.

PAMPEPATO

Glazed Fruit Candy   *Emilia*

½ **cup honey**	½ **teaspoon nutmeg**
¼ **cup powdered sugar**	2 **tablespoons cinnamon**
½ **cup cake flour**	¼ **cup slivered citron**
¼ **cup powdered chocolate**	1 **cup candied fruit, ground**
(bitter preferred)	½ **cup blanched filberts, sliced**
¼ **teaspoon cloves**	½ **cup blanched almonds, split**

Heat honey and sugar in large kettle over low flame, stirring with wooden spoon until well blended. Remove from fire, and add the other ingredients. Mix well, and pour into well-buttered and floured pie pan. Bake in 300° oven ½ hour. When cool, remove from pan, and dust completely with powdered sugar. Store in airtight container.

PANFORTE DI SARDEGNA

Fruit Candy of Sardinia   *Sardegna*

1 **pound seeded dates**	1 **pound blanched chestnuts**
1 **pound seedless raisins**	**(cooked and drained)**
½ **pound figs**	1 **pound powdered sugar**
½ **pound seeded prunes**	¼ **cup fruit brandy (optional)**

Chop or grind fruits and chestnuts fine. Add the other ingredients, mix thoroughly, and knead like bread. Make into 2 long rolls an inch in diameter. Dust in powdered sugar. Store in cool place at least a week before using. Cut into inch slices to serve.

PANFORTE DI SIENA

Fruit Candy of Siena   *Toscana*
          A favorite of Dante, according to legend

½ **cup honey**	¼ **cup slivered citron**
¼ **cup powdered sugar**	1 **cup sliced candied fruit**
½ **cup cake flour**	½ **cup blanched filberts, sliced**
¼ **teaspoon nutmeg**	½ **cup blanched almonds, split**

1 **tablespoon cinnamon**

Heat honey and sugar in large kettle over low flame, stirring with wooden spoon until well blended. Remove from fire, and add the other ingredients. Mix well, and pour into buttered and floured pie pan. Bake in 300° oven ½ hour. When cool, dust completely with powdered sugar. Store in airtight container.

PRALINE DI MANDORLE

Almond Pralines   *Venezia*

3 **cups brown sugar**
1 **cup molasses**
3 **tablespoons powdered chocolate (bitter preferred)**
¼ **cup butter**
1 **teaspoon vinegar**
1 **cup blanched almonds, split**

With exception of almonds, cook all ingredients together over low flame, stirring with wooden spoon until well blended. Continue to cook without stirring until a soft ball is formed in cold water (5 to 8 minutes). Remove from fire, and beat the blend until it begins to thicken. Immediately add almonds, and stir well. Drop by spoonfuls to porcelain surface or metal cooky sheet.

TORRONCINI

Petit Tower-Shaped Nougat Candy   *Campania*
          A delicacy of All Saints' Day, November 1

The same recipe as **Ossi di Morto,** except at the end: Roll the candy in fine **granulated sugar** instead of glazed chocolate icing.

TORRONE DI ALBA

Nougat Candy of Alba　　　　　　　　　　　　　*Piemonte*

1 cup white sugar	2 cups cream
1 cup brown sugar	½ cup blanched filberts, split
1 cup white corn syrup	1 cup blanched almonds, split
¾ cup butter	1 tablespoon vanilla

Heat sugar, corn syrup, butter, and half the cream in saucepan over low flame, stirring with wooden spoon until well blended. Add rest of cream slowly, stirring occasionally. Cook until it forms a hard ball when a bit is dropped into cold water. Add nuts and vanilla, and mix well. Pour into buttered and floured pans (ice-cube trays are ideal), and let cool. Dust completely with **powdered sugar.**

TORRONE DI CREMONA

Nougat Candy of Cremona　　　　　　　　　*Lombardia*
　　　Sold the year around, it is particularly favored
　　　at Easter and Christmas.

1 cup honey	½ cup filberts, split
3 egg whites	½ cup pistachio nuts
1 cup white sugar	1 teaspoon vanilla
¼ cup cold water	1 teaspoon grated lemon rind
1 cup blanched almonds, split	1 tablespoon grated orange rind
¼ cup chopped candied cherries	

Warm honey in heavy, shallow pan. Remove from heat and slowly stir in egg whites with wooden spoon. In a small saucepan, caramelize sugar and water over slow fire. Add to honey mixture, and cook slowly until it forms a hard ball when a bit is dropped into cold water. Fold in the other ingredients, and pour into well-buttered and floured pans (ice-cube trays are ideal), and let cool. Remove, and dust completely with **powdered sugar.**

TORRONE DI FICHI

Fig Nougat Candy   *Abruzzi*

5 cups sugar	2 cups cream
2 cups light corn syrup	1 cup chopped walnuts
3 cups chopped figs	

Heat sugar, corn syrup, and cream in saucepan over low flame, stirring with wooden spoon until it forms a soft ball when a bit is dropped into cold water. Cool, and beat until it becomes thick. Add nuts and figs, and mix well. Pack into well-buttered and floured pans (1 inch deep). Ice-cube trays are ideal. Cut into squares, and dust completely with **powdered sugar.**

B. BISCOTTI (*Cookies**)

AMARETTI

Macaroons   *Piemonte*

    1¼ cups powdered sugar
     1 teaspoon potato or rice flour
     1 cup blanched almonds, ground
     5 or 6 apricot or peach nuts, blanched and ground
     2 egg whites, beaten stiff

Sift powdered sugar and potato or rice flour, and mix them well with finely-minced nuts. Slowly beat mixture into egg whites, mak-

---

* These recipes have been tried and tested at an altitude of 5,000 feet (Denver altitude) with the help and suggestions of my good friend, Al Schneider, distinguished pastry chef.
    Below the altitude of 5,000 feet, *increase* baking powder ¼ teaspoon for each thousand feet lower elevation.
    Above the altitude of 5,000 feet, *decrease* baking powder in the same proportions.

SPECIAL UTENSILS

PIZZELLE IRON
(for waffle cookies)

SFORMATI
(molds)

CIALDONI IRON
(for curled wafers)

CANNOLI FORM
(for little cannon cookies)

ROSETTE IRON
(for rosette cookies)

PASTRY CUTTER

RAVIOLI ROLLING PIN

MORTAR
AND
PESTLE

LAMB CAKE MOLD

ing smooth paste. Form this into little balls, and flatten them with a wet finger. Place them at least 2 inches apart on a heavily-floured cooky sheet in a 325° oven for 15 minutes.

BISCOTTI A NODO

Little Knot Cookies   *Abruzzi*

5 cups flour	3 teaspoons baking powder
1½ cups sugar	¾ cup butter
4 eggs	¾ cup milk
2 teaspoons flavoring (almond, anise, or vanilla)	

Mix all ingredients into a smooth dough. Shape into strips the size of a small finger, and bend them into knots. Bake on buttered cooky sheet in 325° oven till a light brown. Brush with **Glassatura Lustrata** (Chap. IX, D).

BISCOTTI MARUCA

Snail Cookies   *Campania*

3 cups flour	½ teaspoon salt
½ cup sugar	5 large eggs
2 teaspoons baking powder	½ cup butter

Mix all together, and roll out ¼ inch thick. Cut into strips the size of a forefinger. Roll in snail shape. Bake on well-greased cooky sheet in 325° oven, till golden-brown. Make an **icing** of the juice of an orange and enough powdered sugar to absorb the juice. Ice the cookies with a pastry brush.

BISCOTTI RIPIENI

Filled Cookies   *Calabria*

6 eggs	1 tablespoon oil
¾ cup sugar	1 teaspoon vanilla
½ teaspoon salt	5 scant cups flour

Work all ingredients together into a soft noodlelike dough. Roll out thin as a dime.

Filling

1 cup walnuts, chopped	½ cup chopped dates
1 cup white seedless raisins	½ cup grape jam or jelly
	½ cup chopped figs

Grind nuts, raisins, figs, and dates, and stir well into the jelly, which holds mixture together.

Cut dough into small rectangles. Place a teaspoon of filling on each rectangle, and fold it together, pinching edges with fork. Prick each cooky on top with fork. Deep-fry in hot lard till golden-brown. Remove to absorbent paper. Sprinkle with **powdered sugar.**

BISCOTTI RULLATI

Rolled Cookies   *Campania*

3 eggs	4 cups flour
1 cup sugar	3 teaspoons baking powder
½ cup olive oil	½ cup raspberry or strawberry
1 cup orange juice	jam
1 cup chopped walnuts	

Beat eggs, sugar, oil, and orange juice thoroughly. Add flour and baking powder and mix into smooth noodlelike dough. Roll out ⅓ of dough at a time, as thin as a dime. Spread jam over each third. Sprinkle nuts over all. Roll up, and bake all 3 rolls on buttered and floured cooky sheet in 325° oven about 40 minutes. When cool, sprinkle completely with **powdered sugar.** Slice diagonally into ½-inch pieces to serve.

BISCOTTINI DI NOVARA

Small Lady Fingers   *Piemonte*

2 egg yolks	4 whole eggs
2 cups powdered sugar	1 teaspoon vanilla or lemon
2 cups cake flour	flavor

Beat yolks, whole eggs, powdered sugar, and flavoring thoroughly. Add flour, and beat well. Place cookies 2 inches apart on a cooky sheet lined with waxed paper. Either with a plain-hole-tube pastry bag or with a tablespoon, form the little lady fingers ½ inch wide and 2½ inches long. Bake in 350° oven 10 or 12 minutes, until slightly brown. When cool, dust with **powdered sugar.**

CANNOLI

Little Cannon Cookies   *Sicilia*

2 cups flour	**½ teaspoon salt**
2 tablespoons sugar	**2 egg yolks (save whites)**
¼ cup butter	**6 tablespoons wine or whisky**

Mix the ingredients, forming a soft noodle dough; roll it thin as a dime. Cut a number of circles with a large cup or a clean No. 2 can. Roll each circle around a greased tube,° gluing the end to the facing surface with a bit of egg white. Drop 3 or 4 tubes at a time into a saucepan of hot fat and let them brown lightly. Drain, and cool on absorbent paper; slide the baked dough carefully from the tubes. Store in a cool place, and fill only as you use them, with the mixture desired:

> **Crema**
> **Whipped cream, shredded chocolate, and chopped nuts**
> **Budino di Ricotta**
> **Crema Napoletana**
> **Ground glazed fruit, nuts, and cherry cordial to taste**
> **Zabaione**

Dust with **powdered sugar.**

CANTUCCINI

Little Angles   *Toscana*

1 cup butter	**2 egg yolks**
½ cup sugar	**3½ cups flour**

Cream butter and sugar until fluffy. Add eggs, and cream thoroughly. Add flour, and mix into a smooth dough. Form into 2 rolls

° Cannoli forms are 4-inch-long aluminum tubes. Bamboo poles cut into 4-inch lengths, or window-blind rollers, scoured and sandpapered, also can be used.

the size of a half dollar, and flatten them a bit on buttered cooky sheet. Bake in 350° oven 10 minutes. Cut into slanting slices ½ inch thick. Place cookies on cooky sheet in oven for another 5 minutes.

CASTAGNACCIO

Chestnut Tart *Toscana*

¾ **pound chestnut flour**	1 **teaspoon salt**
½ **cup water**	½ **cup pignon nuts**
¼ **cup currants, soaked in warm water and drained**	

Beat all ingredients thoroughly into a thick batter. Pour into well-oiled 10-inch cake pan (copper preferred). Brush top with a little oil and a few pignon nuts. Bake in 350° oven to a golden color, with the sides beginning to leave the pan. Cut as pie, and serve with fork.

CASTAGNOLA DI ROMA

Chestnut Cooky of Rome *Lazio*

> *At Carnevale (Farewell to Meat), the festivity just before Lent, many delicacies such as Castagnola are served with wine.*

2 **eggs**
1 **teaspoon salt**
2 **tablespoons sugar**
1½ **cups chestnut flour (more if necessary)**

Beat eggs, salt, and sugar until creamy. Add chestnut flour and mix into dumplinglike dough. Break off pieces the size of small pullet eggs, and deep-fry them in oil till golden-brown.

CENCI

Ribbon Cookies *Toscana*

¼ **cup butter**	4 **cups flour (cake flour pre-**
4 **eggs**	**ferred)**
⅓ **cup sugar**	1 **ounce whisky or brandy**

Mix like noodle dough; cover to rest 10 minutes. Roll thin as a dime. Cut into diamond shapes, 2 inches in diameter. Deep-fry in oil. Drain; dust with **powdered sugar.** As desired, fill each diamond-shaped piece of dough with a dab of marmalade; fold, and pinch edges together. Deep-fry, drain, and dust with sugar.

CIALDONI

Thin Curled Wafers   *Toscana*

¾ cup cake flour	2 tablespoons butter
¼ cup brown sugar	7 tablespoons ice water

Put flour, sugar, and butter into ice water, and mix thoroughly to form smooth, rather stiff batter. Drop ½ tablespoon at a time into the Cialdoni iron form (see picture page of Special Utensils); close it, and lay it over burner for 1 minute. Turn iron over for another minute. Open, and remove wafer with knife. Immediately, while wafer is still warm (it becomes crisp quickly), form it into cornucopia.

These cookies are used as edible spoons with a bowl of dessert:

1. whipped cream
2. Latte alla Portoghese
3. Crema Napoletana
4. Zabaione

CIAMBELLE DI ROMA

Roman Doughnuts   *Lazio*

  4 eggs
  4 scant cups flour (enough to make batter softer than for
      noodles)
  4 tablespoons oil
  ½ cup sugar (more if desired)

Work ingredients well together, and roll out ½ inch thick. Cut with doughnut cutter. Drop into boiling water. When doughnuts rise to top, remove and lay on dish towel. Bake on greased cooky sheet in 350° oven about 15 minutes, till golden-brown.

COVEZUN' DI SAN GIUSEPPE

Filled Cooky for St. Joseph   *Abruzzi*
Delicacy for Feast of St. Joseph, March 19

Filling

- ½ cup fine bread crumbs
- 3 tablespoons jelly (grape preferred)
- ¼ teaspoon baking powder
- 2 teaspoons cocoa
- ⅓ cup cream (or canned milk)
- 1 cup chopped walnuts
- 1 tablespoon grated orange peel

Mix ingredients well, and cook slowly 10 minutes, stirring constantly. Cool.

Dough

4 eggs	5 cups flour
1½ cups sugar	2 teaspoons baking powder
	1 cup milk

Mix all into soft noodle dough. Roll thin as a dime. Cut circles with a large cup. Place 1 tablespoon filling on each circle of dough; fold over, and pinch edges together with fork. Prick each cooky with fork. Bake in 425° oven about 8 minutes, till light brown. Dust with **powdered sugar.**

CROFANI TIROLESI

Tirolese Fried Cooky   *Alto Adige*

| 2 eggs | 1 tablespoon cream (or |
| 2 cups flour | canned milk) |

Mix into soft noodle dough. Roll thin as a dime. With pastry cutter or knife, cut diamond shapes 2½ inches in diameter. Cut slit in center of each diamond, and pull one corner through slit. Deep-fry in lard. Drain, and dust with **powdered sugar.**

CROSTATE DI FICHI

Fig Tarts   *Sicilia*

4 cups flour	½ teaspoon salt
½ cup butter	1 cake yeast dissolved in
½ cup sugar	½ cup lukewarm milk

1 tablespoon cold water

Mix flour, butter, sugar, and salt as for piecrust. Add yeast and water. Work into a smooth dough. Roll out thin, and cut in rectangles, 2½ to 3 inches in diameter.

Filling

1 cup pitted cooked prunes	½ cup pitted figs
1 cup glazed fruit (optional)	1 cup walnuts
	½ cup honey

½ cup raisins

Grind and mix thoroughly. Drop 1 tablespoon filling on each rectangle of dough, and roll into shape of small finger. With knife make 2 small slits on top of each cooky. Bake in 350° oven 12 minutes, or until delicately brown. When cool, dust with **powdered sugar.**

FOGLIE ARROSTITE

Roasted Leaves   *Venezia*

4 cups flour	4 large eggs
¾ cup sugar	¼ teaspoon salt
1 teaspoon vanilla	½ cup melted butter

1 tablespoon whisky or rum

Mix, and knead well into soft noodle dough. Roll out thin as a dime. With pastry cutter, form strips 4 inches long and 1 inch wide, with one end pointed like a leaf. Deep-fry in hot lard. Drain, and dust with **powdered sugar.**

FRITTELLE

Honey Crinkles   *Lucania*
    Delicacy for Easter and Christmas at Potenza

6 eggs	1 teaspoon vanilla or *spirits* of
4 scant cups flour	anise
½ cup sugar	1 teaspoon salt
½ cup honey	2 teaspoons baking powder

            2 tablespoons butter or oil

Blend all except honey together into smooth noodle dough. Roll out thin as noodles. Cut into strips about 8 inches long and 1 inch wide. Lay these together in pairs (one on top of another). With finger tips, press each pair together down the center. Twist together like doughnuts. Deep-fry in hot lard; drain, and brush tops with hot honey. Dust with **powdered sugar.**

FRITTELLE DI RISO

Rice Tarts   *Toscana*
    Served on the Feast of St. Joseph, March 19

On the night before, cook 1 cup **rice** in 2 cups **milk.** In the morning add 2 **eggs,** 1 teaspoon **baking powder,** 2 tablespoons **fruit brandy** (optional), a few seedless **raisins** and pignon **nuts,** and 2 tablespoons **flour.** Mix well, and drop by spoonfuls into deep **oil** or **lard;** fry till golden-brown. Drain on absorbent paper.

FRITTURA DOLCE

Sweet Fritter   *Piemonte*

½ cup sugar	2 tablespoons melted butter
4 cups rich milk	1 teaspoon lemon juice
½ teaspoon salt	1 cup cream of wheat or yellow
1 egg, well beaten	corn meal

Mix all together well, and cook in double boiler until almost done, but not too stiff. Add egg, and mix thoroughly. Pour into buttered sheet pan. When cool, cut into diamond shapes. Dip each diamond in well-beaten egg, then into finely-sifted **bread crumbs,** and fry in butter till golden-brown on both sides. Dust with **powdered sugar.**

GROSTOLI

Crisp Cookies   *Alto Adige*

3 eggs	1 cup milk
5 cups flour	1 teaspoon salt
½ cup sugar	1 grated lemon rind (optional)
1 teaspoon baking powder	1 ounce rum, brandy, or whisky

Mix into smooth noodle dough, and roll thin as a dime. With pastry cutter, form rectangles 2 by 3 inches; deep-fry in pure **lard.** Drain, and dust with **powdered sugar.**

LE RAVIOLE FRITTE

Fried Filled Cookies   *Emilia*
        Served for Carnevale before Lent, and for Feast
        of St. Joseph, March 19

Prepare **Pasta Frolla** (Chap. IX, C); roll out thin as a dime. With a large glass, cut circles. Fill each circle with apricot or peach **marmalade** or thick Crema (Chap. IX, E). Fold over, and seal with imprint of fork. Deep-fry in pure **lard.** Remove to absorbent paper. Dust with **powdered sugar.**

MEZZE LUNE RIPIENE

Filled Half-Moon Cookies   *Abruzzi*

Dough

6 eggs	½ cup oil
5 cups sifted flour	¼ teaspoon salt
4 level teaspoons baking powder	½ cup milk

Mix into a smooth noodle dough. Roll out thin as a dime. With a large glass, cut circles.

Filling

1 cup wine	½ cup ground raisins
1 cup jelly	1 cup ground fresh apple
1 cup finely-chopped nuts	1 grated orange rind
½ cup fine bread crumbs	

Mix well. Place 1 teaspoon of filling on each circle of dough, and fold together in half-moon. Bake on floured cooky sheets in 400° oven 10 minutes, or until golden-brown.

PALETTA DI MANDORLA

Almond Slices   *Umbria*

Served on Feast of St. Francis of Assisi, October 4

1 cup butter	4 cups flour
1½ cups sugar	1 teaspoon baking powder
4 eggs	1 teaspoon vanilla
2 cups blanched, chopped almonds	

Cream butter, sugar, and eggs. Add other ingredients, and knead until smooth. Form into 2 rolls of half-dollar size, and bake in 375° oven until golden-brown (12 to 15 minutes). When cool, cut into ¾ inch slices, and toast 3 minutes in oven.

PANZEROTTI DOLCI

Fried Pillows   *Lazio*

Prepare **Pasta Frolla** (Chap. IX, C); roll out thin as a dime. With a large glass, cut circles. Fill each circle with 1 teaspoon **ricotta,** ¼ teaspoon **sugar,** and a bit of shredded **chocolate.** Fold together and seal with imprint of fork. Deep-fry in **lard.** Remove to absorbent paper. Dust with **powdered sugar.**

PIGNOLATE

Cookies Shaped Like Pignon Clusters   *Puglia*

3 eggs	3 cups flour
1 teaspoon baking powder	3 tablespoons water
¼ teaspoon salt	½ cup honey

Mix all but honey into noodle dough. With palms of hands, roll pieces of dough to resemble a long pencil. Cut into ¼-inch pieces. Drop a few at a time into saucepan of hot lard. They will come to the top and pop like popcorn. When golden-brown, transfer with slotted ladle to absorbent paper. Put all into a large bowl, pour hot honey over all, and stir quickly. With a tablespoon, scoop out a little at a time and place balls on oiled paper to set.

PIZZELLE

Waffle Cooky   *Abruzzi*

> The cooky iron needed (see picture page of Special Utensils) can be purchased in most Italian delicatessens. I give two basic recipes:

I. 6 eggs
    1 cup sugar
    1 teaspoon vanilla
    1 grated orange rind and ½ its juice
    ¼ cup melted butter
    ¾ cup melted pure lard
    6 cups flour (or less—for soft noodle dough)
    1 grated lemon rind and ½ its juice

II. 6 eggs
    1 cup sugar
    4 cups flour
    ¼ cup melted butter
    ¾ cup melted pure lard
    ½ teaspoon *spirits* of anise

Mix into a smooth dough (softer than noodle-type). Place walnut-size portion in center of iron, and clamp it shut. Heat over gas flame or electric heating unit 1 minute. Turn over for another minute, then open to remove cooky. Proceed with next. Soon the iron becomes hot enough to make cookies rapidly. Regulate heat accordingly.

ROSETTE

Rosette Cookies   *Le Marche*

> *The rosette iron can be purchased in most hardware and department stores. It is a perforated wheel which screws onto a metal handle, similar to a timbale iron (see picture page of Special Utensils).*

2 eggs	**1 cup milk**
½ teaspoon salt	**1½ cups flour**
4 tablespoons sugar	**1 tablespoon whisky or brandy**
1½ cups lard (or more)	**½ cup honey**

Beat all except honey and lard into smooth batter, and place in shallow bowl. In small skillet, melt lard (adding more as used). Dip rosette wheel into hot grease, then into batter—just to the rim of the wheel—and back into hot grease. The cooky will drop off the iron. With fork and slotted ladle, turn it over for a second. Transfer to absorbent paper, and proceed with next cooky. If grease is too hot the iron will sizzle in batter; if too cold, the batter won't stick. Carefully regulate temperature of grease. Brush rosettes with hot honey, and dust with **powdered sugar.**

SAVOIARDI

Savoy Biscuits (Large Lady Fingers)   *Piemonte*

1 egg yolk	**4 whole eggs**
1½ cups powdered sugar	**1½ cups cake flour**

Beat the 5 egg yolks and sugar till light and creamy. In another bowl beat the 4 whites till stiff. Slowly add flour, continuing to beat till well blended and fluffy. Fold into yolks and sugar. Drop batter

onto cooky sheet lined with waxed paper, forming lady fingers
¾ inch wide and 4½ inches long, 2 inches apart. Dust top of each
cooky with **granulated sugar.** Bake in 375 to 400° oven 8 to 10
minutes, until light brown.

SFINGI DI SAN GIUSEPPE

Cream Puffs for St. Joseph   *Sicilia*

½ cup butter	1¼ cups flour
1 cup cold water	2 eggs

Beat eggs with a pinch of **bicarbonate of ammonia** powder. Bring
butter and water to boiling point. When all the butter is melted,
turn heat down, and gradually add flour, stirring well. When almost
cool add egg mixture a little at a time, and mix thoroughly. Drop by
tablespoon onto greased cooky sheet. Bake in 425° oven for 20
minutes.

Choice of filling
Crema al Cioccolato
Panna Montatta
Zabaione
Crema Napoletana
Crema
Budino di Ricotta

"SFRAPPOLE" PER CARNEVALE

Carnival Cooky   *Emilia*
> *Served in Bologna for Carnevale (Farewell to
> Meat) before Lent, and for the Feast of St.
> Joseph, March 19*

Prepare sweet noodle dough (3 cups **flour**, 3 **eggs**, ¾ cup **sugar**,
¼ teaspoon **salt**, 1 teaspoon **vanilla**, ¼ cup slightly melted **butter**,
and 1 teaspoon **whisky** for crispness). Roll out as thin as noodles.
Cut strips 4 inches long and ¾ inch wide, tie them into knots, and
deep-fry them in pure **lard.** Drain onto absorbent paper; dust with
powdered sugar.

SFOGLIATELLE

Eclairs   *Campania*

 ½ cup butter or pure lard 1¼ cups flour
 1 cup hot water   4 eggs

Beat eggs with a pinch of **bicarbonate of ammonia** powder. Bring butter and water to a good boil, melting butter completely. Reduce heat, and add flour, stirring well. Remove from heat. Slowly add eggs, blending thoroughly. Transfer to a pastry bag with a No. 8 tube; squeeze 4-inch strips of paste onto buttered, floured cooky sheet. Bake in 420° oven 20 minutes. Cut horizontally, and fill with one of the following:

 Zabaione
 Budino di Ricotta
 Crema
 Crema Napoletana
 Panna Montata

SFOGLIATELLE RIPIENE

Filled Flaky Tarts   *Piemonte*
     Similar to a turnover

Prepare **Pasta Sfoglia** (Chap. IX, C). Cut rolled dough into 20 squares. Place 1 level teaspoon of ground **fruit** (apple, peach, pineapple, or apricot), or of **marmalade** or jelly in center of each square. Fold into a triangle, and pinch points together. Bake in 425° oven 10 or 15 minutes. Brush tops with ½ preparation of **Glassatura Generale** (Chap. IX, D).

STRABOLI

Funnel Cooky   *Alto Adige*

 6 eggs   ¼ cup sugar
 3 cups flour   3 cups milk
     1 teaspoon salt

Beat ingredients well, making thin pancake-type batter. Hold funnel over a pan of hot lard. Pour batter, a tablespoonful at a time, through funnel into lard, and deep-fry the cookies thus formed until golden-brown. Remove them to absorbent paper. Dust with **powdered sugar.**

TARALLI DI NATALE

Christmas Doughnut   *Abruzzi*

> 1 cup sugar
> 5 cups flour
> ¼ teaspoon salt
> 2 teaspoons baking powder
> 6 eggs, well beaten
> ½ cup oil or melted lard
> ½ teaspoon lemon flavoring
> 1 teaspoon vanilla
> 3 tablespoons milk or whisky (for crispness)

Mix dry ingredients. Add eggs, oil, milk, and flavoring. Knead as for bread dough. Grease your hands, and take ¼ of dough at a time; roll out to ½-inch thickness. Cut in 5-inch lengths, and pinch together as a doughnut. Bake them on slightly-greased cooky sheet in 425° oven 10 minutes, till golden-brown. Brush with **Glassatura Generale** (Chap. IX, D).

TORCERE

Wine Cookies   *Calabria*

> 1 cup sugar   1 cup dry wine
> 1 cup oil   3 eggs
> ¼ teaspoon salt   3 cups flour (more if needed)

Knead well into very soft noodle-type dough. Cut pieces, and roll them like bread sticks. Cut off 2-inch lengths. Roll each out on Gnocchi (dumpling) board or small cheese grater, holding it with your thumb as you press it against grater, and allowing it to drop to the table in form of shell. Deep-fry shells in lard until golden-brown. When ready to serve, stir them in a pan that contains a small amount of boiling **honey;** strain, and place on platter. Dust with **powdered sugar.**

TORTEI

Twisted Sugar Cookies   *Piemonte*

2 cups milk	1 cup butter
1 cup sugar	6 cups flour

½ teaspoon bicarbonate of ammonia powder

Mix ingredients thoroughly into a smooth noodle-type dough. Pull off walnut-size pieces and roll them to resemble a short pencil. Twist and pinch each one together to resemble a tiny doughnut. Cover to rest for an hour. Roll in sugar, and bake in 400° oven 7 or 8 minutes.

TOTOS

Nut Balls   *Sicilia*

4 cups flour	¼ cup milk
1 cup sugar	¾ cup butter or lard
4 egg yolks	½ cup cocoa
2 teaspoons baking powder	2 cups chopped walnuts
	1 grated orange peel

1 grated lemon peel

Mix all ingredients into good hard paste, and roll it into marble-size balls. Bake in 375° oven 12 to 15 minutes. Dust completely with **powdered sugar.**

UCCELLI RIPIENI

Filled Bird Cookies   *Abruzzi*

Dough

7 eggs	¾ cup sugar
4 cups flour	½ cup butter or lard
1½ teaspoons baking powder	1½ teaspoons vanilla

Filling

1 cup honey	2 cups chopped walnuts
¼ cup dark corn syrup	2 grated orange rinds

1 cup fine bread crumbs

Mix dough ingredients into fine soft noodle consistency. Roll out ¼ inch thick, and cut into rectangles 3½ by 2½ inches. Mix filling ingredients well, and cook over slow fire 15 minutes, stirring constantly. When cool again, place 1 teaspoon filling in center of each rectangle, and fold lengthwise. Pinch ends so that one forms head and the other tail of a bird. Bake in 400° oven till delicately brown. Dust with **powdered sugar.**

"ZEPPOLE" DI SAN GIUSEPPE

Puffballs for St. Joseph   *Campania*

1 cup water	**1 cup flour**
¼ cup leaf lard	**4 eggs**

Place water, lard, and flour in double boiler over the fire, stirring constantly until they thicken and work into big hard ball on spoon, leaving side of pan. Remove from fire. Add eggs one at a time, and beat and work until smooth. Transfer to pastry bag with No. 8 tube, pressing out on oiled paper in a circle like a doughnut. With spatula, slide cookies off into hot oil or lard for deep-frying. When golden-brown, drain onto absorbent paper. Cut horizontally through center. Fill with **Crema Napoletana** (Chap. IX, E); top with a **cherry.**

C. TORTE (*Cakes**)

CASSATA NAPOLETANA

Filled Cake, Neapolitan Style   *Campania*
> *For Christmas, a figurine of the Infant Jesus, and for Easter usually a lamb, is placed on the center of the cake.*

Prepare a **Pan di Spagna** and slice it horizontally into at least three ¾-inch layers. Between the layers place filling of **Crema**

---

* *Below* the altitude of 5,000 feet, *increase* baking powder ½ teaspoon for each thousand feet lower elevation.
   Above the altitude of 5,000 feet, *decrease* baking powder in same proportions. See footnote, page 168.

Napoletana (Chap. IX, E) or **cherry preserves,** or alternate the two. Cover top layer with Neapolitan Cream, and garnish with **chopped nuts** and **whole candied fruit** (cherries, pineapple, and the like). Chill at least 2 hours before serving.

CASSATA SICILIANA

Filled Cake, Sicilian Style   *Sicilia*
Christmas and Easter specialty

Prepare a **Pan di Spagna** and slice off horizontally a ¾-inch layer at the top and set it aside. With sharp knife, carefully scoop out center of cake, leaving a ¾-inch shell. Fill this with a blend of

- **1 pound ricotta**
- **4 tablespoons powdered sugar**
- **½ cup chocolate morsels, or shredded bitter chocolate**
- **½ cup candied fruit**
- **½ cup chopped almonds (optional)**
- **1 ounce favorite cordial**

Cover with the set-aside top layer. Frost this with **Glassatura Lustrata** (Chap. IX, D). Place cake in refrigerator until served.

CIAMBELLA

Coffee Cake   *Toscana*

4 cups cake flour	**¾ cup milk**
½ cup butter (slightly melted)	**¼ teaspoon soda**
	1 teaspoon cream of tartar
2 eggs	**1 grated lemon rind**
¾ cup sugar	**½ cup chopped candied peel**

Make a nest in flour, and drop into it the butter, eggs, and sugar. Mix and add milk; work into soft dough. Add soda, cream of tartar, lemon rind, and candied peel; mix until well blended. Place in greased angel-food pan. Brush top with melted butter. Bake in 375° oven about 40 minutes.

CROSTATE DI ALBICOCCHE

Apricot Pie   *Lombardia*

Prepare **Pasta Frolla.** Line a large pie pan with ¾ of the dough. Fill this shell with 2 cups **apricot marmalade.** Cut remaining dough into ½-inch strips, and weave them across the top. Brush with a bit of **egg yolk.** Bake in 375° oven 25 to 30 minutes.

CROSTATE DI VISCIOLE

Cherry Pie   *Campania*

> *True Italian fruit pies are made with marmalades*
> *—apricot and cherry particularly.*

Prepare **Pasta Frolla.** Line a large pie pan with ¾ of dough, and fill with **cherry marmalade.** Cover with woven strips of remaining dough. Bake in 375° oven 25 to 30 minutes.

DOLCE CON LA FRUTTA

Fruit Cake   *Puglia*

1 cup seedless raisins	1 cup milk
1 cup currants	1 cup chopped nuts
3 cups flour	3 eggs
1 teaspoon baking soda	1 teaspoon allspice
1½ cups creamed butter or lard	1 teaspoon cinnamon
	1 teaspoon nutmeg
1 cup sugar	2 ounces brandy

Wash raisins and currants, and dry them a few minutes in oven. Sift flour with soda, and mix all ingredients together. Place in buttered, floured loaf pans, and bake in 325° oven at least 1 hour (until a fork or straw comes clean).

DOLCE DIPLOMATICO

Diplomatic Dessert   *Lazio*

12 lady fingers soaked in rum, fruit brandy, or vermouth
12 lady fingers soaked in coffee
1 recipe of Crema Napoletana (Chap. IX, E)

If scalloped mold is not available, use a deep casserole. Grease well with butter, line first completely with **red marmalade,** then alternately with soaked lady fingers (upright around sides and horizontally on bottom). Add layer of Neapolitan Cream, layer of lady fingers, until full. Chill at least 4 hours. Set mold in pan of hot water for a second. The cake can then be easily removed to a platter for serving.

DOLCETTO DI SAVOIA

Delicacy of Savoy   *Piemonte*

2 dozen lady fingers   **1 preparation of Zabaione**

On each dessert plate place 2 lady fingers. Cover them with a layer of wine custard, add 2 more lady fingers and another layer of wine custard.

MOSTACCIOLO

Spiced Hard-Bake Honey Cake   *Calabria*
              A Calabrian wedding or Christmas cake, made
              several months before the time for use, and aged
              in an airtight container

2 pounds (8 cups) flour   **1 egg yolk**
              1 quart honey

Into a nest of flour on floured board drop egg yolk and honey. Mix well as for a noodle dough—the honey makes it difficult to handle.

Setting aside a generous handful for use as topping, form the remainder into 3 large doughnuts and place them in buttered, floured pie pans. Make 3 tiny ropelike rolls and, wavily, deck top of each cake with one. Sprinkle **confettini** (decorettes) over top of each. Let stand overnight. In the morning, bake cakes in 350° oven ½ hour. At first they are very hard. Wrap them individually in waxed paper, and place in airtight container for at least 2 months. They can be used within 2 weeks if wrapped individually in cloth and placed in an airtight container with a humidor (cup) of wine or whisky, or cut apples; however they must be checked every 3 days, for mold or dry humidor. When serving, cut ½-inch slices.

PAN DI SPAGNA ABRUZZESE

Sponge Cake, Abruzzi Style   *Abruzzi*

10 eggs, separated	**1 cup cake flour**
1 cup sugar	**2 tablespoons white wine**
1 tablespoon vanilla or other flavoring	

Beat egg yolks with sugar until creamy. Gradually add flour, wine, and flavoring, beating constantly in the same direction. Beat egg whites until they are stiff, and fold them in. Pour batter into tube pan which has been buttered and dusted with **powdered sugar.** Bake in 350° oven 45 minutes.

PAN DI SPAGNA ALLA TOSCANA

Sponge Cake, Tuscan Style   *Toscana*

7 eggs, separated	**1 teaspoon grated lemon rind**
1 cup powdered sugar	**1 tablespoon vermouth or other**
1 cup cake or potato flour	**flavoring**

Beat egg yolks with sugar until creamy. Add flour, grated rind, and flavoring, and beat well. Beat the egg whites until they are stiff, and fold them in. Pour batter into deep round cake pan that has been well buttered and then dusted with powdered sugar. Bake in 350° oven 45 minutes.

PANETTONE

Milanese Coffee Cake   *Lombardia*
      There is no Christmas in Milan without Panettone.

- 4 cups flour
- ¼ cup melted butter
- 1 teaspoon salt
- 1 cup of the desired fruit (mixture of raisins, citron, candied cherries, etc.)
- 4 egg yolks
- ½ cup cooking oil
- 1 cake yeast, broken fine into 1 cup lukewarm milk
- ¼ cup sugar

Into a nest of flour on a floured board, drop the other ingredients. Work together well, and shape into a big ball. Cover, and let rise to double the bulk. Work down, and again form into a ball. Place in round deep baking pan or casserole, lined with oiled paper. Let rise again. Brush with **egg white** and **milk**. Bake in 350° oven 1 hour.

PASTA FROLLA

Pie Dough   *All Regions*
      Italy has many pie-dough recipes, of which I
      give two.

- I. 4 egg yolks
- ¾ cup sugar
- 2 cups flour
- ½ cup creamed butter or leaf lard
- 1 grated lemon rind
- 1 tablespoon sherry, vinegar, or liquor

Beat eggs and sugar till creamy. Add a little flour and the butter. Mix well with a fork; add remaining flour, lemon rind, and wine.

Work as little as possible—stopping as soon as you have a smooth dough. If desired, cover, and place in refrigerator overnight, so that it will be flakier. If making a filled pie with complete cover (rather than woven strips), brush top with a bit of egg white to give it a more golden color. Bake in 425° oven 10 minutes; reduce heat to 350° and continue baking till golden-brown.

II. 1 cup (½ pound) leaf lard
     1 teaspoon salt
     ½ cup boiling water
     3 cups flour

Pour boiling water over lard and salt in bowl, stirring well until creamy. Add flour, and mix well. Shape into round ball, and set in refrigerator to cool. When ready to use, let it warm enough to roll out. It will make 4 good-sized single crusts, or 2 filled pies, and will keep several weeks in refrigerator.

PASTA SFOGLIA

Flaky Pastry Dough   *All Regions*

4 cups flour	2 egg yolks
1 teaspoon salt	1 cup cold water
1 pound sweet butter, margarine, or leaf lard	1 ounce liquor or sherry brandy

All ingredients must be cold, and the pastry must be kept cold throughout the procedure. Sift flour and salt onto pastry board. Form a nest in center of flour. Drop into it ¼ pound butter, and work together as for noodle dough. Add egg yolks, water, and liquor, and work into soft, smooth texture. Roll out on lightly floured board to size of a cooky sheet. On half of it, scatter rest of butter in thimble-size chunks.

Fold the whole together, and roll out to original size. Again fold together, and again. Cover dough with a towel, and let it rest in a cold place 15 minutes. Roll it out as before to size of a cooky sheet, and again fold it twice over. Cover; place in the refrigerator another 15 minutes. Repeat twice more the rolling and folding, with two more resting periods. Finally, roll out to thickness of pie dough, and use for tarts or whatever you desire. Bake in 425° oven 10 or 15 minutes for tarts, a little longer for pies.

PASTIERA DI GRANO

Easter Whole-Wheat Pie *Campania*

Prepare **Pasta Frolla,** and line two pie pans with it, saving enough for strips across the tops of the pies.

Filling
- 1 **cup whole or cracked wheat (soaked and boiled till soft)**
- 1 **pint milk**
- 2 **tablespoons melted butter**
- 1 **cup sugar**
- 4 **eggs, well beaten**
- 1 **cup creamed ricotta**
- ½ **cup chopped citron**
- 1 **teaspoon cinnamon**
- 1 **teaspoon grated lemon rind**
- 2 **teaspoons grated orange rind**

Place cooked wheat, milk, butter, and sugar in large saucepan; bring to boiling point, and cook 5 minutes, stirring constantly with wooden spoon. Remove from fire. Add the other ingredients; whip to smooth, creamy consistency, and place in pie shells. Weave strips of dough across top. Bake in 350° oven 45 minutes, or until golden-brown. When cool, sprinkle with **powdered sugar** and **cinnamon.**

PASTIERA DI RISO

Easter Rice Cake *Campania*

Prepare like the preceding recipe (Pastiera di Grano), but instead of the whole (or cracked) wheat and milk, use 1 cup **rice** cooked in 1 quart of **milk.**

PATICA DI BOLZANO

Bolzano-style Feast Cake   *Alto Adige*

2 cakes yeast	1 tablespoon salt
1 cup tepid water	2 cups sugar
8 cups flour	½ pound slightly-melted butter
3 well-beaten eggs	or margarine
2 cups scalded milk (tepid)	1 tablespoon lemon flavoring

Dissolve yeast in water. When yeast begins to float, add 1 cup flour; stir and let rise. After 1 hour add remaining ingredients. Mix into a soft dough, and knead lightly. Cover, and set in warm place to rise for 1 hour. In the meantime prepare separate fillings from the two sets of ingredients that follow, mixing each set well.

I. 2 egg yolks, creamed
    1 teaspoon cinnamon
    ½ teaspoon cloves
    2 tablespoons powdered sugar
II. 1 pound chopped walnuts
    1 cup hot honey
    2 egg whites, stiffly beaten
    1 cup thick cream
    1 teaspoon vanilla

Roll dough out on floured pastry cloth, as thin as noodles. Spread Filling I over it, and then Filling II. Holding near end of cloth in one hand, roll dough away from yourself. Cut through center, making 2 rolls. Grease an angel-food pan well, and place each roll around the tube in it. Let rise to top of pan. Bake in 400° oven 1 hour or longer, till golden-brown.

PIZZA DI SAN MARTINO

Snack for St. Martin   *Abruzzi*
              *Served on the Feast of St. Martin, November 11,
              this is a glorified coffee cake with trinkets in the
              serving.*

2 yeast cakes	5 cups flour
1 cup tepid water	2 well-beaten eggs

1 cup tepid scalded milk   1 teaspoon salt
½ cup slightly-melted butter   1 cup seedless raisins
1 grated orange or lemon rind

Dissolve yeast in water. When it begins to float, add 1 cup flour. Stir, and let rise 1 hour. Then add remaining ingredients, and stir well until blended. Let rise in warm place for 1 hour. Stir down, and beat about 3 minutes. Place in well-buttered large round deep pan or casserole. Bake in 400° oven about 45 minutes. When serving, place wrapped **trinket** (piece of money, ring, or the like) on each serving plate, under the coffee cake.

PIZZA DOLCE

Cheese Pie   *Lazio*

Served on Easter in Rome

Prepare **Pasta Frolla.** Line a rectangular shallow pan (approximately 7 × 11 inches) with ⅔ of it, saving the rest for the top.

Filling

1 pound ricotta
3 egg whites, beaten stiff
¼ cup sugar
1 tablespoon grated orange peel
1 tablespoon citron, chopped fine
½ teaspoon vanilla

Whip ricotta into a fine cream. Add the other ingredients, and mix thoroughly. Place in pie shell, and weave strips of dough across top. Bake in 350° oven about 35 minutes, until golden-brown.

PRESNITZ

Christmas Cake   *Alto Adige*

1 cup seedless black currants
½ cup rum and ½ cup wine
½ cup blanched chopped almonds
½ cup pignon nuts

  cup cake or cooky crumbles
  tablespoon slivered citron
1 tablespoon slivered candied orange
½ teaspoon cloves
½ cup sugar

Let currants marinate in rum and wine several hours. Meanwhile, prepare **Pasta Sfoglia** and roll it out into oblong form on a floured pastry cloth. Add the other listed ingredients to the currants, and mix thoroughly. Spread over entire surface of dough. Holding pastry cloth in one hand, roll dough away from yourself. Flatten the long roll a bit; roll entirety into snail form. Place in well-greased large deep round pan. Brush top with melted **butter** and **egg yolk**. Bake in 400° oven 20 minutes, or until golden-brown.

SFOGLIATA

Flaky Cake with Filling   *Campania*

Prepare **Pasta Sfoglia.** Line a large deep casserole or cake pan with half the dough.

Prepare a filling of

1 pound ricotta	½ cup candied fruit, chopped
4 tablespoons sugar	¼ cup finely-chopped walnuts
½ cup seedless white raisins, chopped	2 egg whites, whipped stiff

Mix well and place in cake shell. Cover completely with other half of dough. Press edges together—don't pinch. Bake in 400° oven 25 minutes, until golden-brown.

SFORMATO DOLCE SQUISITO

Exquisite Sweet Mold   *Emilia*

10 yolks of hard-boiled eggs
1 cup soft butter
1½ dozen lady fingers dipped in vermouth or white wine
10 tablespoons sugar
2 ounces rum or gin

Whip egg yolks with butter until very light and fluffy. Add sugar and rum or gin; again whip until very light and fluffy. In medium-sized deep cake pan, casserole, or mold that has been lined with oiled paper, arrange marinated lady fingers to form a shell for the filling. Pour the fluffy mixture into the shell, and cover with more lady fingers. Chill thoroughly. To serve, carefully turn onto decorative plate, and remove wax paper. Slice as cake.

STRUDEL

Tirolese Flaky Cake Roll   *Alto Adige*

Dough	Filling
½ teaspoon salt	2 cups peeled chopped apples
2½ cups flour	½ cup currants
1 cup warm milk	½ cup powdered sugar
1 egg	1 cup chopped walnuts
1 tablespoon sugar	1 tablespoon grated lemon rind
3 tablespoons melted butter	1 teaspoon cinnamon
	1 teaspoon nutmeg

Prepare dough in warm room, dissolving salt and flour in warm milk, adding the other ingredients, and mixing well until it bubbles. Cover, and let rest ½ hour in warm place. Place dough on clean floured pastry cloth. Carefully stretch it, like a fine piece of rubber, as thin as possible without tearing. Brush melted butter over entirety. Spread filling over surface. Sprinkle with powdered sugar and cinnamon. Holding cloth in one hand, roll dough away from yourself. Cut it into 3 lengths to fit well-greased loaf pans. Bake in 325° oven 45 minutes.

TORTONE DI CIOCCOLATA

Chilled Almond Cake   *Emilia*

2 eggs	½ cup blanched almonds, coarsely chopped
1 cup sugar	
1 cup soft butter	6 hard plain sugar cookies, broken into bits
¼ cup cocoa	
1 ounce whisky or gin	whipped cream

Whip eggs and sugar till very light and fluffy. Cream butter *well* with cocoa and whisky or gin, and add it to the eggs. Beat until very light and fluffy. Add almonds and cookies; mix well. Place in small loaf pan, lined with waxed paper. Pat firmly. Chill. Serve in slices topped with whipped cream. If desired, cover cake with whipped cream, and slice to serve.

TORTA AGNELLO

Lamb Cake   *Abruzzi*

> This Easter specialty makes a beautiful paschal centerpiece. The Lamb Cake mold (in 2 parts) can be purchased in most hardware and department stores.

¾ cup butter	2 teaspoons baking powder
1 cup sugar	¼ teaspoon salt
3 eggs	1 teaspoon vanilla
2 cups flour	¾ cup milk
¾ cup chopped nuts	

Cream butter and sugar. Add eggs, and beat well. Add flour, baking powder, and salt. Mix thoroughly. Add vanilla, milk, and nuts, and again beat well. Grease inside of mold well, and fill face part with batter. Fit the parts together, and bake in 350° oven 1 hour. Remove from oven, and turn face upward to cool for 15 minutes. Remove the cake and set it on a platter. If necessary, re-enforce ears with toothpicks before frosting with **Ghiacciata Bollita** (Chap. IX, D). Sprinkle completely with **coconut.** Use maraschino **cherry** for mouth and **raisins** for eyes.

TORTA AL MOSCATO

Raisin Cake   *Piemonte*

Papa's favorite to serve with wine

1 pound raisins (muscatel preferred)	3 cups flour
	1 level teaspoon soda
2 cups water	3 teaspoons cinnamon

1½ cups sugar
½ cup butter
3 eggs

1 level teaspoon salt
½ teaspoon cloves
½ teaspoon nutmeg

2 cups broken walnut meats (optional)

Cook raisins in water 10 minutes; strain, saving 1 cup juice and adding soda to it. Cream the butter, sugar, eggs, salt, spices, and flour thoroughly. Add the soda and raisin juice. Mix in the raisins and nuts and beat thoroughly. Pour into a well-greased pan. Bake in 325° oven 1½ hours, or until a straw or fork comes out clean.

TORTA MARGHERITA

Daisy Cake   *Toscana*

3 whole eggs plus 5 yolks
1½ cups sugar
1 teaspoon vanilla, lemon, or favorite cordial
2 cups flour (potato, rice, or cake)
½ cup soft butter

Beat all ingredients together at least ½ hour by hand or 10 minutes with electric beater. Pour into 10-inch-deep buttered and floured cake pan. Bake in 350° oven 40 minutes. Frost with desired **icing**.

TORTA RICCIOLINA

Curly Cake   *Campania*

Prepare **Pasta Frolla.** Line a large casserole with half the rolled dough, and fill it with a blended mixture of

1 cup blanched ground almonds
¼ cup creamed butter
3 drops oil of bitter almond
½ cup powdered sugar
2 egg whites, whipped stiff
1 cup chopped candied fruit (optional)

Cut remaining rolled dough in long, very fine strips (if spaghetti machine is available, use finest cutter). Lay them across top in little curls (like coconut). Bake in 400° oven 20 minutes.

TORTA DI CASTAGNE

Chestnut Cake   *Piemonte*

½ **cup butter**	1 **cup sifted cake flour**
¼ **cup sugar**	½ **teaspoon salt**
3 **eggs, separated**	2 **teaspoons baking powder**
	1 **cup mashed chestnuts**

Prepare **Castagne Imbiancate** (Chap. IX, A). Cream butter,
sugar, and egg yolks. Add flour, salt, and baking powder; blend
thoroughly. Add mashed chestnuts and well-beaten egg whites. Mix
thoroughly, and pour into two 8-inch round layer-cake pans which
have been buttered and floured. Bake in 350° oven about 25 minutes.
Let the cake cool before removing it. Place the two layers together,
with filling of **Crema** (Chap. IX, E), and frost top with a little
chocolate swirled into the custard so as to give a marble effect.

TORTA DI FRUTTA

Fruit Cobbler   *Alto Adige*

2 **cups flour**	2 **eggs**
½ **teaspoon salt**	¼ **cup sugar**
2 **teaspoons baking pow-**	¾ **cup milk**
der	

Mix all ingredients together thoroughly, and pour into well-buttered heavy 12-inch skillet. Mix into the thick batter sliced fresh
peaches, pears, or apples. Brush top with butter, and sprinkle with
sugar. Bake in 350° oven 30 minutes, or until a knife comes out clean.

TORTA DI MELE

Apple Cobbler   *Piemonte*
*My school days were happiest when Mamma gave
me this delicacy for lunch.*

4 **cups milk**
½ **cup melted butter**

- **2** cups flour
- **2** eggs
- **½** cup sugar
- **2** teaspoons baking powder
- **12** soda crackers
- **4 or 5** large apples, peeled and sliced

Heat milk to scalding. Add butter, and let cool. Stir in flour, eggs, sugar, and baking powder, and beat vigorously. Pour batter into well-buttered 12-inch skillet. Place crackers on surface and, with tablespoon, carefully push each one to bottom of pan. Scatter apple slices over surface. Sprinkle with sugar and cinnamon and dots of butter. Bake in 350° oven approximately 25 minutes, till top is golden-brown. Serve with cream.

TORTA DI SANGUINACCI

Blood Fruit-Cake *Puglia*
   A delicacy always made during hog-killing season

- **2** quarts fresh, uncoagulated hog blood
- **1** cup seedless raisins
- **½** cup chopped citron
- **½** cup chopped candied orange peel
- **½** cup chopped candied lemon peel
- **1** cup honey
- **1** cup chopped nuts
- **¾** cup bread crumbs
- **½** cup chocolate shavings, or chocolate morsels

Mix thoroughly, and pour into large buttered and floured shallow pan. Bake in 300° oven 1½ hours.

ZUPPA INGLESE

English Trifle *All Regions*

There are many styles of this—basically layers of sponge cake or lady fingers soaked in a desired liquor (often rum), each topped with whipped cream or custard. Here is a recipe of which I am fond: individual servings on dessert plates of

4 lady fingers soaked in cherry brandy or vermouth;
¼–inch layer of Crema or whipped cream;
4 lady fingers soaked in cherry brandy or vermouth;
½–inch layer of Crema or whipped cream, with a swirl of chocolate creating a marble effect.

D. GLASSATURE (*Frostings*)

GHIACCIATA BOLLITA

Boiled Icing   *Abruzzi*

1 cup sugar
1 egg white
1 teaspoon baking powder
1 teaspoon flavoring (almond, lemon, or fruit brandy)
3 tablespoons water
½ teaspoon salt
2 tablespoons white corn syrup

Place all ingredients in top of double boiler, and cook at least 5 minutes, beating constantly, until desired consistency is reached. For a particular color, add drop of food coloring just as icing begins to thicken.

GLASSATURA ALLA CIOCCOLATA

Glazed Chocolate Frosting   *All Regions*

1½ cups sugar
1½ cups hot water
2 ounces unsweetened chocolate shredded

⅓ cup cornstarch
¼ cup cold water
1 teaspoon vanilla or almond flavoring

Mix sugar, hot water, and chocolate in saucepan over fire, stirring constantly until sugar dissolves. Boil 5 minutes, stirring all the while. Dissolve cornstarch in cold water, and slowly stir into the boiling sauce until frosting is thick and creamy. Add flavoring, and beat until cool enough to spread.

GLASSATURA GENERALE

General Frosting *Piemonte*

2 cups powdered sugar   **4 tablespoons cream**
3 drops oil of lemon

Beat all ingredients until creamy. The amount of cream may be varied for the desired consistency.

GLASSATURA LUSTRATA

Glazed Frosting *All Regions*

2 cups sugar   **⅛ teaspoon cream of tartar**
1 cup hot water   **powdered sugar as needed**

Heat sugar, water, and cream of tartar over a slow fire, stirring constantly, until sugar dissolves. Cook quickly *without* stirring, until it reaches thin-syrup stage (sample dropped into cup of cold water readily forms a soft ball). Cool until tepid. Add enough powdered sugar for desired consistency. For a particular color, add food coloring with the powdered sugar.

E. DOLCI AL CUCCHIAIO (*"Sweets for the Spoon":* *Custards, Puddings, and Cream Sauces*)

BUDINO DI PANE

Bread Pudding *Lucania*

2 cups bread crumbs   **½ cup melted butter**
2 cups cold milk   **½ teaspoon salt**
4 eggs   **1 teaspoon lemon flavoring**
raisins and nuts, if desired

Soak bread crumbs in milk. In double boiler, beat eggs into butter Add salt, flavoring, bread, and milk, and stir constantly while cook-

ing. Add raisins and nuts, and pour into butter-lined mold or casserole. Place this in a hot water bath in 350° oven for 1 hour.

BUDINO DI RICOTTA

Cream Cheese Custard   *Campania*

    ½ **pound ricotta**   ¼ **cup finely-chopped walnuts**
    ¼ **cup grated milk choco-**   **2 tablespoons cream (more if**
           late   **needed)**

    Cream the ricotta. Add chocolate and nuts, and blend thoroughly.
Add cream as needed for desired consistency. Vary the taste as de-
sired, perhaps by adding 2 tablespoons chopped candied cherries.
Serve in sherbet glasses, with cookies.

    This custard is also used as a filling for many cakes and cookies.

BUDINO DI RISO

Rice Pudding   *Abruzzi*

Christmas Eve dessert in Abruzzi

In a double boiler place:

    4 eggs, well beaten   **1 cup sugar**
    1½ cups milk   ½ **teaspoon nutmeg**
               1 cup cooked rice

    With wooden spoon, stir the ingredients while cooking in double
boiler until they thicken to a pudding. Pour into sherbet glasses to
cool, then sprinkle with confettini (decorettes) or top with whipped
cream. Or pour the pudding into a baked pie shell, and place in
325° oven till delicately brown.

BUDINO SPUMOSO AL RISO

Velvet Rice Pudding   *Toscana*

    ½ **cup sugar**   **12 egg yolks**
    2 cups flour   **2 cups milk**
    9 egg whites, whipped   ½ **cup soft butter**

¼ cup currants
1 cup cooked rice
¼ cup candied fruit, finely ground

¼ cup maraschino cherry juice
cherries, chopped, from which juice was taken

1 cup blanched pistachio nuts, finely chopped

Line a mold with butter and pistachio nuts. Cream sugar, flour, and egg yolks, blending them. Add the remaining ingredients, except the egg whites and the cherries, and mix thoroughly. Fold in egg whites; pour into mold. Place in hot water bath in 350° oven for 1 hour. Transfer to refrigerator. In serving, set in pan of hot water for a second, then transfer immediately to platter. Sprinkle with cherries.

CREMA

Custard   *All Regions*

6 egg yolks
6 tablespoons sugar
1 tablespoon potato or cornstarch
1 quart milk
1 lemon or orange peel (whole)

With wooden spoon beat egg yolks and sugar until creamy. Slowly add starch and milk, continuing to beat in same direction. Place over slow flame, and when the custard begins to simmer add peel. Now cook the custard about ½ hour, and stir constantly, without letting it boil. When thick and creamy remove peel, and pour it into sherbet glasses or casserole to cool. Use as dessert or as filling for pastries or cakes.

CREMA DI CASTAGNE

Chestnut Custard   *Lombardia*

½ cup butter
3 tablespoons flour
1 cup mashed chestnuts

3 egg yolks, well beaten
1 teaspoon sugar
3 egg whites, whipped

Prepare **Castagne Imbiancate** (Chap. IX, A). Melt butter in top of double boiler. Add flour, mashed chestnuts, egg yolks, and sugar, stirring constantly with wooden spoon until mixture thickens. Remove from heat, and fold in egg whites. Pour into butter-lined casserole, and bake in 300° oven 15 minutes. Serve cold, with or without cream.

CREMA NAPOLETANA

Neapolitan Cream   *Campania*

| 8 tablespoons sugar | 6 tablespoons flour |
| 6 egg yolks | 1 quart milk |

Beat sugar and egg yolks until creamy; blend flour in. Slowly add milk, and stir well. Pour into double boiler, and add desired **flavoring,** which may be 1 orange or lemon peel or 1 teaspoon cherry brandy. Stir constantly with wooden spoon until thick. Remove peel, and whip with egg beater until glossy. Remove from fire, and turn into casserole or sherbet glasses to cool.

FRAGOLE CON VINO

Strawberries with Wine   *Piemonte*

1 quart firm, ripe straw-	½ teaspoon lemon juice
berries	1 cup Marsala or sherry
2 tablespoons sugar	wine

Wash and drain strawberries, and place them in a casserole. Sprinkle sugar and a dash of lemon juice over them. Let marinate ½ hour. Pour wine over all, and stir. Chill at least 2 hours before serving.

GELATO DI TUTTI FRUTTI

Mixed-Fruit Ice Cream   *Campania*

1 cup apricots or peaches
1 cup raspberries or strawberries
¼ cup currants
½ cup candied lemon, lime, or pineapple peel, chopped

1 cup sugar
2 cups water
1 tablespoon gelatin or pectin in ½ cup water
2 cups whipped cream

Pass all fruit through food grinder. Boil sugar and water 10 minutes. Add ground fruits and juice. Cook slowly, stirring with wooden spoon until it coats spoon. Remove, and cool in refrigerator. Add diluted gelatin, and whip vigorously. Add whipped cream; blend, and return to refrigerator trays to freeze.

GRANITA DI CAFFE

Coffee Ice Whip *Sicilia*

½ cup sugar   1 cup strong coffee
1 cup boiling water   2 cups whipped cream

Dissolve sugar in water. Add coffee, and pour into freezing tray. When slushy, scrape into bowl. Fold in whipped cream, and return to tray to freeze.

LATTE ALLA PORTOGHESE

Delicate Portuguese Custard *Toscana*

8 egg yolks, beaten   1 ounce rum or cordial (op-
8 tablespoons sugar   tional)
1 quart milk   rind of 1 lemon

A scalloped mold is preferred; however, a simple mold or angel-food pan can be used. Sprinkle 4 tablespoons sugar into mold. Hold over hot flame until it liquefies. With a circular motion, cause the liquefied burnt sugar to coat the whole inside of the pan.

Cream eggs and sugar; add milk and flavoring and mix thoroughly. Add strips of lemon rind, pour into mold, and cook in a hot water bath in 400° oven until firm (not less than 1 hour). When cool, set in pan of hot water for a second, then turn out onto platter. The burnt-sugar coating gives the custard form a beautiful bronze look. Cialdoni (Chap. IX, B) are often served with this custard, to be used as nibbling spoons and eaten along with it.

MACEDONIA DI FRUTTA

Spirited Fruit Cup   *Lazio*

Choice of Fruits

strawberries: sliced	lemon: peeled and diced
cherries: pitted	raspberries: whole
peaches: sliced	plums: sliced
oranges: peeled and cubed	pears: cored and sliced
watermelon: cubed red	bananas: sliced
meat	cantaloupe: cubed meat

mangoes: peeled and sliced

Using the list above, select firm ripe fruit of the kinds desired, and prepare it as indicated. Make your own combination for a fruit cup.

1 quart mixed sliced fruit   **2 cups vermouth, sherry or Mar-**
¼ cup powdered sugar   **sala wine**
1 ounce cherry brandy, or favorite cordial

In a casserole, cover fruit with sugar. Let it stand ½ hour or more, until sugar is absorbed. Mix one of wines with cherry brandy, and pour over fruit. Cover, and set in cool place to marinate overnight. Serve in sherbet glasses.

MELE FRITTE

Fried Apples   *Piemonte*

Slice unpeeled apples into casserole lined with abundant butter. Place in 350° oven until crisp, turning them occasionally. Serve either plain or with cream.

PANNA MONTATA CON CIALDONI

Whipped Cream with Thin Curled Wafers   *Toscana*
A very fashionable dessert of Florence

Prepare **Cialdoni** (Chap. IX, B) and, with each sherbet glass of **whipped cream,** serve two for the guest to use as a spoon, gracefully biting off a part of the cooky with each dip of cream.

SANGUINACCI

Blood Pudding   *Campania*
         Specialty for Carnevale, preceding Lent

- 1 quart fresh, uncoagulated pork blood
- 2 cups sugar
- ¼ cup melted sweet butter
- 6 tablespoons flour stirred into ¼ cup milk
- 1 quart milk
- 1 pound grated bitter chocolate
- 1 cup pignon nuts
- ½ teaspoon cinnamon

Pour all ingredients into double boiler, and stir constantly with wooden spoon until mixture becomes thick. Pour into casserole to cool.

SORBETTO DI BANANA

Banana Sherbet   *Sicilia*

1½ cups sugar	juice of 1 lemon
2 cups water	1 cup mashed banana

Boil the sugar in water until completely dissolved. When cool, add lemon juice, and mix thoroughly. Add mashed banana. Whip until light and fluffy. Pour into refrigerator tray to freeze.

SORBETTO DI COCOMERO

Watermelon Sherbet   *Sicilia*

1 watermelon	⅓ cup sugar
2 tablespoons cornstarch	½ teaspoon salt
1 teaspoon almond flavoring	1 teaspoon grated lemon peel

Remove the rind and 1 inch of white from melon and put red meat through food chopper, accumulating 4 cups of pulp and juice.

In saucepan over very low flame, cook the other ingredients. When they are well blended, stir in melon and restore to cooking temperature. Beat thoroughly, and place in refrigerator tray to freeze.

SPUMONI

Luxurious Ice-Cream Whip   *Campania*

1 quart strawberries or raspberries	½ cup powdered sugar
juice of 1 lemon	1 cup chopped walnuts
3 tablespoons sugar	1 cup chopped pistachio nuts
	3 cups whipped cream

Mash berries with lemon juice and sugar. Let them marinate ½ hour. Add nuts and powdered sugar, and stir vigorously. Fold into whipped cream. Pour into loaf pans or round ice-cream mold, and freeze. Cut into inch slices to serve.

ZABAIONE

Wine Custard   *Piemonte*

Beat 6 **egg yolks** and 3 tablespoons **sugar** till light and creamy. Add ¾ cup Marsala or sherry **wine** gradually, beating constantly with wooden spoon until all is absorbed. Pour into top of double boiler, and cook over slow fire, beating constantly until mixture thickens. Pour into sherbet glasses. Serve either hot or cold.

CHAPTER X

SPUNTINI E PANE
Snacks and Breads

BRIOCHE

Butter Rolls   *Toscana*

1 cup milk	**¼ cup unsalted butter**
3 tablespoons sugar	**2 cakes yeast, crumbled**
1 teaspoon salt	**5 cups flour**

Scald milk, and remove it from fire. Add sugar, salt, and butter, and stir till all dissolve. Dissolve yeast in 2 tablespoons tepid water, and stir it into lukewarm milk mixture. Add half the flour, and beat until smooth. Add rest of flour, and knead into smooth silky dough. Place in greased bowl, and brush with a bit of butter. Cover, and leave in a warm place free from draft, till dough doubles in bulk (an hour or so). Punch it down, cover, and leave again till double in bulk. Punch it down, cover and leave 15 minutes. Pinch off pieces of dough, and form them into smooth egg-shaped rolls. Place them in greased shallow pan, about 1 inch apart, and cut a diagonal slit across top of each. Brush with butter. Bake in 350° oven about 15 minutes, till golden-brown.

BAGNA CAUDA
(Piedmontese dialect for bagno caldo)

Hot Sauce Snack   *Piemonte*

Bagna Cauda is a veritable base for a New Year's celebration. The natives use it to herald the vin-

*tage season, when large quantities of the new
wines are sampled.*

Prepare large bowl of 1-inch pieces of crisp **green pepper, celery**
or **cardoon**. In small skillet or saucepan, sauté 3 or 4 cloves chopped
garlic in ½ cup **butter** and ¼ cup **olive oil.** When delicately brown,
add 1 small can **anchovies** and stir well. This sauce is served from
the vessel in which it was cooked, and is kept hot over the stove or
electric plate, or in a chafing dish over a spirit lamp. Each partaker
has a fork in one hand and a piece of crusty **Italian bread** in the
other. With the fork, dip a piece of crisp vegetable into the hot
sauce, hold it over the bread, and eat. Add more garlic, butter, oil,
and anchovies as needed.

CROSTINI

Cubed Toast   *All Regions*

Cut **bread** into small squares or other desired shape. Toast in
large skillet with a little **butter** or **olive oil,** stirring constantly until
delicately brown and crisp. If desired add 2 cloves of **garlic** for
flavor, discarding them when delicately brown (if they brown too
much they will ruin the flavor). Many prefer to place cubed bread
with oil or butter in a slow oven, stirring occasionally till brown and
crisp. Use as garnish with green vegetables, or in soup.

FARINATA DI CASTAGNE

Chestnut Bread Snack   *Liguria*

1 pound chestnut flour	**3 cups water**
1 teaspoon salt	**¼ cup olive oil**
1 cup sliced pignon nuts	

Mix chestnut flour, salt, and water thoroughly into thick, smooth
batter, and pour into 10-inch cake pan lined with ¼ cup oil. Stir
again. Sprinkle nuts over top. Bake in 350° oven till golden-brown.

FIATONE DI RICOTTA

Cheese Bread   *Lucania*
> *Specialty of Good Friday and Christmas Eve*

Dough	**Filling**
4 cups flour	1 pound ricotta
8 eggs	6 eggs
3 tablespoons olive oil	½ cup grated Romano cheese
1 teaspoon salt	¼ cup minced parsley
4 tablespoons sugar	salt and pepper to taste

Work and knead the flour and other ingredients into smooth dough. Cover and set aside.

Blend the ingredients for filling together. Roll out ¾ of dough ¼ inch thick. Place in 9 × 13-inch sheet cake pan. Pour filling into dough-lined pan. Cover with remaining dough rolled out ¼ inch thick. Pierce several air vents in dough. Or, weave 1-inch strips of dough as for making a pie. Bake in 375° oven ½ hour. Lower heat to 350° and bake another ½ hour.

FIATONE DI SALSICCIA

Sausage Bread   *Lucania*
> *Also known in Lucania as Easter Bread, because*
> *there is never an Easter without Fiatone.*

2 eggs	salt and pepper to taste
1 cup grated Romano cheese	¼ cup minced parsley
1½ pounds Italian sausage (parboiled and cut into inch pieces)	1 cup diced scamorza cheese

Blend all ingredients together as a filling to be used with the dough of the preceding recipe.

FONDUA

Cheese Pudding Snack   *Piemonte*

1 pound Gruyère or Fontina cheese	¼ cup butter
milk as needed	3 large egg yolks, well beaten

Cube cheese and just cover it with milk to soak 2 hours. Melt butter in top of double boiler. Add cheese and milk, and cook, stirring constantly with wooden spoon until cheese dissolves. Remove from fire, and add egg yolks; stir well. Place over fire for 2 more minutes, stirring constantly until you have a smooth creamy texture, with absolutely no strings or granules. Serve on a platter with garnish of sliced **truffles** or **mushrooms.**

GRISSINI

Bread Sticks   *Piemonte*
     Napoleon called them "dainty batons of Turin."

3 tablespoons leaf lard or unsalted butter, melted	1 cup lukewarm water
	1 cake yeast
1 teaspoon salt	3 cups flour, or more
	2 egg whites, stiffly beaten

Melt lard or butter and salt in half the water; dissolve yeast in rest of water, and mix the solutions. Add 1 cup flour, and beat until smooth. Add egg whites (fold in, as in making waffle batter). Add rest of flour, and knead into soft elastic dough. Place in a greased bowl and brush with a bit of butter or lard. Cover, and leave in warm place free from draft till it doubles in bulk. Punch it down, cover, and leave again till it doubles in bulk. Punch it down, and leave 15 minutes. Divide it in half. Roll out each half ⅛ inch thick. Cut dough into 2-inch squares. Roll the squares to resemble pencils. Cover them, on a greased cooky sheet, to rest ½ hour. Bake in 350° oven till golden-brown.

GUASTIEDDI

Crusty Bun Snack *Sicilia*

- ½ **pound ricotta**
- ½ **pound caciocavallo, provolone, or mozzarella cheese**
- 12 **crusty rolls (preferably topped with sesame seeds), split and brushed with olive oil**
- 1 **teaspoon crushed origano (optional) salt and pepper to taste**

Split each roll. Brush it with olive oil, and insert slice of ricotta and slice of other cheese selected. Salt and pepper to taste, and, if desired, add dash of origano. Set filled buns in roasting pan, cover, and leave in 350° oven for 10 minutes.

MOZZARELLA IN CARROZZA

Cheese in a Wagon *Campania*
This glorified toasted cheese sandwich originated in Naples, but is widely served in Lazio.

Lay a slice of **mozzarella** cheese between slices of **Italian bread.** If desired, remove crusts and prepare miniature sandwiches. Dip each sandwich into **milk,** then into **flour,** and into well-beaten **egg.** Fry in **olive oil** till golden-brown on both sides.

PAGNOTTINI

Crusty Bun Rolls *Emilia*

1 **cup tepid water or milk**	2 **tablespoons melted lard**
2 **tablespoons sugar (optional)**	2 **cakes yeast dissolved in**
1 **teaspoon salt**	2 **tablespoons tepid water**
	4 **to 6 cups flour**

Scald the milk or water; remove from fire. Add sugar, salt, and lard, and stir. Add the dissolved yeast to the lukewarm milk or water mixture. Add half the flour, and beat until smooth. Stir in enough flour to make a medium-stiff dough. Place in a greased bowl and brush with butter or lard. Cover, and leave in a warm place free from draft till it doubles in bulk. Punch it down, cover, and leave it to double again in bulk. Use for one of the following forms:

Pagnottini Tondi (Round Buns)

Pinch off pieces of dough a bit larger than an egg, and form them into balls. Cover, let rest ½ hour; brush with well-beaten egg yolk. Bake in 350° oven till golden-brown.

Pagnottini Ovali (Oval Buns)

Pinch off pieces of dough a bit larger than an egg. Press them into the shape of an egg, and cover them, on a greased cooky sheet, to rest ½ hour. Brush with well-beaten egg yolk, and bake in 350° oven till golden-brown.

Mezze Lune (Half-Moons)

Divide dough, and roll both balls into circles about 10 inches in diameter. Cut into 12 pie-shaped wedges. Beginning at wide end, roll each wedge like a jelly roll, and twist into moon-shape. Place moons on greased cooky sheet, and cover them to stand ½ hour. Brush with well-beaten egg yolk or milk. Bake in 350° oven till golden-brown.

PANE

Bread   *Northern Regions*

3 cakes yeast	3 tablespoons melted lard
3 teaspoons salt	3 cups lukewarm water
3 tablespoons sugar (optional)	8 cups flour (or more)

Dissolve yeast, salt, sugar, and lard in lukewarm water, and mix in enough flour to make smooth medium-textured dough. Work and knead until it readily leaves work board. Brush top with a bit of lard. Cover, and leave in a warm place free of draft, till it doubles in bulk. (When it has reached the peak it will appear to sink a little.) Punch it down, cover, and let rise a second time. When double in bulk, split into three parts. Shape round or long loaves; place on floured sheet pan (3 inches apart to allow for rising). Cover, let rest ½ hour. Brush tops with well-beaten egg yolk. Cut diagonal slit across each loaf. Bake in 350 to 375° oven 15 minutes. Lower heat to 300 to 325° and bake loaves ½ hour longer, or until golden-brown. On removing, tip them against a bread board so that air can circulate freely around each loaf. Newly baked bread will lose its freshness and sweetness and crispness if covered.

PANE A TRECCIA

Braided Bread   *Piemonte*

Split the **Pane** dough of the preceding recipe into nine equal parts. Roll each of these into a strip 14 inches long. Place 3 strips on greased baking sheet, and work them into a braid. Brush top lightly with **milk** or melted **butter.** Cover, and let rise till they double in bulk. Bake in 325 to 350° oven 15 minutes. Lower heat to 300° and bake ½ hour longer, or until golden-brown.

PANE DI SEGALA

Rye Bread   *Alto Adige*

1 tablespoon salt	3 cakes yeast
3 tablespoons pure lard	1 pound dark rye flour
1 quart lukewarm water	6 scant cups white flour

Add salt to half the water over fire, and as soon as it is hot melt lard in it. Meanwhile, dissolve yeast in remaining water. When salt water is almost cool, combine it with yeast solution and mix them thoroughly. Sift rye and white flours together; add half to the liquid, and beat thoroughly. Add remaining flour, and knead into smooth elastic dough. Set it in a large greased pan, cover, and leave it in warm place free from draft 1 hour. Split the dough into sixths. Shape these into round balls or long loaves. Leave them on floured board, covered, for ½ hour. Brush lightly with butter, and bake in 370° oven till done, when fork comes clean.

PANE DI MANDORLE

Almond Bread   *Lucania*

An Easter-time bread

2 eggs	1 cake yeast
2 tablespoons sugar	2 tablespoons tepid water
1 teaspoon salt	4 cups flour
1 tablespoon melted	1 egg yolk
shortening	1 cup blanched almonds

Beat eggs, sugar, salt, and shortening thoroughly. Dissolve yeast in water; add to egg mixture, and stir well. Add flour, and knead into smooth dough. Set it in greased bowl, cover, and leave in a warm place free from draft till it doubles in bulk. Punch it down, and form it into a large round, flat ring. Place in large greased sheet pan. Poke almonds into dough, all over. Brush top with well-beaten egg yolk. Bake in 400° oven till golden-brown.

PANE DI SAN GIUSEPPE

St. Joseph Bread   *Sicilia*

> *On March 19, feast day of St. Joseph, patron saint of the poor, Sicilian women prepare a banquet of varied luscious foods, with the huge loaf of St. Joseph bread as the centerpiece. Thirteen places are set, and 12 poor boys are invited as guests to represent the Apostles.*

3 cakes yeast	1 quart tepid water
1 tablespoon salt	8 cups flour, or more
¾ cup sugar	1 dozen eggs
¾ cup lard	¼ cup sesame or anise seeds

Dissolve yeast, salt, and sugar, and melt lard in water. Form nest of flour on work board. Drop eggs and a few seeds into nest. Work this with one hand, and at the same time gradually add yeast mixture. Finally, work and knead with both hands till you have a smooth elastic dough. Brush top with a bit of lard; cover, and leave in a warm place free from draft till the dough doubles in bulk. Punch it down, cover, and leave it to rise a second time. Punch down, and shape into huge round, flat doughnut. Place on large greased sheet pan, and sprinkle seeds over top. Cover, and let rest ½ hour. Bake in 370° oven till golden-brown.

PANE DI UOVA

Egg Bread   *Calabria*

> *Known locally as Acquadura (hard water), this is an Easter treat. Years ago small individual loaves were made for the children to have blessed in church on Holy Saturday.*

2 cakes yeast	2 dozen eggs
1 cup lukewarm water	1 cup lard, slightly melted
6 cups flour, or more	2 cups sugar
2 teaspoons salt	

On the night before, dissolve yeast in water. Add a little flour, mix, cover, and leave overnight in a warm place free from draft. In the morning form nest of flour on work board. Add 12 of the eggs, yeast mixture, and remaining ingredients. Work and knead into a smooth elastic bread dough. Cover in greased bowl, and let rest till it doubles in bulk. Punch it down, cover, and let rest until it again doubles in bulk. Punch it down once more, and form into a large round flat ring. Place in a large greased sheet pan. At regular intervals press a whole raw egg, shell and all, into the dough, until all the second dozen are used. Brush top of dough with lard. Bake in 350° oven till golden-brown. Serve a part of the bread with a roasted egg enclosed, to be peeled and eaten with the bread.

PANE FRITTO

Fried Bread   *Calabria*

Dialect name, Risped

When preparing **Pane,** pull off chunks of the dough, and spread them out thin. Fry in about ½ inch **lard** till golden-brown on both sides. Remove onto absorbent paper, and dust with **sugar.**

PANZANELLA

Bread Snack   *Sicilia*

Soak slices of dried **Italian bread** in cold water, and squeeze.
Sprinkle chopped **garlic** over top. **Salt** and **pepper** to taste. Top
with **olive oil**.

PIZZA

Neapolitan Snack   *Campania*
> *Neapolitans say, "There is no Pizza without to-
> mato"; and of course they ought to know, because
> Naples is the original home of this snack(not pie)
> enjoyed by all—Italy and America.*

Prepare **Pane** or your own favorite bread recipe; or even buy
dough at the bakery. Roll it out to desired thinness, and arrange
it in well-greased small or large pie pans or cooky sheets. With a
fork, make occasional imprints in dough. Brush completely with
olive oil, and top with slices of fresh **tomato**, tomato paste, or
tomato sauce. Sprinkle as you like with **origano**, chopped **parsley,
garlic**, grated **Parmesan**, or **Romano** cheese. Add **salt** and **pepper**
to taste. Cover it as desired with

    slices of mozzarella or scamorza cheese
    Italian sausage (chopped) or filets of anchovies
    slices of black pitted olives (optional)
    chopped mushrooms (optional)

Bake in 400° oven 25 minutes. Serve hot.

SCHIACCIATA DI CICCIOLI

Crackling Bread   *Lucania*

3 cups yellow corn meal	1½ cups milk
1 tablespoon salt	1½ cups water
3 tablespoons baking	2 eggs
powder	1 cup cracklings

Mix corn meal, salt, and baking powder thoroughly. Add milk and water, and beat until smooth. Drop eggs into batter, and continue beating. Stir in cracklings. Bake in lightly-greased iron skillet or large Dutch oven, about ½ hour in 400° oven.

SCHIACCIATA UNTA

Crackling Snack *Toscana*

To the dough of **Pane,** add 1 cup **cracklings,** 4 well-beaten **egg yolks,** and 1 tablespoon grated **lemon rind.** Work into smooth mixture. Cover, and leave in warm place till double in bulk. Punch down, and roll out ½ inch thick. In well-greased small or large pie pans or on cooky sheets, bake in 400° oven till golden-brown (about 20 minutes).

SFINCIONE DI SAN VITO

Snack for St. Vitus *Sicilia*

Served on the Feast of St. Vitus, June 15

Roll out half the dough of **Pane** and place in greased Dutch oven. Add one of the following **fillings:**

I. ½ **pound ground cooked pork meat**
   ½ **pound caciocavallo or mozzarella cheese, chopped**
   1 **cup grated Romano cheese**
   salt and pepper to taste
   ½ **pound salami, chopped**

II. 1 **cup minced onion browned in olive oil**
    1 **small can tomato sauce**
    1 **small can anchovies, chopped**
    2 **cups diced caciocavallo or mozzarella cheese**

Roll out rest of dough, and cover filling, pressing edges together as in a pie. Cut several slits in top to act as steam vents. Cover with towel, and let rest ½ hour. Bake in 400° oven ½ hour or until golden-brown.

SMACA FAM'

Tirolese Snack   *Alto Adige*
> Smaca Fam' (*this dialect name signifies "smack
> the famine"*) *is as popular among Tirolese as Pizza
> is among Neapolitans.*

1 egg	1 pound luganighe in 1-inch
1 teaspoon salt	slices
2 cups buckwheat flour	½ cup chopped bacon

2 cups water

Beat egg and salt till creamy. Add buckwheat flour and water; mix thoroughly. Pour into butter-lined iron skillet or large Dutch oven. Scatter slices of sausage throughout batter, and scatter bacon over it. Bake in 350° oven 45 minutes, until knife comes clean.

TORTA DI PATATE ALLA GENOVESE

Potato Cake, Genoa Style   *Liguria*

Mix and work 1½ cups **flour**, 3 tablespoons **butter** or **lard**, and ¼ cup **water** as a pie dough. Roll out, and line a 12-inch butter-lined pie pan. Fill with 2 cups chopped **potatoes.** Sauté 2 tablespoons minced **salt pork**, 1 cup chopped fresh **onions** (or ½ cup minced Bermudas), ¼ cup minced **parsley,** and ¼ cup minced **basil** in 3 tablespoons butter, and spread on top of the potatoes. Brush with 1 **egg** mixed with 1 tablespoon **olive oil.** Sprinkle grated **Parmesan cheese, salt,** and **pepper** over all. Bake in 400° oven 25 minutes.

TORTA DI PATATE ALLA TIROLESE

Potato Cake, Tirolese Style   *Alto Adige*

3 large potatoes, peeled	salt and pepper to taste
and grated	1 egg
½ cup milk	½ cup flour

½ teaspoon baking powder

Mix together thoroughly, and pour into butter-lined sheet pan. Dot with butter and a few drops of olive oil. Bake in 350° oven 45 minutes, till golden-brown.

TORTA DI RISO

Rice Cake   *Liguria*

- 1 tablespoon minced salt pork
- 1 tablespoon minced onion
- 2 tablespoons olive oil
- 1 cup uncooked rice
- ¼ cup chopped parsley
- ¼ cup chopped basil
- 1 clove minced garlic
- salt and pepper to taste
- 1 tablespoon water
- 1 cup grated Parmesan cheese
- 1 egg mixed with 1 tablespoon olive oil

Mix and work 1½ cups **flour,** 3 tablespoons **butter** or **lard,** and ¼ cup **water** as a pie dough. Roll out and line butter-lined pie pan.

Sauté minced salt pork and minced onion in olive oil. When delicately brown add rice, and stir until golden-brown. Cover with boiling water. Stirring constantly, cook 15 to 20 minutes. In a bowl mix the parsley, basil, garlic, and 1 tablespoon water. Add with cheese to cooked mixture. Pour the whole into the pie shell. Spread egg and oil mixture over top. Sprinkle with a little grated cheese. Fold edges of dough over to make enclosure. Bake in 400° oven 20 minutes.

TORTA DI SANGUE

Blood Cake   *Piemonte*

- 1 quart fresh, uncoagulated pork blood
- 2 cups milk
- ½ teaspoon allspice
- ½ cup grated Parmesan cheese
- ¼ cup chopped salt pork or bacon
- 1 clove minced garlic
- 2 tablespoons minced onion

Mix all together thoroughly, and pour into oil-lined Dutch oven. Cover, and bake in 300° oven 1 hour.

TORTA DI SEDANO

Celery Cake   *Liguria*

8 eggs	¼ cup melted butter
1 large bunch celery, minced, parboiled, and strained	1 cup grated Parmesan cheese
	¼ cup minced onion
	salt and pepper to taste

Mix thoroughly 1½ cups flour, 3 tablespoons butter or lard, and ¼ cup water. Roll out, and line a 12-inch butter-lined pie pan.

Beat eggs thoroughly; add the other ingredients, and mix well. Pour into dough-lined pan; fold ends of dough over to enclose edges. Bake 20 minutes in 400° oven.

CHAPTER XI

BIBITE
Beverages

BEVANDE STIMOLANTI

Cordials *All Regions*

Flavored extracts are available through Italian delicatessens for various cordials such as:

Anisetta (anise flavor), red
Caffè Sport (coffee flavor), brown
Creme de Cacao (chocolate flavor), chocolate color
Creme de Menthe (mint flavor), green
Rosolio (cinnamon flavor), red
Strega (mystical flavor), golden

Procedure
1 quart water (1½ quarts, if reduced strength is desired)
2 cups sugar
1 pint grain alcohol (188 proof)
   desired food coloring
1 jigger prepared flavoring (for Anisetta, 1 ounce spirits
   of anise from pharmacy can be used)

Boil water and sugar; cool. Add alcohol, coloring, and flavor. Pour into bottles, and seal. Marinate 1 month before serving, in order to realize the true cordial flavor.

BRODO RISTRETTO

Beef Tea   *Toscana*

Remove all fat from 1 pound **round steak.** Chop the steak, and place in sterilized quart jar. Add 1½ cups cold water. Seal and set in large kettle of cold water. Heat water to boiling point, and boil at least 1 hour, until meat is white. Strain, pressing meat to obtain all the juice. Season with salt as desired.

CAFFE ALL'UOVO

Coffee with Egg   *Piemonte*
          A quick energy builder favored by sportsmen

Drop 1 **egg yolk** into an empty coffee cup. Add about 2 table-spoons of **hot coffee,** stirring rapidly so that yolk will dissolve and not cook. Let cool. Add coffee until the cup is properly full, stirring rapidly. This delicious drink resembles malted milk. Add **sugar** to taste.

CAFFE CAPPUCCINO

Coffee and Cream   *Le Marche*
          Italian society enjoys Caffè Cappuccino at breakfast.

- ¼ **cup black strong coffee**
- 1 **teaspoon sugar (optional)**
- ¾ **cup whipped cream, or thick creamy skim from scalded milk**

Pour coffee into soup bowl. If sugar is desired, add immediately, and stir. Then quickly fold in cream. A foam will appear on surface.

CAFFE DI ORZO

Barley Coffee   *Alto Adige*
                    Similar to Postum

Roast fresh **barley** just as you would coffee beans. Grind it like coffee beans. Boil it like coffee. Use half barley coffee and half **milk,** adding **sugar** if desired.

CIOCCOLATA

Hot Chocolate   *Alto Adige*

2 cups milk   ¼ **teaspoon salt, dissolved in a**
2 tablespoons cocoa   **little water**
1 tablespoon sugar

Scald milk in top of double boiler. Add cocoa, sugar, and salt.
Cook all together 15 minutes. Beat well, and serve immediately.

CHIARO D'UOVO AL LATTE

Egg Flip   *Northern Regions*

Scald 1½ cups **milk,** and simmer 10 minutes. Remove from fire,
and add 1 teaspoon **honey;** dissolve thoroughly. Fold in 2 stiffly
beaten **egg whites.** Serve hot or cold.

PONCINO

Coffee Royal   *Northern Regions*
        Served after a sumptuous meal. Smokers say it
        enhances enjoyment of a cigar.

1 tablespoon sugar   **1 ounce rum, grappa, cognac, or**
1 lemon twist (peel only)   **other brandy**
            ½ **cup strong hot coffee**

Place sugar, lemon twist, and spirits in coffee cup. Cover with hot
coffee, and stir.

VINO BRULE

Mulled Wine   *Piemonte*
        Papa always served us this after an ice-skating
        party, or when we had colds.

1 quart wine (preferably   **3 tablespoons sugar**
    red dry wine)   **2 or 3 sticks cinnamon, broken**
4 thin lemon slices with   **4 thin slices of apple (optional)**
    rind   **6 whole cloves**

Place all in large kettle over low heat, and bring to boiling point. Light a match to the vapor, and let it burn 1 minute. Blow out flame. Strain, if desired. Serve hot.

ZABAIONE FRESCO

Eggnog   *Piemonte*

1 egg
1 teaspoon powdered
   sugar

1 teaspoon flavoring (brandy,
   rum, cordial, almond, or
   lemon)

1 cup milk (half cream at desire)

Beat egg, sugar, and flavoring until creamy. Add milk, and beat again. Sprinkle with **nutmeg** if desired.

CHAPTER XII

CIBI CONSERVATI
Preserved Foods

CAPONATA

Canned Appetizer   *Sicilia*

5 large eggplants	1 pint olive oil
15 large ripe tomatoes	5 large onions, peeled and diced
1 cup chopped sweet basil	2 cups green olives, pitted
1 cup chopped parsley	2 cups capers, drained
½ cup vinegar	1 tablespoon salt
½ cup sugar	1 teaspoon black pepper
2 large bunches celery	3 chili peppers, crushed

Peel and dice eggplants, and place in a large kettle. Sprinkle with a handful of salt, and stir well to distribute salt. Place a large plate and a heavy weight over all, in order to draw out the bitter liquid. Let stand at least 3 hours. In the meantime blanch and dice tomatoes into another large kettle; add basil and parsley, and cook slowly (stirring now and then). When cooked into a free juice, add vinegar and sugar, and stir well. While they continue to cook, dice celery and deep-fry it in oil; drain, and place in a third large kettle. Squeeze eggplant, and deep-fry in the same oil; drain and place in kettle with celery. Also deep-fry onions; drain them, and add all the fried vegetables to the thickly-cooked tomatoes. Cook another half-hour. Add olives, capers, salt, pepper and chili peppers. Stir well;

simmer another half-hour. Fill sterilized pint jars, and seal tightly. (Yield, 12 to 14 pints.)

CAVOLFIORE MARINATO IN BARATTOLO

Pickled Cauliflower in Jars   *Calabria*

6 large heads white crisp cauliflower
2 quarts tiny pickling onions, peeled
½ cup chopped parsley florets

¼ cup chopped mint leaves
2 cloves garlic, chopped
2 quarts white vinegar
4 quarts water
½ cup salt

Combine water, vinegar, and salt.

Cut cauliflower into florets, and dice tender whole part into edible pieces. Boil in water for 3 to 4 minutes, drain, and cool. Place in a large bowl with onions, parsley, mint, and garlic. Stir well, and fill sterilized quart or pint jars. Completely fill the jars with the boiling liquid, and seal immediately.

CECI

Chick-Peas   *All Southern Regions*

Wash dried **chick-peas,** and soak them in cold water overnight. Drain, and cover with fresh water, to cook at least 3 hours. Drain, and cover with cold water. Place under a faucet, and allow a fine stream of cold water to wash them for 2 or 3 days, until they are tender and sweet. Drain, and place in jars, adding 1 teaspoon **salt** to each quart. Cover with boiling water and seal. Use as desired either for cooking or, drained and with a dash of salt and oil, for appetizers or snacks.

CETRIOLINI ALLA SENAPE

Mustard Pickles   *Piemonte*

200 midget cucumbers, washed and drained
3 pounds tiny pickling onions, peeled

5 **pounds white crisp cauliflower, cut into florets and slices**
1 **cup salt**

Mix all thoroughly in large kettle; cover with boiling water, and let stand 24 hours. Strain carefully through flour sack; place in large kettle.

½ **pound powdered mustard**	1 **tablespoon turmeric**
1 **tablespoon ginger**	1 **teaspoon black pepper**
½ **cup flour**	½ **cup sugar**
	¼ **cup white vinegar**

Stir all together. In large kettle add 2 quarts white vinegar, and bring to boiling point. Add mustard mixture, and stir constantly till it reaches boiling point. Pour over pickles and cauliflower, and mix thoroughly. Place in sterilized quart jars, and seal immediately.

CILIEGE SOTTO SPIRITO

Brandied Cherries   *Northern Regions*
A cordial favored by the Tirolese

Wash and dry cherries (preferably with stems), and place in pint jars. For black *Bing cherries*, add 1 tablespoon **sugar** to each pint; for fresh *sour pie cherries*, add 2 tablespoons **sugar** to each pint. Cover to brim with good cherry or grape **brandy,** and seal. Shake well, and let cherries marinate at least 1 month. Some people like to bring the brandy just to boiling point before pouring it over the cherries. In serving, place 1 cherry in a jigger glass, and cover with brandy

CONIGLIO PROFUMATO ALL'ACETO

Pickled Wild Rabbit   *Lucania*

Clean **rabbit** well; cut out all blood spots, and soak it overnight in salt water containing 1 teaspoon **baking soda.** In the morning wash again, and cut into serving pieces. Cover these with water in a large kettle. Add **salt** and **hot pepper** to taste. Cook until tender; drain. Remove all bones, and pack the meat well in sterilized jars.

⅓ **part vinegar**   ⅔ **part water, plenty of garlic**
salt, parsley, and caraway seed to taste

Combine the above ingredients and bring to a rapid boil. Pour over rabbit in sterilized jars, to the very top. Seal them immediately.

CONSERVA DI POMODORO

Canned Tomato Sauce   *All Regions*

1 **bushel very ripe tomatoes**   ½ **cup fresh parsley**
1 **cup fresh sweet basil, chopped**   ½ **cup salt**

Parboil tomatoes, and remove skins. Dice into large kettle. Bring to boiling point, and boil ½ hour to remove water content quickly, stirring often to prevent burning. Add sweet basil, parsley, and salt. Simmer till very thick, stirring often. Strain as desired. Pour into sterilized pint jars, and seal tightly. Approximate yield, 16 pints per bushel.

CUORE SOTTO ACETO

Pickled Heart   *Sicilia*

Boil **heart** (of beef, veal, pork, or lamb) in salt water till tender.* Slice or cube, and place in sterilized pint jars. To each jar add 1 clove **garlic** and 1 **chili pepper**. For a pickling liquid, combine ⅓ **vinegar** and ⅔ **water** with **salt** to taste. Bring to a rapid boil, and put into each jar to the very top. Seal immediately.

FUNGHI IN BARATTOLO

Canned Mushrooms   *All Regions*

Soak the **mushrooms** in cold water at least 2 hours. When pleated undercoat opens you can easily wash away any sand. Boil cleaned

* Beef heart is the toughest, lamb heart the most tender.

mushrooms in plenty of water about 45 minutes. Remove them with a slotted ladle (being careful not to stir any sand at bottom of kettle), and drop them into another kettle of freshly boiling water (with 1 tablespoon **vinegar** and 1 teaspoon **salt** for each quart of water). Bring to a rapid boil. Transfer the mushrooms to sterilized pint jars, cover with liquid, and seal.

FUNGHI SECCHI

Dried Mushrooms   *All Regions*

Do not wash the **mushrooms;** but clean and scrape off the whiskers, scrape the stems, and remove all dirt possible. Slice to ¼-inch thickness. Either string slices on heavy cord and hang in light, airy room, or lay them singly on papers and turn daily until they are thoroughly dry. Preserve them in paper bags or large cans, sprinkled with black pepper throughout. Before cooking, soak dried mushrooms in cold water 10 minutes; drain, and wash. Cover them with fresh water overnight, or with hot water 45 minutes. Proceed with the cooking.

FUNGHI SOTTO ACETO

Pickled Mushrooms   *All Regions*

Clean **mushrooms** well, and dice. Boil in salt water 20 minutes. Drain, and boil again in a mixture ⅓ **vinegar,** ⅔ water, with 2 **bay leaves,** 4 whole **cloves** (optional), 1 stick **cinnamon** (optional), **salt** to taste, and ¼ cup chopped fresh **parsley.** When it reaches a rapid boil, empty the kettle into sterilized jars with 1 clove **garlic** to each jar, covering the mushrooms with liquid. Seal.

GELATINA ALLA LIGURE

Pickled Meat, Ligurian Style   *Liguria*

> **2 pig tails, cut into serving pieces**
> **2 pig feet, cut into serving pieces**
> **6 veal or pig ears, cut in two**
> **¼ cup chopped sweet basil**

2 cloves garlic
2 bay leaves
salt and pepper to taste

Wash and clean meat well. Place in kettle with seasoning added. Cover with water, and cook 45 minutes, or until tender but firm. Place meat in casserole. Strain broth, and pour it over meat. Place in refrigerator to jell.

GELATINA DI VITELLO

Pickled Veal *Lombardia*

2 meaty veal shanks   1 teaspoon rosemary leaves
salt and pepper to taste   3 cloves garlic
2 bay leaves

Place meat in kettle with seasoning. Cover with water, and cook at least an hour, till tender but firm. Cut all meat into bite-size pieces, discarding bones. Place pieces in casserole, and cover with strained broth. Set in refrigerator to jell.

LUPINI SALATI

Salted Lupine Seeds *All Southern Regions*

Soak the dry lupine seeds (beans) overnight in salt water. Drain, cover with fresh water, and cook 3 or 4 hours, until skins are puffed. Don't stir while cooking (the skins will shrink). Drain off water, and wash carefully. Cover with cold water, and place under faucet, letting water trickle over them 3 or 4 days, to sweeten. Drain off water, and sprinkle with salt. Serve with appetizers or as condiment. To eat, squeeze shell, eat inner bean, and discard shell.

PEPERONI ROSSI IN BARATTOLO

Pimentos in Jars *Lucania*

Place firm large red bell peppers (thick and meaty) on rack in 375° oven. Turn them occasionally in order to blister evenly. When well blistered, place them in large kettle, and cover, so that the steam will penetrate. Peel peppers, break open, and save juice. Discard pulp and seeds. Place the pimentos in sterilized pint jars, and distribute juice into each jar (don't add any water). Add 1 teaspoon salt to each jar, and seal. Place in pressure cooker at 10 pounds pressure for 15 minutes; or place in hot water bath for 35 minutes. In serving, add chopped garlic and olive oil for seasoning. As desired, use in sandwiches or scramble with eggs.

PEPERONI ROSSI SOTTO ACETO

Pickled Cherry Peppers *Southern Regions*

- 8 quarts cherry peppers
- 3 quarts water
- 1 quart white vinegar
- 1 cup salt
- ¼ cup mixed spices
- garlic

Wash peppers with stems attached, and place them in sterilized jars with 1 clove garlic for each jar. Boil water, vinegar, salt, and mixed spice, and pour over peppers, filling jars and sealing immediately. Allow peppers to marinate 1 month.

PEPERONI UNGHERESI SOTTO ACETO

Pickled Hungarian Yellow-Wax Peppers *Lucania*

Wearing rubber gloves for protection from heat of peppers, slice 1 bushel Hungarian yellow-wax peppers (or other large chili peppers) lengthwise, and discard pulp and seeds. Place slices lengthwise in sterilized quart jars, packing them tightly with knife or a wooden spoon handle.

Pickling Liquid

- 2 quarts white vinegar
- 2 cups white sugar
- 1 cup salt
- 6 quarts water
- 2 cups brown sugar
- ¼ cup whole allspice

Dissolve thoroughly, and bring to rapid boil. Pour over peppers to the very brim of the jars. Seal immediately. Let the peppers marinate at least 1 month.

SALSA AGRODOLCE IN BARATTOLO

Canned Sour-Sweet Sauce   *Sicilia*

2 large cans tomatoes, or   ½ cup minced sweet basil
    15 fresh tomatoes   1 cup olive oil
6 large onions, chopped   salt and pepper to taste
1 cup finely-chopped   1 cup sugar dissolved in ½ cup
    parsley   vinegar

In using fresh tomatoes, parboil and peel; mash in kettle, and stew slowly. Fry onions, parsley, and sweet basil in olive oil, stirring often. When golden-brown add to tomatoes. Salt and pepper to taste. Cook slowly 2 hours, stirring occasionally, till thick. Add sugar and vinegar, and simmer another 10 minutes. Fill sterilized pint or half-pint jars, and seal.

SALSICCE IN BARATTOLO

Canned Sausage   *All Regions*

After making your favorite sausage (Chap. XIV), roast it uncovered in 425° oven until hard and crisp. Place it in sterilized jars, adding about an inch of its own **fat** to each jar. Seal, and place in pressure cooker at 15 pounds pressure for 10 minutes; or place in hot water bath for 1 hour.

TROTA SOTTO ACETO IN BARATTOLO

Canned Pickled Trout   *Lombardia*

Fry **trout** as though for serving, and let it cool. Place it lengthwise in sterilized jars, with 1 stick **cinnamon**, 3 whole **cloves**, 2 cloves **garlic**, and 1 teaspoon **salt** in each jar. Boil **water** and **wine vinegar** (half and half), and let cool. Pour over fish to brim of jar. Seal, and keep in dark, cool place.

TRIPPA MARINATA

Pickled Tripe Campania

Wash honeycomb **tripe** well, and parboil. Wash again, and cut into bite-size pieces. Cover with fresh water, and boil until tender. Drain, and cool. Cover in a bowl with chopped **garlic, parsley, salt** and **pepper** to taste. Sprinkle with enough **olive oil** to season each piece. Add **vinegar** to taste. Stir well, and let marinate at least 2 hours. Serve as appetizer or snack.

UVA SOTTO SPIRITO

Brandied Grapes Piemonte

> *Papa thought a brandied grape was good for whatever ailed us; and, believe me, it was a perfect "warmer-upper" following a skating party.*

The **grapes** (Zinfandel or muscatel) must be perfect, with no blemishes, and each one should have a stem. Wash and dry, and place in sterilized pint jars. Cover to brim with good **brandy,** and seal.

VARIETA DI CARNI IN GELATINA

Jellied Meats in Variety Abruzzi

Choice of Meats

pig feet	**snouts**	**pig tails**
rabbit	**venison**	**pork rinds**
tripe	**pig ears**	

Choose from among the meats listed. Wash well, and cut into small pieces. Boil in water with seasoning of **chili peppers,** fresh **mint, allspice, parsley, garlic, salt,** and **pepper** until tender but firm. Place in refrigerator to congeal.

VERDURE MARINATE IN BARATTOLO

Pickled Vegetables in Jars   *Lucania*

  1 pound pickling onions, peeled
  4 large heads white crisp cauliflower, cut into florets
      and slices
  3 pounds green beans

Clean vegetables, and parboil till heated through. Strain, and place in sterilized jars.

Pickling Liquid

⅓ part white vinegar   ¼ cup chopped parsley
⅔ part water   ¼ cup chopped mint
½ cup whole allspice   salt to taste

Bring to rapid boil. Pour over vegetables to brim, and seal. Allow to marinate at least 1 month.

CHAPTER XIII

METODO PER FARE
IL FORMAGGIO
Method for Making Cheese

Cheese is made in much the same manner as bread. The room must be of sun temperature, and free of draft. Pasteurized milk is not suitable. In fact, if it is possible to make cheese right after the cow is milked, the naturally warm milk is of ideal temperature.

For the homemaker who wishes to experiment with ricotta, I offer the following directions:

Into 1 gallon fresh, lukewarm cow or goat **milk** stir a solution of ¼ **rennet cheese tablet** in ½ cup **cold water.** In about ½ hour the milk will curdle. With a spatula, wooden spoon, or the hands, break the curds; let settle another 15 or 20 minutes. Drain off the whey. Place the cheese in a colander, cheese basket, or cheese form to drain.

For the farmer who has plenty of milk at hand I offer below the true recipe for making ricotta. The name means "recooked"; one makes fresh cheese and saves the whey to recook into ricotta.

FORMAGGIO

Fresh Cheese   *All Regions*

> **5 gallons fresh cow or goat milk**
> **1¼ cheese rennet tablet dissolved in 1 cup cold water**

If freshly given milk (blood temperature) is available, have a large earthen crock full of boiling-hot water before milking the cow. Pour out the water, and fill the crock with warm fresh milk. Pour the diluted rennet into the warm milk, and stir vigorously to distribute completely. Cover, and leave 2 or 3 hours, till curds are formed.

If the available milk is not freshly given, pour it into a large shallow enamel or stainless steel kettle, and heat it over a low flame to blood temperature (mildly lukewarm). Add rennet solution, and stir vigorously to distribute completely. Cover, and leave 1 hour or longer, till curds are formed.

Test coagulation of curd with a finger: if the finger comes out clean the peak has been reached. With a long knife, cut the curds clear through, in many directions. Finally, crumble them thoroughly with the hands. Cover, and leave another hour or two. The mass will sink, and the whey will rise. With the hands, transfer the cheese to a cheese form or cheese basket. *Save the whey for immediate use in making ricotta, using the recipe which follows.* Cover the freshly made cheese with a heavy weight and let it drain overnight in a cool place (to prevent souring). In the morning turn the cheese, and let it drain another day and night. The cheese may be served now, absolutely fresh, or may be aged and ripened into a butterlike consistency as follows:

Remove cheese from its setting and form to a marble slab in a cool, airy room, to dry. Rub top with salt. Next day turn cheese, and rub other side with salt. Turn each morning for about a week, until cheese dries enough to form thin crust. Rub with olive oil, wrap in cheesecloth, and place on rack in cool, airy room to ripen. Turn several times each week, checking oil; if all has been absorbed, add more. Within 5 or 6 months, when a waxlike film forms, the cheese has ripened to perfection.

RICOTTA

Italian Cottage Cheese   *Southern Regions*

Place the kettle of whey (from the preceding recipe) over a medium flame till hot. *Never allow it to boil.* Stir constantly with wooden spoon till a coagulation like cream begins to form on top. At this point, pour a little cold water into the side of the pan, to prevent cooking. With slotted ladle, remove cottage cheese to a bowl. Serve either hot or cold, with salt and pepper to taste.

CHAPTER XIV

METODI PER FARE LE SALSICCE
*Methods for Making Sausages**

The essentials for good sausage are good fresh meat, good casings, a good grinder, and a proper blend of seasoning. If the sausage is to be eaten fresh, or to be frozen, place it in a refrigerator for 1 day to intensify the seasoning. If it is to be preserved in lard or oil for future use, it must be dried properly. The region of Emilia is the home of sausage, but the intricate delicacies come from Bologna and Modena.

BONDIOLA

Stuffed Pigskin Pillows   *Emilia*
Specialty of Ferrara

- **½ pound pork rind, scraped free of fat, boiled, cooled, and ground with medium blade**
- **2 pounds lean pork, ground with medium blade**
- **2 teaspoons salt**
- **1 teaspoon pepper (freshly ground preferred)**
- **½ teaspoon nutmeg**

* See also Salsicce in Barattolo (Canned Sausage), Chap. XII.

¼ teaspoon allspice
2 pieces of pork skin 9 inches square, well scraped and cleaned

Mix the rind, meat, salt, pepper, nutmeg, and allspice thoroughly. Place on one of the pork skins. Cover with the other skin, and sew all four edges together with twine. Prick with fork, and hang to dry in cool, airy room with cross ventilation (not cold enough to freeze). Turn each day so that it dries evenly, for a week to 10 days. To cook, boil with lentils or beans. Slice as sausage.

COPPA

Head Sausage   *Abruzzi*

Similar to American headcheese

1 hog head   **salt and pepper to taste**
1 cup blanched almonds, split

Split and clean head thoroughly; remove jowl (too fat). Cover head in large kettle with cold water. Salt and pepper to taste, and cook till tender. Remove head. Cut off all meat and skin, and grind them with large blade. Add almonds and desired amount of strained broth. Mix thoroughly, and pour into loaf pan to jell. Pour any excess broth into small molds to be used as gelatin (see Chapter VIII C, Sformati).

COTECHINO

Pork-Rind Sausage   *Northern Regions*

Specialty of Modena, Emilia

6 pounds pork rinds
¼ cup salt
½ teaspoon cloves
¼ teaspoon nutmeg
¼ pound pork casings
3 pounds lean pork

  1 tablespoon pepper (freshly ground preferred)
  3 cloves garlic, cracked and soaked in ½ cup red dry wine
     4 hours, and strained

Clean and scrape most of the fat from inner side of pork rinds, and
boil rinds in water 20 minutes; drain, and cool. Grind with medium
blade. Also grind pork meat with medium blade. Mix all ingredients
thoroughly. Stuff into casings. Tie with string every 6 inches. Prick
each link with a fork. Hang sausages to dry for a week to 10 days in
cool, airy room with cross ventilation, turning each day. Place in
refrigerator, and use within the month. To cook, boil with lentils or
beans. Slice as sausage.

FRESSE DI MAIALE

Veiled Pork Patties   *Piemonte*
   For this delicacy the caul fat, a webbed skinlike
   veil around the leaf lard, is saved at hog butcher-
   ing.

  2 pounds lean pork, ground with medium blade
  1 pound pork liver, ground with medium blade
  ½ cup grated Parmesan cheese
  ½ cup fine bread crumbs
  3 teaspoons salt
  1 tablespoon pepper (freshly ground preferred)
  ½ teaspoon nutmeg
  ½ teaspoon cinnamon
  1 cup white seedless raisins, or ½ cup black raisins
     soaked 3 hours in 2 tablespoons water
  1 veil of caul fat, to wrap the patties

With the hands, mix all ingredients together thoroughly, and form
into patties like hamburgers. Wrap each patty in piece of caul fat.
Leave all in refrigerator for at least 1 day before frying, to intensify
seasoning. If caul fat is not to be had, roll the patties in corn meal.
Fry them slowly in butter. If you wish to prepare a sauce for Polenta
(Chap. V), add 1 cup Marsala or red dry wine and 1 cup water
after they are fried. Cover and simmer 15 minutes.

LUGANIGHE
(*lu gáh ni gay*)

Tirolese Sausage Alto Adige

- 6 **pounds choice lean pork and 3 pounds choice lean beef (or all pork, ground with medium blade)**
- 1 **pound pork fat, ground with medium blade**
- ½ **cup salt**
- 1 **teaspoon cinnamon**
- ¼ **teaspoon clove**
- 1 **tablespoon pepper (freshly ground preferred)**
- 4 **cloves garlic, juiced in garlic press**
- ¼ **pound pork or beef casings (pork preferred)**

With the hands, mix all ingredients together thoroughly. Stuff into casings. Tie with string every 6 inches. To cook, prick each link with fork, drop into hot water, and simmer ½ hour; or place in 350° oven for 45 minutes. If cooking with lentils or beans, place in cold water to expel seasoning into broth while cooking. When the cooking starts in hot water, most of the seasoning is retained within the sausage.

PROSCIUTTO
(*pro shoó to*)

Italian Ham Emilia

- 1 **freshly-butchered ham (12 to 15 pounds)**
- 6 **pounds pure rock salt**
- 1 **wooden plank, placed diagonally in a large earthen crock**

In a cool, airy room with cross ventilation (above freezing temperature), rub the ham entirely with 2 pounds rock salt. Leave it on the wooden plank in the crock. After two weeks rub again with 2 pounds rock salt. After a second two weeks rub again with 2 pounds rock salt. Let it marinate two weeks more (40 days in all). Remove ham from brine, and poke several cloves of **garlic** and abundant black ground **pepper** around bone and in all cracks (flies and bugs don't like garlic). Hang salt-cured ham to dry for a year in the same cool, airy room.

SALAME

Spiced Sausage   *Piemonte*

      20 **pounds choice fresh pork**
       8 **ounces salt**
       1 **tablespoon pepper, freshly ground**
       1 **tablespoon cloves (freshly ground preferred)**
      ½ **teaspoon mace**
       1 **teaspoon nutmeg (freshly ground preferred)**
      ½ **teaspoon saltpeter**
      ½ **cup red dry wine in which 3 cracked cloves of garlic
           have soaked 4 hours**
      ½ **pound large pork casings**

  Grind pork with large blade. Add all ingredients, and mix thoroughly. Stuff into casings, and tie with string every 6 inches. Prick each link with fork. Hang sausages to dry 10 days to 2 weeks in well-ventilated room with even temperature (preferably a dark dirt-bottom cellar). They may be eaten fresh, frozen, canned, or put down in oil or lard to use as desired (see Salsicce Sotto Lardo or Salsicce Sott'Olio). To cook, place them in cold water, and let simmer 45 minutes. They may also be broiled, roasted, or fried.

SALAME CRUDO

Uncooked Large Spiced Sausage   *Piemonte*
                    A delicious lunch meat

      20 **pounds choice fresh pork**
      10 **ounces salt**
       2 **tablespoons crushed or whole pepper**
       1 **tablespoon ground pepper**
      ½ **teaspoon saltpeter**
      ½ **cup red dry wine in which 3 cracked cloves of garlic
           have soaked 4 hours**
       1 **extra-large casing, about 1 foot long, from largest
           part of intestine**

Grind pork with large blade. Add the other ingredients, and mix thoroughly. Stuff into casing. Tie well at each end. Prick with fork in several places. Hang to dry at least 2 weeks in well-ventilated room with even temperature. A dark dirt-floor cellar is best for drying. Slice and eat as lunch meat, with crusty Italian bread.

SALSICCE SOTTO LARDO

Sausage in Lard   *All Regions*

Prick freshly prepared sausage with fork and hang to dry for a week to 10 days in well-ventilated room of even temperature (preferably a dark dirt-floor cellar). Cut links, and carefully drop them into large crock of warm melted leaf lard. Keep this in a cold-storage room. As part of sausage is used, avoid uncovering rest under lard.

SALSICCE SOTT'OLIO

Sausage in Oil   *All Regions*

Follow the directions of the preceding recipe; but, instead of lard, use corn oil, olive oil, or a combination of the two.

SALSICCIA ALL'ABRUZZESE

Sausage, Abruzzi Style   *Abruzzi*

> **9 pounds lean pork, ground with medium blade**
> **1 pound pork fat, ground with medium blade**
> **½ cup salt**
> **1 tablespoon pepper (freshly ground preferred)**
> **1 teaspoon crushed chili pepper**
> **1 teaspoon fennel seed**
> **¼ pound medium-sized pork casings**

Spread all the meat on a large enamel or marble-top table, and sprinkle seasonings over all. Mix as in kneading bread, but more lightly so as not to mash meat. Let stand overnight. Stuff into casings in the morning. (It will keep in refrigerator about 2 weeks.) To cook, cut into desired size, and fry slowly, or place in 350° oven for 30 to 45 minutes. If desired, cook with Salsa Parmigiana (Chap. VI) to serve with cooked spaghetti.

SALSICCIA ALLA SICILIANA

Sausage, Sicilian Style   *Sicilia*

> **10 pounds pork meat with fat, ground with medium blade**
> **¼ cup salt**
> **1 tablespoon pepper (freshly ground preferred)**
> **1 tablespoon crushed chili pepper**
> **1 tablespoon fennel seed**
> **¼ cup chopped fresh parsley (optional)**
> **3 cloves garlic, minced (optional)**
> **¼ pound medium-sized pork casings**

Often the Sicilian takes out 3 or 4 pounds of meat and stuffs it with garlic and fresh parsley to eat fresh.

Mix all ingredients thoroughly. Stuff into casings. Let it marinate 1 day in refrigerator before using. Cook as desired; pan-fry or cook with Salsa Parmigiana (Chap. VI). The most popular style is broiled in a large spiral roll (snail-like) on a large grill, till tender.

SALSICCIA DI FEGATO

Liver Sausage   *Alto Adige*

> **1 pork head**   **1 pork tongue**
> **1 pork heart**   **1 pork liver**
> **1 pork kidney**   **salt and pepper to taste**
> **¼ pound medium-sized pork casings**

Split and clean head thoroughly, removing jowl because it is too fat. Soak kidney, after cutting away most of the gristle, in salt water 2 hours. Place head, heart, kidney, and tongue in large kettle of boiling water, and cook till head meat can be removed easily from bones. Take all the meat from the kettle. Remove all blood vessels from liver, and cut several deep slits; scald it in broth about 10 minutes. In the meantime remove all meat and pork rind from head. Remove and discard skin from tongue. Pass all meat, pork skin, and liver through meat grinder with medium blade. Add salt and pepper to taste, and mix thoroughly. Stuff into pork casings (2-foot lengths) tied at one end with heavy twine. Tie together as a large ring. When all are made, return them to kettle of strained broth to cook ½ hour. Strain, and dip into pan of cold water. Strain, and lay them separately on sheet pans in cool place. They can be served as soon as they are cold, but will keep in refrigerator about 2 weeks.

SALSICCINE

Small Sausage   *Piemonte*

15 pounds pork shoulder or butts, ground with medium blade	**1 teaspoon cinnamon**
	¼ teaspoon mace
	¼ teaspoon cloves
½ cup salt	**¼ cup grated onion**
1 ounce black pepper	**¼ cup red dry wine (optional)**
¼ teaspoon nutmeg	**¼ pound sheep casings (very small)**
¼ teaspoon allspice	

Mix all together thoroughly; stuff into sheep casings. Let marinate in refrigerator 1 day before using. Pan-fry or broil. It is delicious with Polenta con Salsiccia e Rape (Chap. V).

SALSICCIOLI

Dry Hot Sausage   *Lucania*
Known in America as Peperoni

4 pounds pork meat	**1 tablespoon pepper**
1 pound salt pork	**3 cloves garlic, juiced in garlic press**
3 pounds beef	
2 tablespoons crushed chili pepper	**1 teaspoon saltpeter**
	⅛ pound smallest pork casings

Grind meat and salt pork with large blade. Mix all ingredients together thoroughly, and stuff into small pork casings. Tie with string every 8 or 10 inches. Prick each link several times with fork. Hang to dry at least 3 weeks in a cool, airy room with cross ventilation (a dark, dirt-floor cellar is ideal). Arrange sausage so that it touches nothing whatsoever while drying.

SCAMPINAI

Little Feet Sausage   *Piemonte*

> Scampinai *is the dialect word for pig trotters.*
> *Butchers in Piedmont prepare these at Christmas*
> *time as presents for their best customers.*

Cut two front pig trotters at shoulder joint. With sharp boning knife, remove meat and bones without puncturing skin. Grind meat with large blade; add equal amount of pork rind (parboiled, cooled, and ground), 1 cup chopped parsley, 2 cloves garlic, minced, salt and pepper to taste. Mix thoroughly, and stuff each leg with foot attached. Sew end together with twine. Prick in several places with fork. Hang to dry 10 days in cool, airy room. To cook, boil with greens, beans, lentils, or just in water, and prepare gelatin with broth (see Chapter VIII, C, Sformati). Slice the little feet as lunch meat.

SOPRASSATA

Supreme Sausage   *Venezia*

> 5 **pounds choice lean pork (loin preferred)**
> 1 **tablespoon salt**
> 1 **tablespoon crushed whole pepper**
> ½ **teaspoon saltpeter**
> ½ **teaspoon nutmeg**
> 3 **cloves garlic, cracked and soaked in ½ cup dry wine,**
>   **then squeezed through a cloth**
> 1 **extra-large casing (about 1 foot long)**

Grind meat with large blade. Add seasoning and wine. Mix thoroughly. Stuff into casing, and tie well at both ends. Prick with fork in several places; hang to dry at least 2 weeks in cool, airy room with cross ventilation (preferably a dirt-floor cellar). If dried correctly, it can be eaten raw like salami.

ZAMPONE DI MODENA

Stuffed Pig Trotter of Modena *Emilia*

This recipe differs from that for Scampinai (p. 250) only in the stuffing:

    3 pounds lean pork meat
    3 pounds pork rind (parboiled, with the fat scraped
        off) ground with large blade
 1½ ounces salt
    1 tablespoon crushed whole pepper
    1 teaspoon nutmeg
    ½ teaspoon allspice

COMPARATIVE TABLE OF
WEIGHTS AND MEASURES

**(Approximate equivalents of European Metric system
and American avoirdupois)**

grams	ounces	grams	ounces
14	½	238	8½
28	1	252	9
42	1½	266	9½
56	2	280	10
70	2½	294	10½
84	3	308	11
98	3½	322	11½
112	4	336	12
126	4½	350	12½
140	5	364	13
154	5½	378	13½
168	6	392	14
182	6½	406	14½
196	7	420	15
210	7½	434	15½
224	8	448	16

453.6 grams	1 pound
1 kilogram	2 lb. 3 oz.
1 liter	1 quart (4 cups)
½ liter	1 pint (2 cups)
¼ liter	½ pint (1 cup)
3 teaspoons	1 tablespoon
5 tablespoons	¼ cup
2 tablespoons	1 fluid ounce
1 cube (butter)	½ cup

ITALIAN INDEX OF RECIPES

(For English index, see pages 260–268.)

253

ENGLISH INDEX OF RECIPES

(For Italian names of recipes, see pages 253–259.)